BLACK FEELINGS

RACE
RHETORIC
& MEDIA

Davis W. Houck, General Editor

BLACK
FEELINGS

Race and Affect in the Long Sixties

Lisa M. Corrigan

University Press of Mississippi / Jackson

The University Press of Mississippi is the scholarly publishing agency of
the Mississippi Institutions of Higher Learning: Alcorn State University,
Delta State University, Jackson State University, Mississippi State University,
Mississippi University for Women, Mississippi Valley State University,
University of Mississippi, and University of Southern Mississippi.

www.upress.state.ms.us

The University Press of Mississippi is a member
of the Association of University Presses.

First printing 2020
∞

Library of Congress Cataloging-in-Publication Data

Names: Corrigan, Lisa M., author.
Title: Black feelings: race and affect in the long sixties / Lisa M.
Corrigan.
Description: Jackson: University Press of Mississippi, 2020. | Includes
bibliographical references and index.
Identifiers: LCCN 2019053595 (print) | LCCN 2019053596 (ebook) | ISBN
9781496827944 (hardback) | ISBN 9781496827951 (trade paperback) | ISBN
9781496827968 (epub) | ISBN 9781496827975 (epub) | ISBN 9781496827982
(pdf) | ISBN 9781496827999 (pdf)
Subjects: LCSH: African Americans—Civil rights—History. | Black
power—United States—Psychological aspects. | Emotions—Social aspects.
| BISAC: SOCIAL SCIENCE / Ethnic Studies / African American Studies
Classification: LCC E185.615 .C673 2020 (print) | LCC E185.615 (ebook) |
DDC 323.1196/073—dc23
LC record available at https://lccn.loc.gov/2019053595
LC ebook record available at https://lccn.loc.gov/2019053596

British Library Cataloging-in-Publication Data available

This book is dedicated to Linda Corrigan
and The Ralph and Claudia Schaffner.

CONTENTS

ACKNOWLEDGMENTS

In all honesty, I began this book as a response to a reviewer who characterized the Black Power movement as an emotionally immature political program led by a bunch of angry kids. I was tired of white reviewers in rhetorical studies dismissing scholarship about radical black activism as juvenile or underdeveloped, even as adjacent disciplines were revisiting the tremendous contributions of Black Power. I was tired of reading reviews that lazily rejected any rhetorical analyses that took seriously the political theory or practical activism of radical black movement organizations. I was tired of hearing that radical black leaders were "too emotional" and weren't pragmatic enough. Mostly, I was tired of the structural racism of the academic review process, where white gatekeepers used their tacit racism to undermine the circulation of scholarship that centered the perspectives of black people, generally, but black men, specifically. Given that the American tradition in the field of rhetoric originally centered on biographical and critical assessments of the "Great [White] Man," producing a body of scholarship about the significant rhetorical contributions of radical black intellectuals has been a challenge that I have (obviously) taken up with much aplomb.

It is my hope that *Black Feelings: Race and Affect in the Long Sixties* provides longitudinal analysis that will help future scholars articulate how feelings have motivated and continue to animate white assessments of black activism and to understand how black activists have used emotions to propel radical and innovative political theory and engagement. I hope that lay readers of this book and the rest of my scholarship will also find utility in thinking through antiblack public policy and radical black activist responses to the failures of liberalism in ways that challenge myths about the civil rights and Black Power movements.

Thanks to Craig Gill and all the wonderful folks at the University Press of Mississippi for their unconditional support. Thanks to Vijay Shah for his diligence, Davis Houck for his vision, Steve Yates for his execution, Courtney

McCreary for logistical support, Todd Lape for his creative genius, and Lisa McMurtray for keeping me on task. Thanks, too, to the good folks at the Mississippi Book Festival, which has been a wonderful venue for my work.

The earliest part of this book was presented at the Public Address Conference (PAC) in Atlanta in 2014 thanks to the kind invitation of the programming committee, including Mary Stuckey, Michael Bruner, David Cheshier, Nate Atkinson, James Darsey, and Carol Winkler. From this wonderful experience, I need to thank respondents to early iterations of these ideas, including Kirt Wilson, Eric King Watts, and Robert Terrill. It would be impossible for me to overstate how this experience changed my career and the opportunities that have followed. In that vein, I need to thank Chuck Morris, Jeff Bennett, Peter Campbell, and Leroy Dorsey, who supported my work as a result of that talk at PAC in 2014.

Various talks from these chapters have been possible thanks to the support of the Vanderbilt University School of Divinity and Black Cultural Center; the Hilliard Research Lecture Committee, University of Nevada at Reno; Department of African and African American Studies at Washington University; Crystal Bridges Museum of American Art; Department of Communication Studies at Davidson College; Department of Communication and Rhetorical Studies at Syracuse University; Department of Gender and Race Studies at University of Alabama; Department of Africana Studies at California State University–Fresno; Department of Philosophy at Texas A&M University; the "Philosophy Born of Struggle" Conference; the Department of Communication at the University of Memphis; and the University of Arkansas Honors College. Portions of this book were written in Stockholm, Sweden, at the International Writers' House with support from the Swedish government; in Helsinki and Turku, Finland, with an invitation from the John Morton Center for North American Studies; and in Coimbra, Portugal, with an invitation from the "Legacies of the Tricontinental, 1966–2016: Imperialism, Resistance, Law" conference and travel support from the Office of the Provost at the University of Arkansas.

In my home department, I was granted a course release to complete the manuscript and have been grateful for the support of chair Bob Brady and dean Todd Shields throughout the conception and execution of this project. I'm also grateful for the support of Stephanie Schulte, Ryan Neville-Shepard, Matt Spialek, Lindsey Aloia, Steve Boss, Sidney Burris, Angie Maxwell, Pearl Ford Dowe, Kathy Sloan, Lynda Coon, Toni Jensen, Geffrey Davis, Lissette Szwydky-Davis, Ryan Calabretta-Sajder, Ana Bridges, Marty Maxwell Lane, and Jo Hsu. I have also been fortunate to have worked with so many wonderful graduate students over the years; in the development of this book, I am particularly grateful for the research skills and friendship of Skye de Saint Felix, Molly McCormack, and Brittan Andres.

For their scholarship and intellectual camaraderie, I'm indebted to Leslie Harris, Ebony Utley, Belinda Stillion-Southard, Gerald Early, Caleb Smith, John Lynch, Tommy Curry, Irami Osei-Frimpong, Stephen Heidt, Steve Herro, Andre Johnson, Amanda Edgar, Vanessa Beasley, Amy Young, Leslie Dinauer, Karma Chavéz, Jessica Pieklo, Doug Dennis, Sam Perry, Jennifer Mercieca, and Ersula Ore.

In Arkansas, I have also been the beneficiary of unwavering support from #surfergirls and forever comrades Jennifer Lowrey, Molly Rawn, Amy Dunn Johnson, Jamie Kern, Jodi Nimmo, and Ginney Norton. William K. Reeder listened to me talk about these ideas and provided (almost exclusively) phenomenological readings of them all. While I wrote, my dear friend Clunk's hourly cable news updates kept me informed. Leigh Wood has been a never-ending supply of good music. And Tony Gray provided countless hours of laughs as I finished the manuscript in a difficult period.

Many of the ideas for this book were first articulated in my *Lean Back: Critical Feminist Conversations* podcast with my cohost Laura Weiderhaft. It would be impossible to overstate how important *Lean Back* has been for my intellectual development and for my emotional sanity. I'm so proud of the work that Laura and I have done critiquing the notion that women (and people of color and LGBTQ people) should "lean in" to capitalism harder, and I am so very grateful for Laura's friendship and intellectual fellowship.

I'm also lucky to have three collaborators who sustain my brain and me. I'm grateful to Susana O'Daniel and Anjali Vats for their unwavering love and total brilliance. I'm also grateful for Phil Elwood, who has been an anchor for years and continues to keep me on my toes.

My mother, Linda Corrigan, continues to champion my work and me. Her love and support have been critical during the writing of this book.

Finally, this book is dedicated to The Ralph and Claudia Schaffner, who sustain me. As a founding #surfergirl member, Claudia continues to enjoy accompanying me to the coffee shop to write and has been nothing but supportive of my chosen profession doing black justice work.

Introduction

RACIAL FEELINGS IN BLACK AND WHITE

"Wait" has almost always meant "Never."
—**Martin Luther King Jr.**, "Letter from Birmingham City Jail"

In the September 1969 issue of *Negro Digest*, a young Black Arts Movement poet then named Ameer (Amiri) Baraka published a piece titled "We Are Our Feeling: The Black Aesthetic." The climax of this poetic manifesto reads: "We are our feeling. We are our feelings ourselves. Our selves are our feelings."[1] Rather than "a theory in the ether," Baraka asserted, "feelings are central and genuine and descriptive."[2] This expression of the centrality of *feelings* to black selfhood provides an important touchstone for understanding how the black liberation movement grappled with its relationship to emotions after the protests and marches in places like Greensboro, Albany, Birmingham, Washington, Selma, and Montgomery. It creates an affective context for the rise of Black Power politics after the passage of the Civil Rights Act of 1964 and the Voting Rights Act of 1965; after Watts, Detroit, and Chicago; after the assassinations of both Kennedy brothers, Malcolm X, Medgar Evers, Martin Luther King Jr., Fred Hampton, and Mark Clark; after the massive escalation of Vietnam and the abdication of President Johnson; and after new conservatism ushered in the soaring popularity of both Nixon and Reagan. Baraka's "We Are Our Feeling" is an important text because it locates *feelings* as the *motive* of Black Power politics as black intellectuals sought new ways to understand the increasingly complicated landscape of black identity in a nation perpetually (re)producing citizenship through antiblackness.

While it would be tempting to read Baraka's manifesto and those like it as articulations of aesthetic feelings, mobilized through artistic practice or appreciation, it was hardly the only documentation of the importance of emotions in understanding black political life in 1969. For example, in the 1969 *Riot Report* (the abbreviated version of the best-selling Kerner Commission's *Report of the National Advisory Commission on Civil Disorders*), Barbara Ritchie writes, "Black Power first articulated a mood rather than a program. The mood was one of disillusionment and alienation from white America, and also one of independence, race pride, and self-respect—or 'black consciousness.'"[3] Ritchie lists the *embodied feelings* that attenuated the shift toward Black Power, characterizing the negative feelings of the time as disillusionment and alienation and the positive feelings as independence, pride, and self-respect. She charts the complex and coterminous relationship between positive and negative feelings as they shaped black liberation as well as white backlash. And as a *mood*, Ritchie is gesturing at a change in disposition, temper, atmosphere, and attitude, clearly marking Black Power as a shift that was as tangible emotionally and physically as it was intellectually. Moods are unique emotional (dis)positions because they always begin "from a specific situation" or are "connected with it (perhaps to a sequence of similar situations)."[4] Moods build what Michael Omi and Howard Winant have famously called "racial formations" that, over time, become structures of property, privilege, and rights.[5] Here perception "determines racialization."[6] In this case, the perception of a new blackness (and also an invigorated whiteness) heralded a new national mood that only grew after 1965 and was amplified by speeches, official documents, and art that articulated Black Power as a new mood.

Indeed, political moods have a *chronopolitics*, or a politics of time, that mark particular movements or political moments around the definition of events. Moods have a chronology and a temporality that can change and evolve across and through time (though not always in a linear fashion). As a mood, Black Power exemplified what Frank Wilderson has called "black time," that is, the idea that black subjectivity is intrinsically connected to experiences of time that mark (anti)blackness in life as well as death.[7] Black memories, remembrances, commemorations, imaginings, fantasies, and counterfactuals all work to resituate black subjectivity within political time in ways that resist erasure and assert new agency. Likewise, moods "identify the cognitive and expressive parameters that have shaped the Black critique of time."[8] Political moods are especially important as black political interventions, particularly as whites say, "Wait."

Black Power was important as a mood because it marked a rupture that fundamentally defined the political feelings that came before its birth and after its decline. Circulated widely in 1966 after a white sniper shot the civil rights activist James Meredith in Mississippi during his March Against Fear,

Black Power was a political slogan that signaled a rhetorical, political, and emotional shift in black ideology and organizing. Meredith described the march as one against a feeling of *despair* and toward a feeling of *empowerment*, saying, "I wanted to drive despair from the frustrated mind of a teenage Negro boy who had only just begun to feel the consequences of being inferior."[9] These rationales are echoed in the Kerner Commission and many of the official reports issued to describe the dynamic shifts in racial moods at midcentury, as we shall see.

When political moods like Black Power emerge, publics justify them through conceptual labor that can shift political moments in the process of deciphering causality and justification. This labor exposes the rhetorical processes where feelings are translated into politics. Thus deep cognitive feelings—these multiple feelings that demand interpretation through contextual lenses—scaffold and amplify to create political moods: for example, a widespread feeling of despair turns into political pessimism. Heller explains, "We feel deeply when we become involved in something with our whole personality, either positively or negatively," and this intensity of feeling precipitates moods that challenge politics as usual.[10] In this way, feelings build the history and emotional constitution of personalities not just of people but of epochs, of generational cohorts, creating what Raymond Williams has termed "structural feelings."[11] In fact, when certain expressions of affect or feeling are not preferred in the given culture at a particular time, "new feelings will be produced by relegating these affects to the background, and the new feelings will be accompanied by new expressions of feeling."[12] In the case of social movements, expressions of new feelings become political action. Here shifts in political action mark the difference between events and plateaus and that blurs the (racialized) distinction, in this case, between white thinking and black feeling, black thinking and white feeling.

As a *mood*, Black Power was precipitated by a series of events and experiences that introduced new structural, political feelings about liberalism (and the reinvigorated belief that promoting social equality served the greater good), political engagement, blackness, civil rights, and segregation to the public with the election of John F. Kennedy. But viewing Black Power as a mood also helps us understand how political feelings expand and constrain political philosophy, phenomenological inquiry, oppositional strategy, and practical activism. Black Power emerged just as formal political rights were both *emerging* and *disappearing* for black Americans as a result of shifting alliances between white conservatives and Great Society liberals.[13] Consequently, Black Power elucidated the tensions formed from the collusion of racial liberalism, newly emergent disciplinary regimes within "law and order" culture,

mass incarceration, global capitalism, and postcolonialism. Former Student
Nonviolent Coordinating Committee (SNCC) chairman Stokely Carmichael
explained that Black Power was the opposite of begging white people to be
humane: "All we had to do was sing *We Shall Overcome* and beg the rest of the
people in the country to have their consciences morally aroused so that we
can get this and this and this. But now with the voting rights act, we can orga-
nize and get political strength and take over county governments which are
run by racists. And that's just what we intend to do, and that's what we mean
by 'Black Power.'"[14] As both a slogan and a political orientation, Black Power
was nothing if not an articulation of changes in *both* feelings *and* politics,
away from hope, accommodation, and moral suasion and toward electoral
and community power.

In his famous Black Power speech at Berkeley in 1966, Carmichael condemned the politics of hope that had defined the decade's beginning and
explained to a mostly white crowd, "You cannot form a coalition based on
national sentiment. That is not a coalition. If you need a coalition to redress
itself to real changes in this country, white people must start building those
institutions inside the white community."[15] Asking white people to disavow
hope in favor of dismantling antiblack institutions is one way in which black
intellectuals engaged with white political feelings. Carmichael added a critique of Martin Luther King's moral suasion as well, saying that coalition
building had failed because "we've always moved in the field of morality and
love while people have been politically jiving with our lives. And the question
is, how do we now move politically and stop trying to move morally?"[16] Carmichael's comments articulate Black Power as a fracture in politics, one that
asks black activists and white eavesdroppers to move beyond the affective
politics of the Great Society and embrace the labor of movement organizing to confront the inadequacies of midcentury liberalism. Black America
embraced Black Power "because it captured their *feelings* about the status quo
in nondeferential *tones* that few had ever heard expressed publicly," explains
Hasan Kwame Jeffries.[17]

Robert E. Johnson, editor of *Jet* magazine, compared Black Power's emotional repertoire to jazz, calling it "a strange sound rolling from the lips of
militant Negroes and directed at the eardrums of segregationist whites."[18] In
calling attention to the content as well as the vocalization of Black Power
demands, Johnson highlights the uniqueness of what I have previously called
the Black Power vernacular.[19] The Black Power vernacular employed a new
emotional and rhetorical repertoire critical of liberalism and the civil rights
movement that was amplified as a result of black frustrations with the Senate
filibuster to kill the Civil Rights Act of 1966 in September of that year. The

death of the bill was a major defeat for the Johnson White House and for the movement, since it marked the first time that a civil rights bill had been killed in Congress since Johnson assumed the presidency, and marked a change in political will to guarantee black equality. Martin Luther King Jr. prophesied that the Senate vote "surely heralds darker days for this social era of discontent," clearly demarcating a new, darker mood that coincided with the bill's defeat and with the wide popularity of Black Power in its wake.[20] Commenting on the affective dimensions of Black Power in 1966, Floyd McKissick, national director for the Congress of Racial Equality (CORE), described Black Power as an emotional prophylactic for despair, saying that rather than a call for black supremacy (as whites consistently articulated it), Black Power was "a drive to mobilize the Black communities of this country in a monumental effort to remove the basic causes of alienation, frustration, despair, low self-esteem and hopelessness."[21] These feelings propelled a new reservoir of stances, tones, arguments, metaphors, feelings, and futures for black citizens that demanded white accountability and black liberation.

In *Black Feelings*, I trace the surging optimism of the Kennedy administration through the Black Power era's powerful circulation of black pessimism to understand how black feelings constituted a terrain of political struggle for black meaning, representation, and political agency. *Black Feelings* provides an account of the dynamism of racial feelings at midcentury and provides a rationale for Black Power as a mood and a repository of rhetorical, political, and affective discourses necessary to process and resist the constant physical violence directed against black activists and the psychological strain of movement disappointment, particularly with liberals (both black and white).[22] *Black Feelings* demonstrates how racial feelings emerged, ebbed, flowed, disappeared, and reemerged as the long sixties unfolded and finally ended.[23] With a particular focus on the important political consequences of mobilizing negative feelings—what Sianne Ngai calls "ugly feelings"—to Black Power intellectuals, *Black Feelings* exposes the paradoxes of liberalism that promoted and foreclosed freedom and equality as black activists grappled with the twin pillars of modernity as articulated by Marx and Foucault: capitalism and disciplinarity.[24] Black Power was a response to a historically contingent articulation of white hope, and it interrogated the social and political norms of feelings-talk under the newly emergent terrain of racial liberalism, particularly as, say, integration fell short of the goals of even its most ardent supporters. Rather than treat Black Power as epiphenomenal, it seems paramount to understand the *intentionality* of Black Power as a political program and as a mood formed in response to antiblack political feelings in a moment where racial liberalism was influencing and producing new racial assumptions and policies. By racial liberalism, I mean the rewriting of the tenets of liberal democracies through race policy as a way of shaping the discursive logics of the state, particularly around the notion of equality.[25] Indeed, Black Power acknowledged the sentiment central to Frederick Douglass's 1852 speech "What to the Slave Is the Fourth of July?," namely, that black Americans have always been ambivalent about the often impossible feeling of US national belonging even before racial liberalism began to formally characterize public policy. While many scholars have been critical of black pessimism as a political invocation, assessments of Afro-pessimism often rely on positive assessments of race relations in America and a continued reliance on racial liberalism as a guiding light for political discourse, particularly as it pertained to integration as a possible solution to segregation. In the words of Harold Cruse, "Racial integration [is] a great myth which the ideologues of the system and the Liberal Establishment expound, but which they cannot deliver into reality.... The melting-pot has never included the Negro."[26]

Although the book's conclusion considers Afro-pessimism as the emergent political mood of the Obama era (after Ferguson and the birth of #BlackLivesMatter), *Black Feelings* as a whole considers black emotional inventions in opposition to white hope, particularly in critiques of civil rights discourses during the Kennedy and Johnson years, from 1960 to 1968. As integration became the prevailing discourse of racial liberalism shaping midcentury discursive structures, so too did racial feelings mold the biopolitical order of postmodern life in America. By examining the discourses produced by Malcolm X, Stokely Carmichael, Eldridge Cleaver, Huey Newton, and other radical black leaders and movement icons like Martin Luther King Jr., who were marshaling black feelings in the service of black political action, *Black Feelings* traces how black activists mobilized new emotional repertoires to build black political culture while also chronicling how those repertoires were used simultaneously to discredit black activism. I consider how political feelings bound and broke racial bodies in the production of black activism, and uncover how the intimacy of shared feelings (re)arranged black bodies. I demonstrate how black feelings created the spatial and temporal movement, or *motion*, of this phase of the black freedom struggle. By motion, I mean to chart how black rhetors have moved against the process by which black life "was nothing but inert matter, waiting to be molded in the hands of a superior race."[27] Using new rhetorical innovations and vocalics allowed Black Power intellectuals to express feelings prohibited from public display and to manage the pain that accompanied the systemic violence enacted through the inventions of white superiority and black inferiority. How else to combat the literature, politics, and ontology of modernity that positioned white culture as civilization and black culture—and by extension all of Africa—as primitive?

In this mode, black interlocutors before but especially during the Black Power era used the language of *feelings* to offer a new black *reason*. I mean black reason in the sense that Mbembe does, as "forms of knowledge; a model for extraction and depredation; a paradigm of subjection, including modalities governing its eradication; and finally, a psycho-oneiric complex. Like a kind of giant cage, Black reason is in truth a complicated network of doubling, uncertainty, and equivocation, built with race as its chassis."[28] Black Power engaged in the (re)production of black reason via black feelings as an antidote to the erosion of black potential, and it responded to white hysterics mobilizing racism to undermine black emancipation; consequently, black vernacular speakers mobilized "a fabulous machine whose power resided in its vulgarity, in its remarkable capacity for violence, and in its indefinite proliferation."[29] Mbembe explains that the primary activity of black reason has been "fantasizing. It consisted essentially in gathering real or attributed traits, weaving them into histories, and creating images" to resist the (il)logics of antiblack domination.[30] Through Black Power fantasizing, black reason used ideas, myths, and feelings to politicize articulations of black being in new ways to build different political moods that documented the centrality of antiblackness to the American Dream.[31] Whether fantasizing that white racists could be compelled through moral suasion or about black community control, liberation activists relentlessly offered black reason as a testament to their creativity and political savvy, even when white supremacist institutions blocked their path, imprisoned them, assassinated them, or erased them. Thus black reason is and was an interrogation of the "logics of pain in the subject formation processes of late modern politics."[32] Particularly when cultural traumas dislocate time as well as black identity, black subjectivity must be reimagined as it was in the Black Power era. Thus is Black Power a major inventional moment in what we now call Afro-pessimism.[33]

While this book does not offer an exhaustive account of midcentury racial feelings, it certainly charts how politicos, activists, and artists articulated the relationship between *feeling black* and *black feelings*. In doing so, *Black Feelings* investigates the affective energies that animated the rhetorical and political shifts of the 1960s to understand how they troubled liberalism's tropes of progress, equality, exceptionalism, perfection, and colorblindness. In doing so, I describe the ways in which vulnerability, intimacy, and violence shaped new political orientations toward political hope, melancholy, rage, alienation, and suicide. Accordingly, I see Black Power as an enduring assemblage and as a racial formation that exposed the pathways of white power while reconstituting blackness (and masculinity) in sometimes contradictory or shortsighted ways, but always with the goal of manufacturing new political attachments. For example, in much of the racial trauma that accompanied the black freedom struggle, hope and mourning are intertwined, despite being seemingly opposite political feelings. Although black reason attempts to stabilize black subjectivity and resist domination, political moods shift over time as populations respond to material reality and the emergence of history. This is apparent in studies of black political action after the assassinations of, say, John F. Kennedy or Martin Luther King Jr., when black political moods indicated different *feelings* about *politics*. Although I take up these moments in later chapters, it is clear that public grief was one major vector that influenced new rhetorical and emotional paradigms in the black freedom struggle as it operated with and against liberal hope. In Sara Ahmed's words, "harm has a history," and black activism was nothing if not an articulation of the history of harm and, by extension, the feelings produced by that systemic harm, particularly as the hope framework ebbed.[34] We might think of black activism, especially Black Power activism, as a kind of rhetorical and historical excavation of black pain, as well as a series of polemics about how to both mine and mobilize that history for new emotional and political strategies of resistance. If we begin this archaeology of black pain with Malcolm X's proto–Black Power pedagogies of pride and rage, for example, it becomes clear that one distinct feature of Black Power rhetoric was centering the slave experience as a fundamental source of knowledge in what Jeffrey Santa Ana has termed "feeling ancestral."[35] This rhetorical work engaged black time differently by charting the contours of slavery in contemporary black public life. Likewise, understanding the economic and political investments in the plantation economy created a vivid space for reassessing contemporary black life in the United States through the lens of property rights. In this way, Black Power intellectuals worked to circulate structures of feeling that reoriented black and white auditors and readers toward new modes of self-expression rooted in the economic, physical, and psychic traumas of American slavery and the African diaspora as a way of destabilizing narratives of American political progress and egalitarianism and as a mode of establishing global Third World solidarity.

Rather than political gradualism, Black Power provided a series of futurist imaginings and an alternative chronopolitics to weaken antiblackness as a foundational political project in the United States. Martin Luther King Jr. described this dynamic eloquently in 1956 after the Montgomery boycott:

> The enlightened white Southerner, who for years has preached gradualism, now sees that even the slow approach finally has revolutionary implications. Placing

straws on a camel's back, no matter how slowly, is dangerous. This realization has immobilized the liberals and most of the white church leaders. They have no answer for dealing with or absorbing violence. They end in begging for retreat, lest "things get out of hand and lead to violence."[36]

King notes how gradualism, as a chronopolitics of white political stasis, undermines the possibility of racial equality, and he is clear that the incremental pace and scope of federal desegregation would ultimately precipitate rioting and rebellion, guaranteeing Black Power discourses. The civil rights marches, in particular, disrupted racialized time and functioned as both chronopolitical and spatial challenges to segregation. Watching huge columns of black civil rights activists and their white allies walk from Selma to Montgomery, for example, helped to demonstrate that black freedom participants could *move*, that is, *march* into the future with a new vision for American life. In fact, the march, as a movement tactic, put the *move* in *move*ment as a way of embodying a different kind of chronopolitics that moved from (white) nostalgia for a calcified past to a newly emergent, dynamic (black) future. King even called marches a "technique of the future," explaining that "marching feet announce that time has come for a given idea. When the idea is a sound one, the cause a just one, and the demonstration a righteous one, change will be forthcoming."[37] While black pessimists railed against the political hope of civil rights to transform white feelings and practices connected to antiblackness, the optimism of the sit-ins and marches nonetheless focused on how they would disrupt and reshape racial politics and racial time, demonstrating "how patrolling the boundaries of affect can have authorizing functions in public discourse."[38] And while King and Malcolm X, for example, were not Black Power orators per se, both textured Black Power discourse as antecedent intellectuals and, in King's case, as both supporter and foil. That is to say that Black Power is indebted to both King and Malcolm for discursive interventions that built Black Power as a mood, even when there were divergences in ideology. Nowhere is this more evident than in Barack Obama's discourses, which I take up at length in the book's conclusion.

This history of black feelings is also one deeply concerned with *black existence* and the possible productions of black selves in antiblack nation-states. As Achille Mbembe has argued, the "fundamental meanings of Blackness and race have always been existential."[39] The sociologist James Turner elaborates, describing how the black citizen in the United States "lives in a symbiotic relationship with the white man and is held in subordinate position by the caste system. Furthermore, he is governed by the secondary institutions imposed or sanctioned by the white dominant group, especially in the

areas of religion and social morality."⁴⁰ This relationality fundamentally shapes
the production of black (and white) subjectivity. As such, the co-constitutive
relationship between feelings and politics in the United States pivots on the
possibility for (both political and personal) agency within a schema that
nods to ideal liberal notions of equality but fundamentally revolves around
exclusionary citizenship based on race, gender, sexuality, class, ability, and
immigration status. Thus do these chapters engage issues of ontology as they
arise in anticolonial articulations of black American subjectivity in ways that
discursively produce new political subjects in the face of the dominations that
racial liberalism has enacted on its citizens of color, but uniquely on black
citizens—what Wendy Brown has called "domination liberalism."⁴¹ Domination liberalism, particularly as it is exercised through racial power, "operates
affectively: it is exercised through and is reproduced through our *feelings*, and
it is forceful and effective precisely because of that," adds Deborah Gould.⁴²

These forceful and effective new ontological orientations articulated a
longing to *share power* as the loss of freedom became an object of intense
scrutiny and as *practices of freedom* became the rhetorical and political goal
of new black agitation. That is, Black Power rhetors were preoccupied with
doing freedom in opposition to the institutionalization of freedom through
the passage of laws securing rights. Indeed, the social movement struggles
at midcentury managed the paradoxes of freedom in ways that attempted
to develop and deploy new modes and styles of freedom enacted through
the body and through intimate bodies, thinking and feeling in tandem and
in opposition. "Freedom is a project suffused not just with ambivalence but
with anxiety, because it is flanked by the problem of power on all sides: the
powers against which it arrays itself as well as the power it must claim to
enact itself."⁴³ Because, in Calvin Warren's words, "the American dream . . .
is realized through black suffering," black freedom is an impossibility.⁴⁴ This
impossibility is what makes the imperative of political hope so toxic: it holds
out for a black political future that is fundamentally foreclosed on by the very
structures through which black Americans are expected to petition for freedom, although these forms of redress have not emerged since emancipation.

Following Ann Cvetkovich's lead, my method of inquiry in tackling these
objectives involves "an exploration of cultural texts as repositories of feelings
and emotions."⁴⁵ I trace how discourses increasingly depicted Black Power as
a bodily sensation propelled by intense feelings that created racial moods.
Black Feelings provides a style of reflection that attends to descriptions of
both the *physicality* and the *rhetoricity* of feelings in discourses about Black
Power. Where some of the newly emergent literature on affect or feelings is
concerned with primary drives and the affects that emerge from them, I am

interested in the production and circulation of cognitive feelings. Cognitive feelings are language dependent; they are "social, historical, and individually specific emotions."[46] Cognitive feelings function as pedagogical tools in building identification with and against objects of affection and derision. They create the foundation for political grievances, and they shape political norms as well as resistance to normative political structures. The cognition of sensations and their arrangement into social meaning are what makes them *feelings* as opposed to *affects*. Because, as Heller explains, "to feel means to be involved in something," I am interested in how the *language of feeling* propelled citizens to become involved in various ideas, organizations, acts, and productions of the black liberation movement.[47] In doing so, I untangle competing political feelings to understand how they marked different political strategies, geographic localities, and rhetorical tactics as activists managed political success, disappointment, grief, and impasse.

In providing a rhetorical account of these feelings, I hope to recenter feelings as a critical component in the rhetorical assessment of both civil rights and black liberation. Consequently, this book makes a major intervention into the field of rhetorical studies that, I hope, will demonstrate the utility of racial feelings in projecting claims about citizenship, belonging, rights, and sovereignty, particularly in confrontational rhetorical postures like that of the Black Power movement. In providing this rhetorical account of the political feelings surrounding black activism, I seek to explicate how black intellectuals described, animated, located, solicited, and projected feelings that shaped their political affiliations and their rhetorical strategies. Contributing to literature in the fields of rhetoric, cultural studies, African American studies, and social movement studies, *Black Feelings* moves the criticism of affect from literary studies into rhetorical studies to understand the complex tapestry of emotional discourses that accessed and mobilized new public sentiments around race and resistance in the long sixties. Thus I hope to describe how black political feelings like rage, shame, resentment, disgust, betrayal, and melancholy created a structural coherence in Black Power discourses to manage the increasingly narrow possibilities for black dissent and to invigorate new black ontologies.

Feeling and Moving: Early Social Movement Studies

In early protest studies, emotions were central to understanding the emergence, development, and resolution of social movements, but they have unfortunately receded from the scholarly literature. Early accounts of emotions within social movements pathologized social movement activists as being inflamed by either ideology or passion. In this tradition, emotions are the product of mob mentality or demagogues and thus have no relationality to the needs or goals of community members. In this scholarship, emotions are the product of internal conflict and not structural violence, so only damaged people with inappropriate needs or drives participate in movement politics.[48] With a focus on demagoguery, mob rule, brainwashing, and cults of personality, this literature saw political emotions as fundamentally damaging to communities and protest as a form of obedience to "outside agitators."

Social movement scholars have mostly moved beyond the assertion that mob psychology was primarily responsible for protests; consequently, modern scholars generally describe social movements as intentional political and rhetorical interventions. Several studies stand out, though, for demonstrating that *feelings* are an intrinsic part of modern movement organizing. For example, Neil Smelser's influential 1968 essay observed that protest has a psychological function, "since the deepest and most powerful human emotions— idealistic fervor, love, and violent rage, for example—are bared in episodes of collective behavior."[49] Smelser's assessment of emotions in the development of social movements follows Freudian psychology, which has mostly passed out of vogue for social movement scholars; however, his work demonstrated how political resistance "permits the expression of impulses that are normally repressed," particularly to build support for charismatic leaders.[50]

Given midcentury concerns about mobs and demagogues, social movements in the 1960s "did not always arouse sympathy, since they could be dismissed as the work of confused youngsters suffering from Oedipal fantasies."[51] As we shall see, the fearful psychological language about social movement protests shaped white criticisms of black activism, since white critics could not read how black social networks and organizations negotiated shared cultural meanings, including their navigation of political emotions. Likewise, descriptions of black activism using the language of the mob or the demagogue often displaced white political mobilization onto black activism. In this literature, black "protestors were not rational agents with purposes of their own. The more emotional an individual (or crowd) became, the less rational she (or they) became, ipso facto. The actual stuff of contentious politics— moral principles, stated goals, processes of mobilization, the pleasures of participation—was ignored."[52] The inverse relationship between feeling and thinking was a major assumption advanced even by early social movement studies that considered how (racialized) political feelings emerged as part of social movement identity. These studies saw political feelings as a negative remainder of political action, propelling people into authoritarianism and groupthink, which rendered black activism illegible or dangerous rather than preserving any space for recuperative readings of political feelings. Thus did antiblack political theorizing collapse into the language of black feelings to discredit movement activism as the *opposite* of "real" political action, replicating the "(white) reason / (black) feeling" dichotomy that shapes colonial race relations and undermines racial equality.

While this vein of scholarship demonized political emotions, groundbreaking theorists like Ruth Searles and J. Allen Williams argued that black activism in the 1960s was a result of unmet individual needs.[53] In addition, black psychologists William Grier and Price Cobbs described how white supremacy forced black people to repress their emotions, giving rise to new politicized feelings. They argued that black people cultivate "a lack of feeling" as a form of self-protection in response to the intense violence and brutality of black life in white America.[54] "For black people, the ability to divorce oneself emotionally from an object is necessary for survival," which has consequences for black identification with racial liberalism, as we will see.[55] Grier and Cobbs also provided a template to narrate black anger and black pain, particularly black rage.[56] Indeed, the literature of black psychology and psychiatry, which I take up in later chapters, documented the *erasure* of black feelings and legitimized their political expression in response to white panic about projections about black emotional contagion, which is the subject of Chapter Four.

The rhetorical excavation of emotional content in the political realm has been sparse, perhaps because the field of rhetoric continues to be populated mostly by white scholars who continue to demarcate (racialized) reason from (racialized) feeling. Lucaites and Hariman, for example, argue that "emotions have become rhetoric's major liability."[57] This position is due, in part, to the fact that rhetorical scholars have distrusted emotions in the transmission of political messages because of the close association with contagion. Likewise, some scholars are just uncomfortable trying to describe things that they perceive to be unquantifiable, like emotions. Nevertheless, emotions figure prominently in social movement discourses, particularly as activists and antagonists tussle over the meaning of national symbols. Sara Ahmed remarks, "Histories are bound up with emotions precisely insofar as it is a question of *what sticks*, of what connections are lived as the most intense or intimate, as being closer to the skin."[58] And because feelings about the proximity of bodies are the stuff of politics, it makes sense that the social *movement* of bodies produces political emotions. But as Martha Nussbaum's extensive scholarship on political emotions has argued, liberalism's political feelings "take as their object the nation, the nation's goals, its institutions and leaders, its geography, and one's fellow citizens seen as fellow inhabitants of a common public space. Often ... emotions directed at the geographical features of a nation are ways of channeling emotions toward its key commitments—to inclusiveness, equality, the relief of misery, the end of slavery."[59] In the United States, political commitments require emotions—particularly antiblack feelings—to sustain them and to cultivate initiatives that build public culture.

However, as a movement and as an assemblage of arguments and feelings, Black Power highlighted the multiple ways in which American life has been characterized by antiblack hostility, violence, and death through new emotional repertoires that emphasized the connection between emotions and nationalism, between feelings and justice. Anne Cheng's *The Melancholy of Race* demonstrates how black grief in America is difficult to quantify because it cannot be "definitively spoken in the language of material grievance."[60] Cheng is concerned with experiences and losses that cannot be ameliorated through juridical institutions *precisely because* they are tools of violence and persecution. As a movement forged through the production of discourses that meditate on the inaccessibility of either material comfort or judicial redress, civil rights and Black Power discourses mapped the contours of racial exclusion in every major institution in the country, highlighting how, in Cheng's words, "racialization in America may be said to operate through the institutional process of producing a dominant, standard, white national ideal, which is sustained by the exclusion-yet-retention of racialized others."[61] While activists differed in their approaches to articulating antiblack harm and antiblack exclusion, they had in common a desire to challenge midcentury political hermeneutics.

In navigating the linguistic and material processes of racial exclusion, black activists wrote and spoke about the complex web of feelings they were negotiating during the civil rights era, and their discourses are alive with feelings that often seem opposed but are, in reality, fused together for survival. So, throughout this book, hope emerges alongside melancholy. Pleasure and pain intermingle. Rage and joy coexist. And often, political feelings emerge in diachronic clusters, sometimes indistinct and sometimes in tension with one another as activists and interlocutors navigate the politics of racial time: past, present, and future. Ultimately, black activism is steeped in a distinct temporal vulnerability, marking how black Americans are bound and broken by white power that persistently undermines the production of stable and inclusive identities and institutions. This vulnerability shapes the feelings that black interlocutors accessed, provoked, deployed, augmented, and shaped, meaning that black feelings as political feelings are rhetorical productions for audiences both amenable and hostile that seek to reshape public culture with and against white feelings.

A Note on Method

Using statements from presidents Kennedy, Johnson, and Nixon, as well as administration officials; speeches and writings from movement leaders; manifestos from movement participants; and autobiographies, interviews, and recollections from activists and artists, *Black Feelings* provides a dense analysis of the rhetoricity of feelings that characterize the debates surrounding black citizenship in this period. Because emotional density is a marker of political climate, the book tends to pile on textual evidence to showcase the range of spaces and places where orators echo and amplify feelings as those feelings emerge and decline as frameworks for understanding black reason and black action. As a result, the book is a primer for how to read emotions in the political realm, and it provides a template for other rhetoricians to offer rhetorical histories of political emotions. Documenting the density of feelings demonstrates the ways that these midcentury figures articulated their political feelings for multiple publics in polysemic and complex ways, which is important for me, especially since I am a white scholar.

Black Feelings follows scholars in cultural studies and affect theory by using keywords as a strategy for organizing critical observations, emotional experiences, and appeals that reshaped black political life during this era. Keywords like *hope, despair, trauma, melancholy, optimism, cruel optimism,* and *pessimism* provide catalysts for new interpretive schemas for activists and for scholars of social movements, but they also anchor political moments because of intentional rhetorical choices by politicians and activists. *Black Feelings* asks: How do fear, pain, betrayal, disgust, revulsion, disappointment, resentment, rage, melancholy, grief, love, pessimism, and optimism function to maintain or disrupt power? And how did black activists manage the impasses that marked the movement, from tactical setbacks and political plateaus to governmental disruption? The book also charts how the language of black feelings shaped interventions into the public sphere to agitate white listeners while simultaneously building black in-group solidarity through new appeals to black subjectivity.

Certainly pain is a central occupation of justice movements, and the civil rights movement was no different, particularly as early southern activists trained to bear, and bear witness to, police brutality, imprisonment, and torture. *Black Feelings* asks: How does pain (re)arrange the bodies of the black freedom struggle? One way that pain (re)arranges bodies (both black and white) in the black freedom struggle is through the rhetorical disidentification with whites, white norms and values, and white supremacy. Another way is in the rearrangement of black organizations toward revolutionary embodiment and revolution.[62] Given the centrality of political assassination and murder in the civil rights struggle, *Black Feelings* also asks: How do we understand grief as a motivation of social movements or as a repository of rhetorical action, especially in an era where political assassinations were so common? How does unbearable vulnerability motivate political action or strategic recalibration? How can political reflection and deliberation reorient a movement sagging under the weight of feelings of betrayal and disappointment in allies, particularly white liberals? In the words of Judith Butler, what happens when "certain forms of grief become nationally recognized and amplified, whereas other losses become unthinkable and ungrievable"?[63] The grievability of black lives is particularly salient as #BlackLivesMatter activism continues to focus attention on the publicness of black death in the United States.

While *Black Feelings* explicitly takes up the production and circulation of black emotions, it does not neglect the dynamics that also articulate white feelings, especially those feelings that motivate and frame antiblack public policy, social commentary, and violence. Alongside black feelings, white pain, white rage, white resentment, and white backlash form a pathological economy that shapes racial culture and accentuates the colonial character of race relations in the United States. I suggest that the gradual shift to Black Power prompted white fears about the actual possibility of black equality due to this new vernacular of agitation as well as to civil rights gains, catalyzing white backlash. White anxiety about blackness intensified and, in some cases, overwhelmed the possibility of other kinds of emotional commitments and attachments to black citizens, particularly black men. This is especially true since, as Mbembe argues, "The Black Man is above all a body—gigantic and fantastic—member, organs, color, a smell, flesh, and meat, an extraordinary accumulation of sensations. If he is movement, it can only be a movement of contradiction while stuck in one place. . . . And if it is strength, it can be only the brute strength of the body, excessive, convulsive, spasmodic, and resisting thought: a wave, rage, nervousness all at once, whose domain is to incite disgust, fear, and dread."[64] If the black body is understood *as black* as a way of cultivating and maintaining *white feelings and sensations about power*, and as *male* as a pathological justification for antiblack violence, then we can see antiblack policy as the manifestation of these feelings against black people, but especially against black male leaders exerting political rights. Consequently, *Black Feelings* is concerned with how the black imagination functions as a space of rhetorical invention, to prompt new ways of resisting racial domination through the articulation of black emotions. It suggests that negative emotions like disgust, revulsion, disappointment, betrayal, and pessimism are just as invigorating to political action (if not more so) than positive feelings like hope, joy, and optimism, in part *because* they are keyed to black masculinity.

Discourses that characterize black feelings as infantile or nihilist rely on the assumption that traditional governmental discourses of whiteness are *rational*, and black political fantasies, ideologies, strategies, and tactics are *emotional*; but this formulation denies the power that governmentality has exercised to patrol the border between rationality and feeling via antiblack violence from slavery to the present. As Mbembe has explained, "It is on the basis of a distinction between reason and unreason (passion, fantasy) that late-modern criticism has been able to articulate a certain idea of the political, the community, the subject—or, more fundamentally, of what the good life is all about, how to achieve it, and, in the process, to become a fully moral agent."[65] The manufactured space between reason and feeling is where communitarian and national norms are delineated. For black activist intellectuals, the articulation of the Black Power vernacular as a temporal shift as well as a mood meant an articulation of blackness as a moral location that was able to expose how antiblack violence (particularly in the mundane expressions of state governmentality like the police) shaped the political feelings propelling new forms of black subjectivity.

To hone interpretations of political feelings, I turn to emotional pedagogy, a method of inquiry that acknowledges *learning* is connected to *feeling*. Rather that bowing to or borrowing from the historical dialectic between reason and emotion, emotional pedagogy sees emotion as central to knowledge.[66] To understand what Laura Micciche calls "emotion's rhetoricity," we must examine the ways in which rhetors *teach feelings* as pedagogical exercises in building the heuristics for new epistemologies and ontologies.[67] This responds to "a real need to examine the complex relations among emotion, pedagogy, rhetoric, and violence, and how affective relationships are imbricated with representations of cultural differences."[68] Since emotional pedagogy is part of the process of cultivating, maintaining, and transmitting political emotions, it fundamentally deals with futurist imagining and the possibility of inhabiting, or Being, in the Heideggerian sense, in the future. "Emotion and imagining work together; our imaginings are intensified by our loves and hates, and implicated in our fears and hopes."[69] But in a culture characterized by antiblackness, political feelings are inherently racialized, since both the *presence* and the *absence* of blackness shape whiteness and white privilege. As Warren explains, "The logic of the Political—linear temporality, bio-political futurity, perfection, betterment, and redress—sustains black suffering. Progress and perfection are worked through the pained black body and any recourse to the Political and its discourses of hope will ultimately reproduce the very metaphysical structures of violence that pulverize black being."[70] As such, *Black Feelings* answers Thomas West's call: "Making real critical connections between affect and violence among pedagogy, rhetoric, and emotions is all the more important in light of neoconservative positions that seek to erase difference as a motivation for violence and, as a result, (re)mystify the pedagogic work of violence in policing dominant interests."[71]

Précis of Chapters

Black Feelings proceeds somewhat chronologically to make arguments about how racialized feelings about time, violence, identity, and resistance emerge and recede as a response to the discursive field of American political life in the long sixties. Because racial feelings are recursive—emerging, disappearing, and reemerging over time—I do move back and forth in this period to demonstrate how black feelings circulate in the past, present, and future simultaneously to undermine white notions of linear futurity that are fundamentally antiblack. And because the *Brown v. Board of Education* decision itself demanded that desegregation occur "with all deliberate *speed*"—a vague notion that allowed segregationists to stall segregation efforts—I am interested in rhetorics of time and the language of magnitude as they pertain to racialized political feelings.

Chapter One tackles the resonance of hope as a central theme of 1960s liberalism and contextualizes hope as a (white) futurist impulse shaping public policy as well as radical organizing during the Kennedy years. As a shift away from postwar nuclear anxiety, the Kennedy administration's mobilization of hope reasserted liberalism as a panacea for national feelings about the United States that were grounded in white masculinity. Relying on Arthur Schlesinger Jr.'s writings on hope, as well as the Kennedy administration's articulation of that chronopolitical feeling, I argue that hope and hopefulness help ground racial hierarchies and segregation, making it, in Berlant's words, a cruel attachment. The attachment to hope is cruel because, as I discuss later in the book, it is permanently wedded to fear. Thus are hope and fear co-constitutive, especially in American race politics.

In Chapter Two, I take up King's critiques of white hope and of liberalism to understand how he conceptualized "the beloved community" as a goal in overcoming antiblack feelings through shame appeals and interracial intimacy. I look at the complicated rhetorical production of black hope in a time of American political crisis, particularly as Kennedy stumbled on civil rights early in his administration. While Kennedy's civil rights legacy changed in the wake of his famous address in June 1963 and after his assassination prompted passage of the Civil Rights Act of 1964, nonetheless the racial struggle of his presidency hinged on a chronopolitics that was constantly in flux as black leaders fought white political stasis. Thus did King both use the (white) rhetorical tropes of hope popularized by Kennedy and simultaneously criticize their reliance on white political norms as the crisis of hope emerged in 1963.

Chapter Three examines the "damage thesis" that continues to circulate in racial discourses and helps to propel black rage. This chapter looks at Malcolm X's rhetorical career to understand how he used negative feelings to teach black listeners new modes of being and reason that helped to shape Black Power before and after his assassination in 1965. Malcolm's pedagogy of racial contempt was scaffolded on new black psychology and psychiatry, especially as it emerged in Harlem, and it offered what I am calling an "American Negritude" that reinforced African psychologists, academics, and diplomats who offered a new posture of blackness critical of subservience and accommodationism. Malcolm's pedagogy of rage and contempt was often intentionally misread as hate by white pundits to justify his containment and repression, and it formed the backbone of what we now call Afro- or black pessimism as it lampooned white liberals and the false promises and inherent racism of contemporary liberalism.

The assassination of Malcolm X created a leadership vacuum to the left of King, and Chapter Four charts the proto–Black Power philosophies and feelings that emerged from the urban rebellions that shaped American public life from 1964 to 1968 as hopelessness replaced hope in American public life. While the rebellions themselves were an embodied language of disappointment, frustration, and despair, the language of explosiveness characterized assessments about the riots from black and white interlocutors. But riots complicated liberalism's racial politics by impugning the exceptionalism that mystified antiblack violence as a permanent feature of American life. Examining the language of riots as explosions in the writings of activists, pundits, and government officials, I discuss the ways in which white assessments of urban rebellion pathologized black mass politics to discredit structural analyses of power.

Chapter Five meditates on the assassination of Martin Luther King in 1968 to understand how black pessimism and melancholy came to define the Black Power era. The recollections and memories of his assassination and funeral pronounced the death of nonviolence and the movement, foreclosing political feelings anchored to white feelings, white liberalism, and integration. With the death of King, his beloved community receded, and Black Power displaced it as a space for a radical disavowal of moral suasion and an embrace of revolutionary politics because King's death exposed hope as a dangerous attachment and nonviolence as a form of cruel optimism.

In the final case study in Chapter Six, I examine how the absence of hope and the collapse into black pessimism were driven by the exposure of white liberalism's collaborations with antiblack political rhetoric through the language of "law and order," through the expansion of the FBI's harassment and surveillance of Black Power activists, and through the expansion of mass incarceration. Using Huey Newton's writings, I explore the meme of revolutionary suicide as a repository of feelings about black Being in a colonial state where blacks have been denied both thinking and feeling as avenues of expression. Revolutionary suicide is an attempt to reconcile assassination and repression with possibilities for black agency, but it demonstrates how little room black activists had to politically maneuver by 1971 as the nation consolidated racial feelings around law-and-order politics and the new conservatism.

In the book's conclusion, I linger on the significance of racialized feelings of hope and hopelessness in the age of Obama to underscore how hope mobilized the Obama coalition while foreclosing it as an accessible political emotion in an era of massive police brutality, continued mass incarceration, and increasing antiblack state violence in the United States and abroad. Taking up Eric King Watts's notion of the "postracial fantasy," I chart how black feelings have shifted since the nation elected its first biracial/black president to demonstrate similarities and differences in the circulation of black feelings. I demonstrate the recursivity of political emotions surrounding racial liberalism to underscore how futurity, chronopolitics, political mobilization, and co-optation continue to function as the arguments about time continue to obscure discourses of freedom and about how they undermine substantial critiques of racial liberalism. In charting the articulation of hope by Obama, I'm also interested in the concomitant emergence of scholarly defenses of black nihilism in the wake of the 2012 killing of Trayvon Martin and the dozens of high-profile killings of unarmed black youths by police after George Zimmerman's acquittal of Martin's death.

In many ways, *Black Feelings* is an exploration of the dialectic of hope and fatalism in the American tradition as it takes up the very real material prohibitions that undermine racial equality through the promotion of antiblack public policy. Thus does *Black Feelings* expose the hope of democratic optimism to be both racialized and deeply ironic as a political discourse, given that its optimism is especially predicated on black suffering. Each of these case studies contributes to a robust assessment of the political feelings of the 1960s to understand how black feelings shaped the futurism of the milieu. In this way, the book offers a series of texts that provide what Daniel Innerarity has called "futurologies."[72] In choosing these moments where rhetorical feelings emerge, control, or conceal, my aim is to demonstrate how feelings mark the appearance and disappearance of futurist imaginaries as they accompany and drive political resistance to antiblack state power. For the black rhetors at midcentury, the language of feelings helped them to articulate the choice between movement and stasis in ways that mobilized new political futures. Responsibly managing capital and its deployment in the present and very near future hardly ameliorates the kind of suffering that prompts social movements like the black freedom struggle, and this is precisely why time is such an important rhetorical battleground. Black activists struggled over whether to wait or to push for a more radical futurism that saw the struggles over black life and death as necessitating radical speech acts that reoriented auditors toward new futurist possibilities and new subjectivities. In fact, white arguments about waiting serve to obscure arguments about freedom and mobilize a language of neutrality to recuperate liberalism against racial equality. These processes, both political and rhetorical, are exactly where the limits of liberalism are contested and where meaning is orchestrated through political feelings that are both coterminous and in tension.

BLACK FEELINGS

Chapter One

POSTWAR FEELINGS
Beyond Hope

From Birmingham to Watts, Detroit to Memphis, the 1960s had no shortage of domestic tumult. But the nation's political upheaval was produced, in part, by competing feelings that defined the era. As the Eisenhower administration receded (along with postwar tension and euphoria) and gave way to the youth and optimism of the Kennedy administration, the cultural politics of the nation shifted. John F. Kennedy's New Frontier signaled changes in America's identity and role in the world as a Cold War superpower. In his acceptance speech at the 1960 Democratic National Convention, Kennedy opined: "We stand today on the edge of a New Frontier—the frontier of the 1960s, the frontier of unknown opportunities and perils, the frontier of unfilled hopes and unfilled threats. . . . Beyond that frontier are uncharted areas of science and space, unsolved problems of peace and war, unconquered problems of ignorance and prejudice, unanswered questions of poverty and surplus."[1] Kennedy's New Frontier was an innovative progressivist program that reoriented postwar American identity away from nuclear anxiety and toward social and economic welfare.[2] Among New Frontier legislation, Kennedy included bills to raise the minimum wage, decrease the age for Social Security eligibility, introduce fair housing, augment highway funds, introduce food stamps, expand farm subsidies, safeguard civil rights, encourage youth civic participation, and fund space exploration, reflecting "Kennedy's affinity for heroic causes."[3]

Kennedy's fresh, new American political vision reshaped national expectations beyond the cloud of war.[4] Central to this refashioning of the American imaginary was the deployment of a constellation of political feelings about

Kennedy himself and Camelot (as his administration came to be known) that reinforced optimistic nationalism at the nadir of atomic anxiety. With Frank Sinatra crooning about Kennedy's "High Hopes" during the campaign and a bevy of new, young politicos entering the White House after the election, hope reigned supreme as the new feeling of American politics. In fact, the word "most commonly associated with Kennedy's leadership was hope."[5] Crafting the White House statements projecting this new mood was Arthur Schlesinger Jr., special assistant to President Kennedy, who occupied a singular space as the resident intellectual in the Kennedy administration. Schlesinger privately influenced the president's articulation of policy, but publicly his essays framed the emotional purpose of the administration as a departure from the austerity of the 1950s. Kennedy's speeches captured a deep cultural longing for a shift in public feelings, and they exhibited an "existential quality, the sense that he was in some way beyond conventional politics, that he could touch emotions and hopes thwarted by the bland and mechanized society."[6] And Schlesinger's unrestrained public praise of Kennedy crafted a narrative of the man and the administration that was unflinchingly positive, rooted deeply in a distinctly American optimism, and central to the administration's utopian longings.[7] Schlesinger pronounced Kennedy "the first President since Franklin Roosevelt who had anything to say to men and women under the age of twenty-five, perhaps the only President with whom youth could thoroughly identify itself—and this at a time when there were more young people both in the population and in the colleges than ever before."[8] As Schlesinger notes, by 1966 (the birth of Black Power), more than *half* of the nation's population was under the age of twenty-five.[9]

The baby boomer generation would come to redefine politics by challenging the Silent Generation's passivity about political participation. Schlesinger wrote, "We no longer suppose that our national salvation depends on stopping history in its tracks and freezing the world in its present mold. Our national leadership is young, vigorous, intelligent, civilized, and experimental."[10] Preaching a gospel of innovation, idealism, pragmatism, irreverence, and skepticism, Schlesinger's writings were critical of millennialism, self-congratulation, self-righteousness, hyperindividualism, and the ideologues of the past. Schlesinger's prose helped set the emotional tone for the administration as a radical and progressive departure from the past and framed Kennedy as youthful and vigorous, which explains the appeal of "Camelot" to the liberal intelligentsia.

As Schlesinger characterized the youth politics of the administration, he noted the role that *emotions* played in the protracted generational struggle within liberalism: "Having seized power themselves from a resentful former generation, the Kennedys understood the emotions of the young crowding into a capricious and incomprehensible society."[11] The Kennedy administration created the framing and the conditions for the youth revolution that would crescendo with organizations like the Student Nonviolent Coordinating Committee (SNCC), the Black Panther Party (BPP), the Young Lords, and Students for a Democratic Society (SDS). This emphasis on the potential of America's untapped *youth* propelled students to sit in, be jailed, march, and protest to promote progressive values on issues ranging from civil rights to the war in Vietnam. In his inaugural address, Kennedy delivered the line that would define this generation: "And so, my fellow Americans: Ask not what your country can do for you—ask what you can do for your country."[12] Kennedy's call to service evoked political feelings about the citizen's civic duty to the nation and evoked a sense of *responsibility* for cultivating interdependent futures, particularly abroad. Particularly for young people, the call to service aroused fidelity to a vision of nationhood firmly rooted in futurity and notions of technological progress. Kennedy's language articulated demands of the future on the present and prioritized futurist accountability for young people in a way that had not been part of the rhetorical corpus of the presidency before.

Kennedy's focus on the nation's youth helped to propel young people into politics in novel ways, leading to the creation of the Peace Corps, Youth Conservation Corps, the Mobilization for Youth programs, and Volunteers in Service to America (VISTA). The New Frontier was, at least in part, driven by an emotional appeal to young people to reorient themselves toward a progressive vision of international political participation in the aftermath of McCarthyism. While the notion of shared sacrifice was certainly promoted during the war years, Kennedy's articulation of collective struggle centered youth through an emotional lens that encouraged them to shape the future as political agents. Given Kennedy's own youth, the potential existed for this strategy to backfire, but as his presidential campaign closed, Kennedy championed the idea as an antidote to nuclear anxiety and political stagnation.[13] Throughout his administration, public service formed the cornerstone of his managerial liberalism as he encouraged the nation's youth toward political action.

While it makes sense that New Frontier programs would activate the political feelings of white Americans who saw Kennedy as a role model and leader, the mobilization of political hope spilled out beyond white communities, in part because the generational call to service was colorblind. As BPP minister of information Eldridge Cleaver recalled, "The accent on youth that had been key to the Kennedy Administration helped to define youth as a relevant political condition that was not to be despised—and that could be used."[14]

Cleaver astutely describes Kennedy's emphasis on youth culture as one that drove tremendous numbers of young people to embrace new modes of political engagement. Certainly this was true of the black freedom struggle, but over the course of the decade, black youth involvement was demonized, in ways that were distinct from disdain for the New Left. Kennedy's colorblind hope propelled black and white youth to engage with political futurity, even if it was flawed and incomplete.

This chapter discusses the Kennedy administration's emotional repertoire since it set the tone for youth dissent for the decade. Here I examine the co-constitutive nature of hope and despair in the postwar period to understand how these competing political feelings expressed generational and racialized disputes about the nature of the polis, the uses and abuses of power, the role of political institutions in guaranteeing social and political equality, and the role of dissent as an emotional sphere of public discourse. My guiding texts on discourses of hope include Kennedy's speeches, Schlesinger's writings on Kennedy, and Norman Mailer's responses. While talking about white feelings first in a book titled *Black Feelings* may seem odd, I suggest that much of the black struggle in the United States has been aimed at producing new political feelings that worked both in tandem with and against feelings being culti-vated by the white establishment. In this case, "hope" was not a background feeling or an incidental emotion. Instead it was what Agnes Heller has called "an orientational feeling" that is a priori and originates from institutions that want it to undergird cognitive processes.[15] Hope reoriented Americans toward a different kind of racialized chronopolitics regarding their personal commitments, but also toward the way the administration wanted them to think about the nation's futurity, since Kennedy himself was asking for a dif-ferent kind of relationality to citizenship and problem solving.

Although I return to these themes throughout the book—especially in the conclusion, where I discuss President Obama's discourses of exception-alism and the birth of black nihilist scholarship—*Black Feelings* as a whole grapples with how hope is temporalized and racialized in political dis-courses that shape the materiality of American life as hope structures social movements and reconfigures power. But when the political future is always already foreclosed through antiblack structural violence, hope is a cruel attachment for black people and other people of color rather than a feeling that can fully emancipate, the way, say, Paul Ricoeur describes.[16] Thus the following chapters aim to understand how feelings about civil rights and black activism "fit together" in political systems where rhetors, white and black, sought to label, define, and make social sense out of new assemblages of political emotions.[17]

Pedagogies of Feeling: Producing Postwar Hope

The 1960s were a swirl of many political emotions, but at the beginning of the decade, no emotion was more intentionally deployed by the state than hope. Why hope? As Casey Nelson Blake has noted, "Settlement houses, progressive schools, social-gospel churches, and cross-class advocacy groups once provided an extraordinary infrastructure for Progressive politics. Today's pragmatists have almost nothing comparable to support their political and intellectual activity. No wonder then that the word 'hope' figures so prominently in their writing. Even as it recalls the social-gospel roots of Progressivism, the recourse to 'hope' reveals the distance traveled since that distant era of confident reform."[18] Absent these spaces for the cultivation of progressive politics, hope became a repository of *longing* in the second half of the twentieth century because it focused on the futurity of political action and because the confidence of New Deal progressivism had faded. Hope in the 1960s signaled a semantic shift in political language, demarcating a microcohort for whom feelings defined their youth in explicitly political terms. Because orientational feelings like hope create expectations, they are particularly useful in organizing new political moments.

As a corollary of democratic practice, political hope is an *active* emotional disposition that undercuts hopelessness through action and requires a certain level of engagement: thinking, speaking, dreaming, doing. Citizens "engage in politics because they hope for improvement in their lives, for cooperative relations with others, and for stable and just social structures in which to live."[19] In Paulo Freire's estimation, "Hope is an ontological need," one that exists in opposition to fatalism.[20] Freire makes the case for operationalizing and mobilizing political hope, particularly in the face of a crisis of feeling or an age of anxiety. In their repetition of feeling, Kennedy administration officials demonstrated how the performance of hope, as Gilles Deleuze has written, is certainly a "repetition of the category of the future."[21]

The mobilization of hope was particularly salient for the Kennedy administration, which, as Ted Windt reminds us, was fundamentally "a *crisis presidency*" that needed to manage the fallout from overexposure to urgent emergencies.[22] So the persistence of hope as an affective frame is interesting given how frequently Kennedy himself (or his surrogates like Schlesinger or speechwriter Ted Sorensen) characterized political encounters *as crises*. Windt notes that Sorensen accounts for no less than fifteen crises in just the first eight months of the administration, *with the exception of civil rights*. Kennedy spoke infrequently of civil rights, and when he did, Windt explains that he "strove to *defuse* the powerful emotions" aroused by desegregation.[23]

Nonetheless hope and crisis were co-constitutive discourses that shaped an intense discursive period as the Cold War unfolded. Stan van Hooft makes the case that "political hope is motivated by felt needs or some degree of anxiety or concern as opposed to fantasy or desire," and this dynamic encompasses much of the administration's rhetoric, suggesting that hope was understood as a curative for anxiety or at least a political feeling that would help to shore up political support in a political moment characterized by extreme uncertainty.[24]

Resisting what Schlesinger called the "conformism and homogenization" of the 1950s,[25] the emotional field of the Kennedy administration addressed the fears and anxieties of the postwar milieu and harnessed the economic boom that Tom Kemp has called the "climax of capitalism," by proposing new ways of imagining American political possibility.[26] These administration discourses were pedagogical exercises in political hope, teaching Americans how to think about their futures in soaring language that sought to inspire populism. While hope here retains a bit of its religious connotation, it is firmly secured in the political arena. As Ricoeur writes, this sense of "hope, in spite of the secular character that it shares with utopia, is intended to pro-vide a clear alternative to utopia."[27] While I take up this point in Chapter Five, Ricoeur delineates between hope and utopia in the political idiom:

> Whereas utopia tends to elude the constraints of efficient and durable action and the hard paradoxes of institution, authority, sovereignty, law and coercion, hope is addressed to the very possibility of dealing responsibly with these constraints and paradoxes. Religious hope and utopia seem to share a common presupposition, namely that a complete resolution of historical contradictions is possible above or beyond history. The politics of hope relies on the opposite presupposition, i.e., the recognition of the ultimate incompleteness of discourse and action.[28]

The incompleteness of both political discourse and action is managed, in part, by political emotions like hope, which help to institutionalize politi-cal feelings as a way of making any political change *gradual and stable*. As a specific political emotion and practical alternative to utopia, hope represents the possibility of managing political conflict through historical debate (rather than, say, faith). Ricoeur underscores how "hope is not a statement but an interpretation" of possible solutions and outcomes.[29] "Applied specifically to political action, hope implies the confidence that a *responsible* political action can be conducted *in spite of* the perversions, the dangers, and the paradoxes of political action, and as a plausible alternative to some other interpretations which compete with hope on the basis of the same recognition of the incom-pleteness of political action."[30] Thus does political hope function to short-circuit radical social change in the name of incrementalism. Hope habituates a preference for gradual change, demonstrating its relationship to futurity in terms of pace and scope.

On the one hand, Kennedy's use of hope as an emotional and political frame was prefigured by Eisenhower's attack on the New Englander's youth and inexperience in a world defined by atomic insecurity. However, given its religious connotations, hope also resonated with Catholics who supported Kennedy's narrow win. Still, the use of hope as an emotional frame had origins before his presidential campaign. Consider Kennedy's speech nominating Adlai Stevenson at the 1956 Democratic National Convention: "The time is ripe. The hour has struck. The man is here; and he is ready. Let the word go forth [a phrase that would reappear in his inaugural address] that we have fulfilled our responsibility to the nation."[31] The emphasis here on new beginnings demonstrates the temporality of hope as a construct, which Kennedy develops in later speeches and which amplifies the heroic frame that Kennedy honed in his Pulitzer Prize–winning book *Profiles in Courage* (1956). For example, when he accepted his party's nomination in 1960, Kennedy introduced the New Frontier: "It is time for a new generation of leadership—new men to cope with new problems and new opportunities. . . . We stand today on the edge of a New Frontier—the frontier of the 1960s—a frontier of unknown opportunities and perils—a frontier of unfulfilled hopes and threats."[32] This call for new men signaled a generational shift in power that sought to reimagine US leadership in the mold of young, vigorous masculinity rather than the tired and worn masculinity of earlier generations.[33] But it also centered hope as a civic virtue delivered by this new brand of republican man.

Kennedy himself articulated this new emotional frame for politics in many speeches, referring to it on the stump as well as in the White House. On the campaign trail, for example, in Bangor, Maine, Kennedy elaborated on his conception of presidential leadership: "The President of the United States represents not only the Democrats of this country, he represents all of the people around the world who want to live in freedom, who look to us for hope and leadership."[34] Kennedy himself became the embodied repository for hope as a political emotion mobilizing the boomer generation, but he also saw himself as an international symbol of hope. Just as in his inaugural address, Kennedy promoted political service to the nation and the world, but he also reflected on the massive political transformations happening across the globe after the war. Acknowledging the emergent postcolonial movements worldwide, Kennedy launched the Alliance for Progress with these words: "To our sister republics south of the border, we offer a special pledge—to convert our good words into good deeds—in a new alliance for progress—to assist free men and free governments in casting off the chains of poverty. But this peaceful revolution of hope cannot become the prey of hostile powers."[35] Although Kennedy's military responses to anticolonial movements in the hemisphere arguably diverged from this sentiment, it demonstrates how hope directed the American policy of constructive engagement through Kennedy's Alliance for Progress, indicating that *progress* is the rhetorical frame for political hope.

Thus does hope have a temporality (preference for the present and future aimed against the past), as well as a geography (of or against colonialism or empire even when in the *service* of empire), extending the possibility of political futurity. Political hope demonstrates "its indebtedness to the past, its opportunity in the present, and its supercession in the future."[36] In this way, "The temporality of hope is a time 'not-yet-realized,' a future tense unmoored from present-tense justifications and pragmatist evidence, [and] the politics of hope cleverly shields its 'solutions' from critiques of impossibility or repetition."[37] The "not-yet" and "could-be" of political hope mystifies solutions for large-scale structural inequalities like poverty or white supremacy but promises a freedom from anxiety that can galvanize stasis. Political hope holds out for a point in the future, where conditions will be more ripe, while also pointing to the exceptionalism of hope's interlocutors as symbols of progress. Political hope is self-aggrandizing as all the while it holds within it the fact of impossibility.

Hope Is Hip

Given the narrowness of the 1960 election and the threat of nuclear war (one that only increased during Kennedy's presidency), hope was a frame shaped in the aftermath of war and success. But as Ricoeur notes, hope "is the expectation that mediation between the rulers and the ruled *can* still be managed, that the situations of hegemony and of subordination are not necessarily incompatible with mutual recognition between the rulers and the ruled."[38] Consequently hope makes risky political action tolerable because it "implies that man may be the *mediator* required by the definition of freedom as a relational freedom."[39] As the foregoing evidence suggests, Kennedy certainly saw himself as the ideal mediator. However, as both Ricoeur and Bernard Dauenhauer suggest, hope as a political emotion has many interpretive possibilities, "ranging from active pessimism to tragic optimism."[40] It is precisely this range of interpretation that concerns this book's argumentative arc.

For their part, Kennedy administration officials articulated hope as an emotional and rhetorical arc that functioned as an assemblage of "dreams, the whimsical, longing, failure, inclusions and exclusions."[41] Their expressions of hope positioned Kennedy and the nation's youth as the interlocutors of a new political vocabulary. And Kennedy himself was a fount of this language, as Schlesinger writes:

> His "coolness" was itself a new frontier. It meant freedom from the stereotyped responses of the past. It promised the deliverance of American idealism, buried deep in the national character but imprisoned by the knowingness and calculation of America in the fifties. It held out to the young the possibility that they could become more than satisfied stockholders in a satisfied nation. It offered hope for a nation drowning in its own passivity—passive because it had come to accept the theory of its own impotence.[42]

Schlesinger described Kennedy as a magical man, whose cool, virile powers grew from the emotions that he activated and the language of investment that he used. Schlesinger also depicts hope as an emotional sword for a new model of heroic leadership and political redemption. Kennedy became the archetype for this paradigm, though Schlesinger acknowledges ambivalence in the "great man" model, writing that "the common man has always regarded the great man with mixed feelings—resentment as well as admiration, hatred as well as love."[43] The assertion of hope in this moment, then, exposed how language, in Foucault's words, "speaks only from something essential that is lacking," in this case, a vision for a new mode of (white masculine) belonging and power.[44] Kennedy's virile (white) masculinity was the centerpiece of the New Frontier. Where Kennedy had "stood as a symbol of male regeneration" during the campaign, his presidency sought "to actualize this impulse."[45] Offering himself as an antidote to the "masculinity crisis" that had paralyzed the country in the 1950s, Kennedy provided a vigorous, assertive, futurist image of man that was supposed to lift middle-class American men out of their lethargy and malaise.[46]

With the birth of television, Kennedy's movie star cool challenged the bland, industrial landscape of postwar America. Kennedy "had a beautiful wife, and a heroic military past; he projected an aesthetic detachment that combined elements of noir cool, jazz cool, and existential cool," and "his victory over the well-meaning intellectual Adlai Stevenson for the nomination—and then over the uncool Richard Nixon—marked a sea change at the symbolic level."[47] These kinds of descriptions articulated Kennedy as the anti-Eisenhower and anti-Nixon, whose bodily performance of cool disrupted white masculinity in a way that marked significant generational differences. Norman Mailer described Kennedy through an extended contrast with Eisenhower: "Eisenhower has been the anti-Hero, the regulator. Nations do not necessarily and

inevitably seek for heroes. In periods of dull anxiety, one is more likely to look
for security than a dramatic confrontation, and Eisenhower could stand as a
hero only for that large number of Americans who were most proud of their
lack of imagination."[48] Mailer continues by describing "the incredible dullness
wreaked upon the American landscape in Eisenhower's eight years," during
which America saw "the triumph of the corporation":

> A tasteless, sexless, odorless sanctity in architecture, manners, modes, styles has
> been the result. Eisenhower embodied half the needs of the nation, the needs
> of the timid, the petrified, the sanctimonious, and the sluggish. What was even
> worse, he did not divide the nation as a hero might (with a dramatic dialogue as
> the result); he merely excluded one part of the nation from the other. The result
> was an alienation of the best minds and bravest impulses from the faltering his-
> tory which was made. America's need in those years was to take an existential
> turn, to walk into the nightmare, to face into that terrible logic of history which
> demanded that the country and its people must become more extraordinary
> and more adventurous, or else perish, since the only alternative was to offer a
> false security in the power and the panacea of organized religion, family, and the
> F.B.I., a totalitarianization of the psyche by the stultifying techniques of the mass
> media which would seep into everyone's most private associations and so leave
> the country powerless against the Russians even if the denouement were to take
> fifty years, for in a competition between totalitarianisms the first maxim of the
> prizefight manager would doubtless apply: "Hungry fighters win fights."[49]

This scathing critique of Eisenhower and the early Cold War years demonstrates the brand of white masculinity that helped define Kennedy's presidency in opposition to the war years. Mailer's comments on the emotional
attachments to Kennedy highlight a redemption narrative, where Americans longed for a new (white and male) futurism that took them beyond the
survivalism of the Great Depression, the horrors and triumphs of the war,
and far away from the conformity of the postwar golden age. Nelson George
described this kind of white, masculine vision (found most disturbingly in
Mailer's 1957 essay "The White Negro") as a fetishizing of whiteness and masculinity that functions "as a strange, often unintentional rape of black ideas
and styles."[50]

While the United States needed a fresh framework for reengaging with
nationalism, hope was universal enough as a liberal feeling to cement Camelot
as a space for both presentism and futurist longing, but it also fossilized white
masculinity in the form of Kennedy cool, providing an emotional rationale
for the rejection of blackness as an antidote to postwar stagnation in public

life. Racialized masculine discourses, then, were fashioned with and against Kennedy's prototype, suggesting that the New Frontier was a demarcation of gender performance as much as it was of policy. As a disciplinary technology, then, Kennedy's white masculine cool functioned as a discursive space through which to fashion the aesthetics and politics of masculinity. It also served as a visual boundary for preferable masculinity, setting Kennedy up as a foil for Black Power aesthetics under Johnson.

Kennedy and Black Hope

While it is easy to talk in generalities about Kennedy's hope as a new paradigm of political engagement, it is also true that Kennedy's identity politics began a brief period of optimism for black Americans. Kennedy's 1960 intervention in Martin Luther King Jr.'s arrest with fifty-two other black protesters at a sit-in demonstration in Albany, Georgia, created space for black hope. Though King was sentenced to four months' hard labor, Kennedy halted his campaign to call Coretta Scott King to express his concern. The following day, he called the judge to object to King's sentence while privately pressuring Georgia governor Ernest Vandiver to release King. In *The Making of a President*, Theodore H. White underscored how Kennedy's intervention in Albany shifted black perceptions of his presidential ambitions. White describes the moment thus: "In the Negro community the Kennedy intervention rang like a carillon."[51] White's description of black sentiments regarding Kennedy's advocacy for King are *sonic*, suggesting that the *sound* of this feeling was both municipal and religious, signaling how Kennedy's intervention operated on several emotional registers simultaneously. In his account of the moment, Steven Levingston has written eloquently about Kennedy's "high wire act": balancing "the support of racist politicians against a civic obligation to fight for racial justice," where the tension between these two impulses "drove the politician to cozy up to Southern bigots, equivocate on civil rights, and then scramble to justify, or deny, his actions to the black community."[52] This was particularly true after King shrewdly refused to endorse Kennedy in the 1960 election, despite protestations from his own father, who saw Kennedy's action in Albany as one that needed repayment. Nonetheless the black press endorsed Kennedy, and in spite of his brother Bobby's resistance to any action that would alienate southern Democrats, especially in the election, the campaign courted the black vote. Despite Kennedy's inaction on issuing an executive order to end housing discrimination "with one stroke of a pen," King met with Kennedy at the White House and asked him to sign a Second

Emancipation Proclamation to end institutional segregation in every walk of American life.[53]

Although he had negotiated civil rights demands with King for three years, Kennedy's major foray into the rhetoric of civil rights did not occur until his major address on June 11, 1963, after the dramatic confrontation between his administration and Governor George Wallace over the desegregation of the University of Alabama. It preceded his introduction of civil rights legislation that was arguably weaker than even Eisenhower's 1957 civil rights bill. The administration fought any efforts to strengthen the bill and demonstrated that Kennedy's vocal support for civil rights was not matched by executive action until events pushed him to intervene. This was hardly surprising, since the administration (like its predecessor) refused to go to court in school cases. The US Commission on Civil Rights (USCCR) reported in 1963 that the Department of Justice entered only *one* school desegregation case.[54] Additionally, Kennedy refused to support legislation, advanced by northerners in Congress, to require districts to develop plans for "first-step" compliance with *Brown.* "In so doing, he helped pave the way for a controversial initiative linking federal financial aid to a district's progress on desegregation."[55] Because of the volatility of school desegregation, particularly among southern Democrats, "Kennedy and Johnson never identified themselves with the issue. Only under external pressure did they back greater statutory authority for the executive branch to enforce *Brown.* Even afterward, their hesitancy did not vanish; Title VI trapped liberal policymakers into making a choice, between either desegregating schools or funding education, that many of them wished not to make."[56] I argue that JFK was never a figure of hope for black folks politically, even though he was rhetorically. His public support for civil rights, despite lacking a substantive executive record (especially on school desegregation), helped LBJ cement Kennedy in public memory as a civil rights leader. But a closer examination of the policy initiatives, or lack thereof, demonstrates that black hope in Kennedy as a policy figure was misplaced.

Kennedy's 1963 civil rights address offered his first public response to the desegregation of higher education, and it is arguably the most important presidential discourse on race since Lincoln's Emancipation Proclamation. Still, although the speech functions in the same emotional register as hope, it notably does *not* invoke hope. Kennedy implores:

> It ought to be possible for American consumers of any color to receive equal service in places of public accommodation, such as hotels and restaurants and theaters and retail stores, without being forced to resort to demonstrations in the

street, and it ought to be possible for American citizens of any color to register to vote in a free election without interference or fear of reprisal.

It ought to be possible, in short, for every American to enjoy the privileges of being American without regard to his race or his color. In short, every American ought to have the right to be treated as he would wish to be treated, as one would wish his children to be treated. But this is not the case.

The speech's crescendo points to a *lack of hope* in the nation's ability to provide equal citizenship for black citizens. Kennedy's repetition of the phrase "It ought to be possible" is important because he is speaking of the possibility of racial equality that is already always foreclosed because of white supremacy, southern white Democrats, and the spatial density and economic incentives of segregation. Nonetheless, "ought" functions simultaneously as a call to future moral responsibility and as a recrimination about present action while also *demonstrating the impossibility of desegregation*. While Kennedy insists that the time has arrived to fulfill this promise, his use of "ought" invites shame of those *outside the administration* for their role in preventing inequality. "Ought" signals a civic obligation, linking it to the hope of the New Frontier, but that obligation does not acknowledge the administration's own role in actively undermining the civil rights movement. Universalizing the issue by resisting the urge to characterize civil rights as a southern issue helps to distribute the responsibility more equitably across the country, but it also speaks to a broader understanding of what it means to fulfill the promises of liberal democracy. Kennedy wags his finger at conservatives and southern Democrats for preventing equality. This is augmented, however, by where Kennedy thinks the questions of civic equality should be debated. He says, "It is better to settle these matters in the courts than on the streets, and new laws are needed at every level, but law alone cannot make men see right." Kennedy's frustration with the situation in Alabama is palpable, but the speech does not indulge in sweeping optimism precisely because there is no political will to solve the problem. Instead his major civil rights address points to the limitations of democratic liberalism in transforming attitudes and beliefs. As Wendy Brown writes, "The optimism of the radical social democratic vision is fueled by that dimension of liberalism which presumes social and political forms to have relative autonomy from economic ones, to be that which can be tinkered with independently of developments in the forces of capitalism."[57] Somehow law should be able to end racial hierarchies despite the financial architecture of antiblackness and the administration's own unwillingness to use the courts to intervene in desegregation efforts.

While the Kennedy administration pushed hope as a new national sentiment to redefine citizenship and nationalism on every issue *except* civil rights, we might ask: What happens when hope fractures? When there is not enough hope to go around? What happens when the racial politics of hope expose the fissures in the liberal notion of universal citizenship? Ghassan Hage suggests that when not enough hope exists to generate inclusive civic participation, the result is the circulation of paranoid nationalism.[58] Paranoid nationalism describes white impulses to restore confidence in government officials through an emotional field steeped in worrying. "It is an essentially narcissistic response, based in the worrier's sense that the nation cannot protect them from the object of their fears."[59] This is particularly compelling in time of political crisis (real or perceived) because it highlights the contingencies of national belonging. In other words, paranoid nationalism uses political feelings of anxiety and concern to move people in support of or against national policies by scapegoating others. The rhetorical practice is marked by a rhetoric of scarcity and the feeling of political precarity. Values are under attack. The threat is everywhere. No one is safe. However, as a field of political emotions, paranoid nationalism obscures how nations facilitate precarity for both citizens and noncitizens, for ideal citizens and for those whom the nation attempts to exclude formally or informally. In promoting a collective worrying, paranoid nationalism makes it difficult to create and sustain identifications based on racial solidarity, since it is precisely that kind of racial solidarity that is described as destructive to whiteness and conventional articulations of nationalism. Considering that Kennedy's messages of hope were ubiquitous in every discourse except civil rights and that the administration was also characterized by crisis talk about everything from the Berlin Wall to the Bay of Pigs to the Cuban Missile Crisis (the latter, of course, being the closest the United States has come to nuclear war), it does seem possible that the language of hope is ironic, given the contemporary political events that were undermining hope for so many Americans as well as for citizens outside the United States. While I return to the irony of hope in the book's conclusion, it bears repeating that hope contains its own impossibility, the tonality of which is apparent in Kennedy's civil rights address.

The End of Hope: The Kennedy Assassination

Although Martin Luther King's assassination in 1968 marked what Todd Gitlin, former president of the Students for a Democratic Society, called "the last black hope" (I take up this event in detail in Chapter Five), hope circulated as a distinct political commitment even as the nation slid into Vietnam and found itself mired in a battle about racial equality. Through the botched job at the Bay of Pigs, through the construction of the Berlin Wall, and through the Cuban Missile Crisis, the administration continued to articulate hope as a political vector, at least until Kennedy's assassination on November 22, 1963. John Kennedy was the youngest man elected president and the youngest killed in office, so it "makes perfect sense that most Americans told pollsters in the wake of November 22 that they were grieving as though they had lost a member of their own family."[60] Theologian James W. Douglass has written elegantly about the relationship between hope and Kennedy's assassination, particularly in posterity. Douglass argues that "Kennedy's murder can be a profound source of hope to us all."[61] He adds, "In a time when the Cold War has given way to a war on terror, hope comes from walking through the darkness of our history. We can find hope from that point of total denial and darkness where we don't want to go. Hope comes from confronting the unspeakable truth of the assassination of President Kennedy."[62] Douglass's perspective highlights how the confrontation with the president's death transformed hope and provided a test for America to confront its political violence when targeting white liberals.

Gitlin, on the other hand, writes that Kennedy's assassination marked the death of liberal hope. He discusses the competing emotions that percolated after the president's death:

> Fatalism flourished; the power of the will to prod history was blunted. One common conclusion was that even the steadiest of institutions, the august presidency, was fragile indeed. . . . From the national mélange of rational optimism and free-floating paranoia, and in the face of widely cited mysteries drifting foglike from cracks in the official accounts of the assassination, there emerged conspiracy theories galore.[63]

The commingling of surging optimism and trenchant paranoia, the fragility of the moment as a political watershed, and the concern about the stability of political institutions rendered the political hope of Camelot ironic. Gitlin continues: "The educated young felt his call, projected their ideals onto him. His murder was felt as the implosion of plenitude, the tragedy of innocence. From the zeitgeist fantasy that everything was possible, it wasn't hard to flip over and conclude that nothing was."[64] In Gitlin's estimation, forged from hindsight, "panic, rancor, [and] recrimination" created "a situation tailor-made for the Republican politics of racial resentment."[65]

But black leaders across the country felt Kennedy's loss acutely. Before Kennedy's assassination, the sit-in movement, the Freedom Rides, and James Meredith's desegregation of the University of Mississippi tested the nation's commitment to desegregation and prompted federal commitment to black freedom in small but significant ways as pressure mounted for the Kennedy White House to take a more forceful position supporting civil rights. Martin Luther King's success in Birmingham in May 1963, though, stood alone as a milestone in broadcasting the seriousness of civil rights activism and succeeding in both challenging the business establishment in Birmingham and raising the movement's profile to transform white attitudes about segregation beyond Alabama. It was followed, however, by the murder of NAACP field secretary Medgar Evers at his home in Jackson, Mississippi, an event that marred the jubilance of Birmingham as a political win for black activists and reminded all that white southerners saw black activism as punishable by death. As 1963 ended, the bombing of the Sixteenth Street Baptist Church in Birmingham, killing four little black girls, immediately undermined the emotional climax of the March on Washington for Jobs and Freedom. And Kennedy's assassination less than two months later provided an opportunity for the nation to grapple with the relationship between hope and grief as political emotions that coexist in a heterogeneous liberal democracy. As van Hooft reminds us, "Political hope's object is an occurrence or a policy outcome that is considered to be possible. If we need hope because social progress is not guaranteed, we are also led to hope by the belief that it is possible."[66] Hope, then, was ironic because while it holds out the possibility for enactment, it recognizes impossibility as a feature of the feeling, particularly in the context of political assassination.

Hope was displaced by the wave of death that permeated public life in the United States during the long sixties, beginning with the president's assassination. The animosity about civil rights was increasing in intensity and volume. However, Kennedy's death had an unequal emotional legacy, for "if Kennedy's death turned dreams to dust for some, others remained faithful to the image they had formed of him, including his hope for a better future. . . . This sentiment seemed especially strong among African Americans" and "helps explain why they were so drawn to him in life, why they suffered so at his death, and why images of the fallen leader could still be found, years later, adorning the walls of their homes."[67] Vivian J. Malone Jones, one of the two black students who integrated the University of Alabama in 1963, explained that Kennedy "gave hope to black people after so many years of hopelessness."[68] Likewise, after her husband's assassination, Myrlie Evers-Williams praised Kennedy's eloquence and his commitment to civil rights, saying that she "began to believe a new day was coming, one that would give us our legitimate place in American society."[69] These kinds of sentiments dominated public accounts of the president's death and shaped black memory and nostalgia about the slain president.

The Johnson administration thus began in a moment of crisis about the utility of hope as an orientational feeling. Mary Dudziak explains that Johnson's embrace of Kennedy's civil rights legacy cemented Camelot:

> Kennedy friends and family would place a heroic gloss on the youthful image of the departed leader. Johnson himself, an outcast during the Kennedy presidency, would aid that construction by elevating civil rights as a Kennedy legacy. Civil rights had not been at the top of Kennedy's agenda while he lived. In death, however, his motives and priorities were transformed. He was now above politics. He became a symbol of public mortality, as well as the youthful vigor, that an anxious national longed for.[70]

The national anxiety that underwrote the white backlash cycle would last into the Reagan administration as Kennedy's presidency was framed through the lens of his martyrdom for civil rights. But "within a few weeks it became apparent that Johnson was committed to Kennedy's domestic policies, if anything with greater vigor and a more sweeping popular mandate. But the tension between radicalism and managerial liberalism was fundamental and outlived the martyred Kennedy."[71]

More than one activist sought to connect Kennedy to Lincoln via their legacies for black emancipation. Nonetheless Kennedy's assassination "touched off widespread feelings of fear, anxiety, and disorientation, all feelings associated with a period of collective cultural trauma."[72] As a collective and extremely public trauma, Kennedy's assassination marked the limits of hope as a rhetorical frame for liberalism, since it exposed the co-constitutive relationship between hope and progress, on the one hand, and loss, suffering, disappointment, cruelty, and death, on the other. The violence that has accompanied hope in the United States, with emancipation being the ultimate expression of this dualism, was unavoidable after Kennedy's assassination as paranoid nationalism began its public resurgence in the new conservatism.

Political Optimism and Presidential Assassination

Kennedy attempted to demonstrate a diligent responsibility for the political future in the face of decades of presentism while also articulating a new relationship among action, knowledge, feelings, and responsibility. His was a repoliticizing of nationalism for the largest youth generation that the country had seen, and it activated new emotional fields connected to civic participation. But his death both amplified his messages about hope as a political feeling and constrained that vector of political engagement (particularly for Johnson, whose rhetorical skills were very different). Young people, in particular, felt Kennedy's murder deeply, in large part because he had become a repository of "hope that seemingly untractable problems could be solved."[73]

In hindsight, Kennedy's assassination marked a turning point in the affective politics of American political life. Where his administration had promoted political hope as the civic orientation of the early 1960s, his death transformed that hope and optimism into something more complicated. This should not be surprising, since Arthur Schlesinger's essay "The New Mood in Politics" cheerily opined, "The 60's will probably be spirited, articulate, inventive, incoherent, turbulent, with energy shooting off in all directions." But as Sean Wilentz notes in his introduction to the newest collection of Schlesinger's essays, by early 1963, "Events were already proving him correct—more so than he could have expected. But the final outcomes would break liberals' hearts."[74] Hope and heartbreak go hand in hand, and this relationality became plain after the president's assassination.

Still, Kennedy's popularity in black America was only enhanced after his assassination, since, in the estimation of many, he had paid the ultimate price for his association with civil rights activism. Matthew Holden explains that it is rather surprising that Kennedy's presidency cemented him as a hero in the black community:

> There was, of course, a broad public perception of a moral-psychological crisis associated with race. If there was such a crisis, however, it was one with which John Kennedy was very reluctant to entangle himself. He was perhaps more cautious than anyone except FDR and he was reluctant to act administratively. . . .
> The ultimate reality was that Kennedy, with his remarkable political caution and his strong sense of exposure to Southern pressure in Congress, deemed himself obligated to act in ways that were equivalent to a posture of a standstill.[75]

Holden is right that Kennedy's position on civil rights was stasis; this is particularly true in light of more recent scholarship by Kenneth O' Reilly documenting the administration's support of FBI disruption of the Freedom Rides and surveillance of the Southern Christian Leadership Conference.[76] But Holden's remarks support my conclusion that Kennedy became an icon because people admired his rhetorical commitment to liberal racial politics even if the administration would not push either Congress or the courts to secure black political rights for fear of alienating the Dixiecrats in the South.

Nonetheless, this discussion of the Kennedy administration's circulation and production of hope as an emotional and political pedagogy helps us understand the kind of new framework being proposed by the state as a way of understanding postwar political challenges. Gitlin explains, "To think about the enormous repercussions of the assassinations of 1968, we need to backtrack to the imagery and mood of a more general Armageddon, of which the triggering moment is the assassination of 1963. Kennedy, King, Kennedy, they sometimes felt like stations in one protracted murder of hope."[77]

The next chapter picks up this story to understand how hope was interpreted as a public emotion and as an organizing principle of rhetorical invention among black activists, especially Martin Luther King, during the Kennedy administration and after King's assassination. As we shall see, hope was a much more complicated political emotion for black Americans who had seen the pitfalls of liberalism and the betrayal of white liberals long enough to be suspicious of white proponents of civil rights actions. And their critiques of Kennedy's inaction on civil rights blamed his administration for undermining civil rights efforts even as Kennedy himself publicly supported civil rights as an ideal.

Chapter Two

CONTOURING BLACK HOPE AND DESPAIR

Where the emotional repertoire of Kennedy's New Frontier centered hope as an emotional anchor and optimism as a new mood in American politics, it began to falter early, despite the administration's relentless public relations campaign. In a retrospective essay in the *Nation* on March 3, 1962, titled "Fumbling on the New Frontier," Martin Luther King Jr. portrayed the White House's commitment to civil rights thus:

> The year 1961 was characterized by inadequacy and incompleteness in the civil-rights field. It is not only that the Administration too often retreated in haste from a battlefield which it has proclaimed a field of honor, but—more significantly—its basic strategic goals have been narrowed. Its efforts have been directed toward limited accomplishments in a number of areas, affecting few individuals and altering old patterns only superficially. Changes in depth and breadth are not yet in sight, nor has there been a commitment of resources adequate to enforce extensive change. It is a melancholy fact that the Administration is aggressively driving only toward the limited goal of token integration.[1]

King suggested that 1961 exposed the progressive narrative of hope as incomplete, partial, woefully inadequate, and unsettling as it pertained to the black freedom struggle. He invoked black *melancholy* in opposition to Kennedy's hope to describe how "blacks have responded to rejection and marginalization" through strategies that often fuse political disappointment with a resilient and distinctly racialized *black hope* focused on emergent moments of political action.[2] Joseph Winters explains that melancholy is not always pessimistic; rather, melancholy can also be understood as a continual engagement with the disappointment intrinsic to narratives of progress as they are inevitably punctuated by "painful, fragmented accounts" of inadequate resources coupled with social violence.[3]

Additionally, King had concerns about Kennedy's lack of *emotional knowledge* about racism, writing in his memoir that the president "knew that segregation was morally wrong and he certainly intellectually committed himself to integration, but I could see that he didn't have the emotional investment then. . . . He had never really had the personal experience of knowing the deep groans and passionate yearnings of the Negro for freedom, because he just didn't know Negroes generally and he hadn't had any experience in the civil rights struggle."[4] King worried that Kennedy's insufficient emotional knowledge about discrimination and segregation and his social distance from actual black people, particularly those residing in the South, would make him an ineffectual collaborator on the legislative issues that the Southern Christian Leadership Conference (SCLC) was supporting in Congress.[5] Kennedy's lack of commitment influenced the tactics of the civil rights struggle, particularly as it engaged the terrain of *time*. Because King understood the emotional temporality of the civil rights struggle, he centered *impatience* as a dominant black political feeling, as we shall see. Impatience is an important chronopolitical feeling deeply connected to hope. It expresses dissatisfaction with pace and timing, which was especially important, since the Birmingham campaign in spring 1963 occurred one hundred years after the signing of the Emancipation Proclamation, and activists articulated the continuities of oppression across the century.

In the February 1961 issue of *Harper's*, for example, James Baldwin analyzed King's attention to the temporality of feelings and the importance of interracial intimacy thus: "What he says to Negroes he will say to whites; and what he says to whites he will say to Negroes. He is the first Negro leader in my experience, or the first in many generations, of whom this can be said: most of his predecessors were in the extraordinary position of saying to white men, *Hurry*, while saying to black men, *Wait*. This fact is of the utmost importance."[6] Baldwin praises King's ability to manage the chronopolitics of the moment and harness the rhetorical space of *black hurry* while the white nation said to *wait*. Baldwin saw this confrontation over temporality as a major factor in King's iconicity, praising King's ability to manage it for blacks and whites alike.

King understood that the federal government is prone to stasis, and he recognized the desperation of black activists who could not afford to wait any longer for full social equality. King explained, "The paradox of laudable limited progress on the one hand, and frustrating insufficiency of progress on the other, is understandable if it is realized that the civil-rights struggle can be viewed from two quite dissimilar perspectives."[7] King delineates progress as a goal and demonstrates that it functions as a rhetorical expression of political time, suggesting that there is a racial framework for understanding the rapidity or slowness of social change. Daniel Innerarity's work on futurism helps us to comprehend how "the asymmetry that characterizes all forms of power is also found in the concept of time," which helps us to "determine what is important or urgent, as well as our priorities and the distribution of scarce temporal resources."[8] But even this assessment misses the racialized dimension of time as it pertains to public policy.

Given Kennedy's tendency to forestall civil rights initiatives, as well as his incomprehension of the civil rights struggle as an emotional as well as discursive terrain, King's temporal politics had the potential to be ineffective through no fault of his own. Pushing for legal change faster than attitudes could change in the public might change the law but could not change the sentiments governing human interaction. Nonetheless, in a 1962 sermon, King pointed to the importance of *time* by dubbing integration a "revolt against the myth of time," adding: "We hear this quite often, that only time can solve this problem. That is we will only be patient, and only pray—which we must do, we must be patient and we must pray—but there are those who say just do these things and wait for time, and time will solve the problem. Well the people who argue this do not themselves realize that time is neutral, that it can be used constructively or destructively."[9] King urged activists to reject calls for patience, explaining that they "must come to realize that it is necessary to aid time, that without this kind of aid, time itself will become an ally of the insurgent and primitive forces of social stagnation."[10] Thus was the civil rights movement a revolt against the myth of linear time and the call to wait. As a mobilization of political rights, the movement's success was marked by the ability to resist the passivity of waiting by assembling chronopolitical embodied feelings like impatience, indignation, and urgency to challenge white political stasis through direct action. This is because direct action dramatized the political stakes of racialized conceptions of time.

To create the conditions for equality, King saw that white political time must be disrupted with intimate *black* feelings (particularly impatience) that highlighted how political hope is racialized. King described the civil rights movement as one "based on faith in the future" animated by "a philosophy, the possibility of the future bringing into being something real and meaningful" and "based on hope."[11] That (black) hope sprouted from the idea of "We Shall Overcome." The slogan and song encompass the chronopolitical intervention of intimate citizenship as it emerged in social movement activism. King explains, "Before the victory is won some may have to get scarred up, but we shall overcome. Before the victory of brotherhood is achieved, some will maybe face physical death, but we shall overcome."[12] Even in the face of brutality and death, the notion of overcoming that was popularized in direct action discourse helped to fuse activist suffering and hope into a distinctly black chronopolitics that resisted white political inaction. In "Pilgrimage to Nonviolence," King wrote that he often "felt the power of God transforming the fatigue of despair into the buoyancy of hope" through the "suffering, frustration, and agonizing moments" of his activism.[13] This hope was the *product* of his transformation through pain and suffering. This kind of black *political feeling* was a *goal* of early nonviolent direct action, demonstrating the fungibility and polysemy of hope within American liberalism.

In addition to invigorating a discussion of chronopolitics as a measurement of political commitment and as a rationale for continued black activism, King's critiques in 1962 speak to his assessment of the president's inexperience with black people or black intimacy. Because Kennedy shared neither time nor space with black people in any meaningful way, King's observations about Kennedy contrasted with accounts of King's own ability to perform the same kind of intimacy. For example, writing of his first encounter at King's Dexter Street Baptist Church, James Baldwin waxed poetic: "It is rare that one *likes* a world-famous man—by the time they become world-famous they rarely like themselves, which may account for this antipathy. Yet King is immediately and tremendously winning, there is really no other word for it and there he stood, with an inquiring and genuine smile on his face, in the open door of his hotel room."[14] Baldwin was surprised at the affinity he felt when the two men met in King's hotel room, describing King as "likeable. Genuine. Winning."[15] Impressed by King's connection to the problems of black America, Baldwin praised him for being devoid of the "hideous piety which is so prevalent in his profession," and he wrote that King's secret was his "intimate knowledge of the people he is addressing, be they black or white, and in the forthrightness with which he speaks of those things which hurt and baffle them."[16]

King's likability stemmed from his ability to perform intimate citizenship. Ken Plummer has defined "intimate citizenship" as a series of citizenship practices that bridge the personal and political spheres through rhetorical and spatial proximity.[17] Intimate citizenship is useful in thinking about the disconnect between black melancholy and white hope because it points, as King's comments on Kennedy demonstrate, to the inability of whites to feel empathy and social concern for black citizens. It also speaks to intimacy as a necessary ingredient in social movement success because it highlights how emotional closeness builds trust and camaraderie in social movement organizations. Given that King's campaigns relied on moral suasion to arouse feelings of white guilt and shame, the relationship between public and private feelings is salient when civil rights leaders attempted to leverage black public suffering to help pass federal legislation.

This chapter examines King's performance of intimate citizenship as he articulated the rationale for the "beloved community" that he wanted to produce through direct actions in places like Birmingham, Selma, and Chicago. It evaluates how hope, disappointment, indignation, and despair framed King's direct action and the SCLC's intimate relationship with the black middle class, the White House, and white liberals. King's faith and optimism were shaken by the end of 1963, and after Kennedy's assassination, King's own language about emotion *shifted*. King was forced to reconsider and respond to the use of *rage* as a black political emotion because the decade gave way to a more militant black posture about the white political and emotional inadequacies, as we shall see in the next chapter. I argue that white failure to perform intimate citizenship limited the civil rights movement and fueled rhetorical expressions that engaged a very different emotional repertoire for both whites and blacks. As high-profile black assassinations dominated the news, Black Power became a foregone conclusion that harnessed oppositional feelings to reorient black politics and ontologies. Consequently, many of King's own discourses, especially in relation to Birmingham, focused on the relationship between hope and despair as he attempted to translate black feelings about civil rights to white publics as the crisis of hope deepened in 1963. Ultimately, though, King's observations about hope and despair were much more aligned with Black Power rhetors than many scholars care to admit, mostly because they are not tracing the emotional timbre or range of these black leaders.

The "Beloved Community": Political Emotions and Social Action

The SCLC's nonviolent direct actions aimed to produce what King called the "beloved community," an intimate, loving interracial brotherhood that would overcome destructive racial feelings to produce a new public culture. In his first SCLC manifesto, titled "Nonviolence and Racial Justice"—written after being elected by one hundred black clergy at Ebenezer Baptist Church in Atlanta in January 1957—King explained that nonviolence

does not seek to defeat or humiliate the opponent, but to win his friendship and understanding. The nonviolent resister must often express his protest through noncooperation or boycotts, but he realizes that noncooperation and boycotts are not ends in themselves; they are merely means to awaken a sense of moral shame in the opponent. The end is redemption and reconciliation. The aftermath of nonviolence is the creation of the beloved community, while the aftermath of violence is tragic bitterness.[18]

This "beloved community," born of a "new age" and a "new [social] order,"[19] was to emerge through the manifestation of white shame while avoiding white humiliation. It was a community built *explicitly* on the production and management of political feelings that were fundamentally racial in character. King's understanding of the beloved community was an exercise in political imagination where an antiracist belonging could be enacted through a process that intentionally provoked negative white feelings both as a corrective to shame and as an invocation of shame as a curative for feelings of "indignity, of defeat, of transgression, and of alienation."[20]

Simultaneously prophetic and pragmatic, always dynamic and changing, the beloved community was an imaginary terrain where black activists could propose alternative emotional structures of connection among Americans without disrupting the exceptionalism that is intrinsic to American liberalism. Fusing John Dewey's democratic ideal with Alain Locke's cosmopolitan unity, the beloved community emerged as a space that offered new communitarianism fusing both *memory* and *hope* in the service of a new national loyalty.[21] Here, self-transforming personal risks could be undertaken with the goal of building a new relationality to one's community, but these tasks were fundamentally *emotional* in character, hence King's assertion of the transformation of *consciousness* as a goal of nonviolent direct action. King saw the beloved community as emotional and social sustenance for a new America, with memory and hope being the constitutive devices that propelled it forward. King's notion of the beloved community fused together what Peter Coviello has called "operative fantasies of intimacy, mutuality, and belonging."[22]

King's notion of the beloved community—coming as it did before the Kennedy candidacy and amplifying the metaphors of the New Frontier— assumed that "*only shared hopes are stable.*"[23] Thus did early civil rights activism shape hope via the language of shared futures. However, as Judith Green notes, "Losers within adversarial struggles move or mutate, but they do not change their minds," making the moral suasion of the beloved community potentially ineffective, particularly as King and others used the "battlefield" metaphor that opened this chapter.[24] Clearly the goal of the beloved community was to create conditions for a mutual willingness; however, Green argues that the processes of social building "must be *carefully nurtured* in a suspicious, power-structured world within which communities of memory have some major past and present problems with each other to overcome if their trust is to be elicited and their hopes are to be progressively intertwined." She adds, "The imperative quality of feelings that are connected to past harms and suspicions of present motives should not be passed over too quickly on the path to cosmopolitan unity."[25] But the relationality between past, present, and future was complicated at midcentury because the movement was asserting simultaneous claims about the past (slavery), the present (segregation), and the future (the beloved community) within a political field characterized by suspicion and violence. Nonetheless the beloved community assumed the possibility of white people's transformative power through the production of social love and the possibility of forgiveness, if not reparation.

In 1958, early in the movement, King elucidated the *emotional goals* of nonviolent direct action, preaching that "the struggle in the South is not so much the tension between white people and Negro people" but rather "between justice and injustice, between forces of light and the forces of darkness."[26] In attempting to reframe the civil rights struggle beyond race, King contends that "at the center of our movement stood the philosophy of love," of *agape*, the "understanding, creative, redemptive good will for all men" because God loves them.[27] In focusing early movement attention on agape as the kind of emotional fortitude to love people in a polyglot nation founded on slavery, King was advancing a potentially radical conception of national belonging, one that had distinct emotional vectors that helped build what he called "a deep sense of somebodiness," or the membership in a deeply transformative democratic community that valued black pride and saw blackness itself as beautiful.[28] This position, of course, stood in opposition to the race-neutral humanism that did not identify black pride as a precondition of democratic practice. Almost ten years later, in a 1967 speech in Ohio, King explained that *the feeling of belonging* matters, saying, "We must feel that we count. That we belong. That we are persons. That we are children of the living God. And it means that we go down in our soul and find that somebodiness and we must never again be ashamed of ourselves. We must never be ashamed of our heritage. We must not be ashamed of the color of our skin. Black is as beautiful as any color and we must believe it."[29] For black people, the refusal of the antiblack shame produced by white supremacist policies was paramount to their somebodiness, and King asserted *pride* as a curative for the emotional practices that undermine black agency and prevent a sense of national or community belonging. Black *pride*, particularly as it was articulated by Black Power activists and then recirculated by King, as we shall see, forms an important recursive structure of feeling to combat the despair that marks black time in the United States.

Birmingham, 1963

While King was committed to a deeply democratic ideal of racial plurality, he was also aware of the paradoxes of liberalism that undergird racial oppression in the United States, where fear of black and brown people justifies white supremacy. In a section titled "The Liberal Dilemma" inside a 1956 pamphlet titled "Our Struggle" describing the Montgomery Boycott, King prays: "Let us pray that God shall give us strength to remain non-violent though we may face death." He follows the prayer with an assessment of the likelihood of violence: "And death there may be. Many white men in the South see themselves as a fearful minority in an ocean of black men. They honestly believe with one side of their minds that Negroes are depraved and disease-ridden. They look upon any effort at equality as leading to 'mongrelization.'"[30] This assessment, coming as it did before the sit-in movement, the Freedom Rides, and the direct actions of Albany and Birmingham, is striking for its honest confrontation of racial feelings about miscegenation. In describing white self-concept as well as white assessments of black Americans, King acknowledged the likelihood of antiblack violence as a result of white *fear* about miscegenation. This recognition highlights how the brutality of white supremacy and the fears of racial mixing shaped black responses to structural inequality in the years after *Brown*. Likewise, this perspective informed the SCLC's decision to use the lessons from its most notable direct action protests in Alabama.

The SCLC descended on Birmingham in April 1963 to demonstrate how to disrupt structures of white supremacy through the production of black abjection via police violence. But SCLC cofounder Rev. Fred Shuttlesworth, in many ways, was a much more compelling orator than King. "In blunt, unembellished terms, his expression of raw emotionality captured [the] feelings [of the rank-and-file blacks in Birmingham] in ways that even King, with his oratorical polish, sometimes did not. More important, however, his bold confrontations fundamentally embodied the feelings of poor and working-class blacks."[31] The combination of King's easy intimacy with Shuttlesworth's populism was a winning combination because it created social trust among black Alabamians who had never participated in direct action. Preaching on the eve of the Birmingham protest, Shuttlesworth explained, "These are the days when men would like to kill hope ... when men in Mississippi can be declared 'not guilty' of murder, when men can be shot down on the steps of the courthouse. These are dark days. But hope is not dead. Hope is alive here tonight."[32] Shuttlesworth's comments invoke an immediate form of hope as a mobilizing feeling for black intimacy, fortifying activists against inevitable police violence while also recognizing the darkness and impossibility of the task.

King called Birmingham "the largest city of a police state" and "the most segregated city in America," and he chose it intentionally for this SCLC protest.[33] He described passivity and silence in the city, where the violence led black people to "abandon hope," and he depicted an emotional landscape where

> the silent password was fear. It was a fear not only on the part of the black oppressed, but also in the hearts of white oppressors. Certainly Birmingham had its white moderates who disapproved of [Bull] Connor's tactics. Certainly Birmingham had its decent white citizens who privately deplored the maltreatment of Negroes. But they remained publicly silent. It was a silence born of fear—fear of social, political and economic reprisals. The ultimate tragedy of Birmingham was not the brutality of bad people but the silence of the good people.[34]

One goal of the Birmingham protest, then, was to bridge racial silence and fear through both *speech* and *action* to overcome how the anticipation of social violence controlled the political possibilities of potentially "good" citizens, black *and* white. Because institutions seek to gain compliance from citizens by coercing them to obey institutional authority as a moral obligation of citizenship, people defer to institutional actors to avoid feelings of guilt or shame that emerge from the impulse to resist authority. Nonetheless the SCLC shamed institutions (municipal employees and local business owners, as well as the police) to create political cover for residents to *speak* as a means of undermining the shame and guilt that had historically foreclosed black political action. Birmingham was an articulation of voice in Eric King Watts's sense, where voice "is constitutive of ethical and emotional dimensions that make it an answerable phenomenon."[35]

The breach of silence via embodied protest in Birmingham represented the most successful political moment where the voice of *moral suasion* emerged in opposition to a feeling (fear). However, the protest intentionally aroused shame and guilt in both whites *and* blacks who were not already participating in the desegregation struggle (as a result of physical terrorism from whites or their economic relationships). In *The Color of Our Shame*, Christopher Lebron writes eloquently about how shame streamlines deliberation and shapes narrative and material coherence between ideals and actions.[36] As shame forms and disrupts normative deliberation, it creates the conditions for treating black people as moral equals. Moral suasion, as a *rhetorical strategy*, is about the pedagogical function of assessing *temperament*: political as well as moral. As a *political strategy*, moral suasion is about *coercion* and the application of public pressure, since King used it in tandem with boycotts. In

Birmingham, activists sought to evoke defiance in black residents, and both shame and guilt in local and national white viewers who were forced to confront the brutality as police attacked black children with fire hoses and dogs.[37]

Thus was Birmingham fundamentally an exercise in political shame where civil rights activists functioned as *witnesses*, exposing the shame of a nation through their mediated confrontations with overwhelming corporeal public violence. In his "Letter from Birmingham Jail" and again to Kenneth Clark in a 1963 interview, King described the importance of nonviolent direct action because it "arouses a sense of shame within [the white community]. . . . I think it does something to touch the conscience and establish a sense of guilt."[38] White guilt was an emotional vector that, for King, had tremendous potential to motivate white political change through a new politics of responsibility. This is, in part, because shame is a communal feeling. And because it is so closely associated with failure and relies on being *seen* in order to emerge, shame is a lingering (political) feeling. The magnitude and proximity of political *feelings* to political *identity* are precisely why King and Malcolm X are so often positioned in a dialectic about black identity; the relationship between *feeling* and *citizenship* is where the two leaders marshaled opposing political feelings. Citizenship is predicated on a series of filiations that confer national belonging and evoke idealized feelings that are harnessed for social action. Ahmed explicates, "Being like the nation that has failed to live up to the ideal hence confirms the ideals as the proper desire of the nation. The fear of being seen as 'like them' structures this shame narrative."[39] Shame, then, structures citizenship and feelings of national belonging; consequently, the replacement of shame with intimacy is what undergirds King's beloved community. Still, as King's "Letter from Birmingham Jail" demonstrates, sympathy for black protesters can easily be destroyed by the perception that protesters deserve punishment. As such, to be successful, white shame must rhetorically displace antiblack fear.

In Birmingham, the political shame *did* seem to frame the racial tableau. The vicious corporeal police violence enacted on black children with billy clubs, fire hoses, and German shepherds in Birmingham created a profound confrontation with Alabama's failure to live up to national ideals, producing dissonance as the nation managed its imagined idealness for a larger international community and creating pressure for social change. However, the problem with the evocation of shame in the context of social movements is that it is *fleeting* as a political feeling rather than *permanent*, thus making shame difficult to sustain. "Shame 'makes' the nation in the witnessing of past injustice, a witness that involves feeling shame, as it exposes the failure of the nation to live up to its ideals. But this exposure is temporary, and becomes the ground for a narrative of national recovery. *By witnessing what is shameful about the past, the nation can 'live up to' the ideals that secure its identity or being in the present.* In other words, our shame *means that we mean well,* and can work to reproduce the nation as an ideal," writes Ahmed.[40] The intended audience here "is implicitly 'international civil society.' Messages evoke this imagined witness: 'The eyes of the world are upon you. One hundred years from now how do you want to be remembered?'"[41] Thus does witnessing create the conditions for political leverage against a racist police state via an *emotional temporality,* a calculated chronopolitical intervention that demonstrates how witnesses will be perceived in their lifetime and for posterity. Shame harnesses time to push bystanders into action through an encounter with possible (and possibly shared) futures.

However, Thandeka complicates Ahmed's discussion by charting how *whiteness itself* is made up of thick, interlocking patterns of shame where white complicity is elicited and produced through shame appeals that expose how privilege can be stripped away from white people (by other whites as well as by people of color, particularly black Americans) who do not comply with white norms around race.[42] Whiteness, as a product of multiple discourses, is fundamentally derived from and through shame about fidelity to antiblackness, but it is also produced through claims about being aggrieved *by black people.* Whiteness is also a discourse of white victimage, where whites redeploy the language of oppression to expose the shame of whiteness as a way of consolidating white power against people of color. Robin DiAngelo coined the term "white fragility" to describe how white people are shielded from racial stress, so that any racial tension is unbearable to them.[43] The complexity of this dynamic, where black activists provoke white shame and white rhetors assert shame and fragility as the justifications for racist domination, complicated the political success of the civil rights movement in the long sixties. Shame, according to Silvan S. Tomkins, is one of the primary negative affects intensely felt *within the body.* But shame also has a co-constitutive relationship with *pride,* which is where the political function of both emerges as a predictable affective consequence of racial power, particularly in countries with the legacy of slavery of colonialism.[44] So the backlash against black activism designed to elicit *white shame* often takes the form of *white pride,* a dynamic that bears itself out across time.

Where rhetors like Malcolm X resisted the reassertion of the nation as ideal in articulating national shame (and pride), integrationists saw the national ideal as attainable and staged interventions designed to evoke shame and create national belonging for black activists and for white bystanders. This is not surprising, since dressing in their Sunday best and performing nonviolent direct action helped to position civil rights activists as *ideal citizens* in ways that did not disrupt the idealization of the nation. However, this embodiment did not fundamentally dislodge whites from their pursuit of financial and political supremacy. "The national ideal is shared by taking some bodies as its form and not others. The pride of some subjects is in a way tautological: *they feel pride at approximating an ideal that has already taken shape*," writes Ahmed.[45] Thus did image events like Birmingham seek to evoke shame and then *reintegrate* black and white subjects into the nation beyond the moment where they failed to live up to racial equality as part of liberalism's national ideal. Nonetheless, King described the emotional volatility of black Birmingham: "A leader who understands this kind of mandate knows that he must be sensitive to the anger, the impatience, the frustration, the resolution that have been loosed in his people. Any leader who tries to bottle up these emotions is sure to be blown asunder in the ensuing explosion."[46] King's language about both the chronopolitics and the volatility of racial confrontation there echoed other black leaders like Malcolm X, who used the topoi of explosives to describe the range, temporality, and intensity of emotions in the desegregation struggle (as we shall see in chapters 3 and 4).

"Letter from Birmingham City Jail"

King's letter from Birmingham, the most famous and arguably the most important discursive production that emerged from SCLC protests in the city, explicitly addressed the relationship between these volatile public feelings and the promises of direct action. King's letter described how, if "repressed emotions are not released in nonviolent ways, they will seek expression through violence."[47] In the letter, we encounter an indignant King, whose initial politesse is followed by a reprimand to white clergy and their criticisms of SCLC's tactics in the city. More aggressive here than in many of his public speeches, King described his own feeling as one of disappointment, although perhaps he also means anger and is treading gently as he begins his rebuke. Nonetheless, as Rieder explains, "Disappointment is not without furies of its own. It is an emotion of dashed expectations. You have to expect something from someone before he can let you down."[48] King's admonishment to the clergy provides his critique of American exceptionalism through his indictment of the moral turpitude of white supremacy, but his expression of disappointment is meant to invoke shame.

While King's letter amplified the shame intended by the protest, it also intensified perceptions of the chronopolitics in Birmingham. Birmingham became a central image event because the clash between activists and police, interpreted by King from jail, threw the temporality and the violence of the moment into stark relief for white audiences inside and outside of the American South. As Klinke has written, "Notions of familiarity, recurrence, repetition and regularity are crucial alongside modern linear progressive and declining constructions of time," and King's own rhetoric marked the permanence of racism, the irony of the desegregation fight one hundred years after emancipation, and the importance of understanding political time as a white construct.[49]

In the letter, King noted that freedom is never given but must be demanded, highlighting both federal inaction and the paradoxes of liberal claims of equality. King explained that the persistence of black pain underscores that

> freedom is never voluntarily given by the oppressor; it must be demanded by
> the oppressed. Frankly, I have yet to engage in a direct-action campaign that was
> "well timed" in the view of those who have not suffered unduly from the disease
> of segregation. For years now I have heard the word "Wait!" It rings in the ear
> of every Negro with piercing familiarity. This "Wait" has almost always meant
> "Never." We must come to see, with one of our distinguished jurists, that "justice
> too long delayed is justice denied."[50]

King's account of the linearity of black resistance and white immovability on racial equality is significant because, as he explains, blacks "have waited for more than 340 years for our constitutional and God given rights. The nations of Asia and Africa are moving with jetlike speed toward gaining political independence, but we still creep at horse and buggy pace toward gaining a cup of coffee at a lunch counter. I guess it is easy for those who have never felt the stinging darts of segregation to say 'wait.'"[51] King's indictment of white inaction shapes the discursive terrain of civil rights around *white resistance* to black equality, producing what King calls the "corroding despair" propelling "legitimate and unavoidable impatience."[52] Indeed, King describes how *white feelings* about black equality push a *white time* that denies black agency through appeals to *slow down* black time by means of mundane brutality like lunch counter discrimination, which is designed to undermine black political efficacy, to *prevent* black equality, and to undermine black justice.

Citing the history of lynching in America, the arbitrary police brutality, the suffocation of black poverty, the bitterness produced by the broken dreams of black children, the degradation of being called degrading names, the humiliation of being called degrading names, and the "inner fears and outer resentments" of a precarious existence, King concludes: "When you are forever fighting a degenerating sense of 'nobodyness'—then you will understand why we find it difficult to wait. There comes a time when the cup of endurance runs over and men are no longer willing to be plunged into an abyss of injustice where they experience the bleakness of corroding despair. I hope, sirs, you can understand our legitimate and unavoidable impatience."[53] With an extended focus on *waiting* and the feelings that it engenders—despair, hopelessness, and resentment—King equates waiting with a preference for injustice. Likewise, King illustrates how white chronopolitics distort black selfhood to undermine black agency, producing antisocial feelings that inhibit national identification (a process that propels riots and suicide, as we shall see).

For King, the antidote to this culture of violence, subjugation, and despair lies within the intercommunalism of the beloved community. In Birmingham, King describes it thus: "We are caught in an inescapable network of mutuality, tied in a single garment of destiny. Whatever affects one directly, affects all indirectly." As an oppositional account of both connectivity and intimacy, King's words here direct attention to the kinds of relationality that should supplant segregation. Describing the tensions produced by direct action, King describes the goal as being "to create a situation so crisis-packed that it will inevitably open the door to negotiation. I therefore concur with you in your call for negotiation. Too long has our beloved Southland been bogged down in a tragic effort to live in monologue rather than dialogue."[54] Seeing *rhetorical engagement* as a solution to the unidirectional authority of segregation, King sees political negotiation as the best possible outcome of the Birmingham protests, demonstrating how leverage creates opportunities to (possibly) rearrange power via affective racial provocations that demonstrate the hyperviolence of whiteness. In doing so, King also calls out the hypocrisy of white liberals and admits to being "gravely disappointed with the white moderate," stating that he has "almost reached the regrettable conclusion that the Negro's great stumbling block in his stride toward freedom is not the White Citizens' Counciler or the Ku Klux Klanner, but the white moderate, who is more devoted to 'order' than to justice."[55] In expressing his feelings here, King invokes accountability and responsibility for white *liberals*, a position that still hinges on guilt and shame but also demands action as reparation, amplifying the critiques of Malcolm X and prefiguring Black Power.

King's letter leveraged the political feelings created by the scenes in downtown Birmingham that shook the nation, reframing white stasis and black impatience for Americans shocked by the brutality of the confrontation. Marking the exigency of Birmingham as a turning point in addressing antiblack violence and structural inequality, King says:

Human progress never rolls in on wheels of inevitability; it comes through the tire-
less efforts of men willing to be coworkers with God, and without this hard work,
time itself becomes an ally of the forces of social stagnation. We must use time cre-
atively, in the knowledge that the time is always ripe to do right. Now is the time to
make real the promise of democracy and transform our pending national elegy into
a creative psalm of brotherhood. Now is the time to lift our national policy from the
quicksand of racial injustice to the solid rock of human dignity.[56]

In answering the white call to "wait," King offers the black "now" as the creative temporal antidote to the discomfort of emotional and national failure
via shame and guilt. Black time ameliorates social stagnation and provides
human dignity. In moving between two rhetorical forms (elegy and psalm),
King suggests replacing what Du Bois called the "sorrow songs" with the lyri-
cal engagement of the beloved community, the only place he sees dignity as
possible. In doing so, King's affective orientation and his invocation of a particular politics of time demonstrate how he foresaw emotional leverage at this
critical moment in the black freedom struggle.

King's letter was first published in the *Nation* in August 1963, coinciding
with the March on Washington for Jobs and Freedom, under the title "The
Negro Is Your Brother," suggesting Christian agape, or goodwill, as the frame
for the intimate citizenship of the beloved community. King himself describes
agape as a kind of unconditional political love predicated on God's love for
all of humanity and not the specificity of the individuals involved.[57] But in
thinking about brotherhood as a rhetorical frame of the civil rights struggle,
it is hard to read that intervention as anything other than a specific form of
intimate citizenship, one predicated on social forgiveness that can ameliorate
the political shame produced as racial violence is exposed and condemned.
Additionally, the melodrama in Birmingham helped create visual and narrative identification with black protesters that clearly defined them as victims
of violence and evoked pity in northern whites. Birmingham produced feelings of outrage and shame, especially among whites not living in the South,
demonstrating that a goal of moral suasion is to produce political feelings
that influence behavior.

After Birmingham

After Birmingham, King elaborated on the disappointment he felt with the
white clergy.[58] King's disappointment stemmed from their refusal to acknowledge the civil rights movement as a humanist cause steeped in the Gospels.

But while King preferred political liberalism to, say, religious fundamental-
ism, ultimately he was also quite critical of what he called "liberalism's super-
ficial optimism," which "failed to see reason by itself is little more than an
instrument to justify man's defensive ways of thinking."[59] He added that "liberalism had been all too sentimental concerning human nature and it leaned
toward a false idealism."[60] King's indictment of liberalism's sentimentality is
noteworthy because he also describes his refusal to engage with pessimism
while nonetheless preserving a critical appraisal of liberalism's own self-righ-
teous optimism.

Aware of the impact that Birmingham had on the national conscience
while managing the desegregation of the University of Alabama in the spring
of 1963, President Kennedy acknowledged the political feelings that were producing black activism as well as resistance to civil rights. In his now-famous
"Civil Rights Address" of June 11, 1963, Kennedy echoed King's own sermons
and speeches and described the "fires of frustration and discord" that were
"burning in every city," using contagion language that I assess in Chapter
Three. Kennedy was clear that desegregation was "a moral issue. It is as old
as the Scriptures and is as clear as the American Constitution. The heart of
the question is whether all Americans are to be afforded equal rights and
equal opportunities. . . . Those who do nothing are inviting shame as well as
violence. Those who act boldly are recognizing right as well as reality."[61] Recognizing the paradox of liberalism, Kennedy's condemnation of segregation
was a moral one predicated on white shame and responsibility for violence.
The president saw violence in Birmingham as the result of white refusal to
comply with federal law and with moral imperatives enshrined in the country's founding documents. Kennedy suggested that nonviolent resistance was
congruent with the national ideal, and segregationist politics were not.

For his part, King described the summer of 1963, crescendoing with the
March on Washington, as "a revolution because it changed the face of America. Freedom was contagious. Its fever boiled in nearly one thousand cities,
and by the time it had passed its peak, many thousands of lunch counters,
hotels, parks and other places of public accommodation had become integrated."[62] King's "I Have a Dream" speech provided an extensive meditation
on the tension between hope and melancholy as the paradox of liberalism,
exemplifying what Jeffrey C. Alexander has called "the drama of civil repair,"
where interlocutors perform reparative work as a means of ameliorating
social conflict.[63] In the exordium of the speech, King explained, "In a sense
we've come to our nation's capital to cash a check." King accused the US government of refusing to honor the debts of justice, claiming, "It is obvious
today that America has defaulted on this promissory note insofar as her citi-

zens of color are concerned."[64] Using the debt metaphor implicates capital-ism as a primary failure of American race relations, but it also suggests that economic safety and security exist for some of America's white citizens at the expense of the rest of the culture. It is an illustrative metaphor, an accusation shadowed by implications in the Declaration of Independence and assured in the Emancipation Proclamation, that black Americans should be granted meaningful freedom. But as King reminds us, the promise was never fulfilled; the reparations were never made. "Instead of honoring this sacred obligation, America has given the Negro people a bad check, a check which has come back marked 'insufficient funds,'" King exclaimed.[65] This indictment of the nation's inability to live up to its ideal followed the politics of shame invoked in Birmingham, and as the basis of much of the twentieth century's racial liberalism, the speech is circulated most often for its fidelity to the idea of meritocracy, especially evidenced in King's discussion of the importance of the content of character rather than the color of skin.

Nonetheless, King's *tone* in his most famous speech often amplifies feel-ings of indignation. Indignation is anger that invokes shame as its goal. Rather than consummatory rage, indignation often focuses on the revocation of rights or privileges that are expected owing to the promises of a social con-tract. As a form of outrage, indignation has an object, a party responsible for the indignity of legal or social rejection despite the normalized ideals. This dynamic makes indignation a useful political emotion for mobilizing dissent because indignation is an emotional recourse against cultural exclusion. For integrationists, however, the organizational problem with mobilizing indigna-tion as a vector of shame is that assimilative politics are deeply connected to *unacknowledged shame*. This relationality is significant because assimilation is fundamentally about the rejection of *flaws*, often expressed as intrinsically biological or as part of moral and social character, which creates self-hatred.[66]

This is why Malcolm X and Black Power activists were so critical of King's attachment to integration; they saw it as a *rejection of blackness*, as a form of false black pride, and as a sign of deep political shame that undermined black political efficacy. Malcolm was extremely critical of King's advocacy of nonviolence, regularly calling King an Uncle Tom for teaching black people to suffer for integration. In his 1963 address "Message to the Grassroots," Mal-colm discusses the way that King and his colleagues promoted black suffer-ing, explaining:

The white man does the same thing to you in the street, when he wants to put the knots on your head and take advantage of you and not have to be afraid of your fighting back. To keep you from fighting back, he gets these old religious

Uncle Toms to teach you and me ... to suffer peacefully. ... As Rev. [Albert]
Cleage pointed out, they say you should let your blood flow in the streets. This
is a shame. You know he's a Christian preacher. If it's a shame to him, you know
what it is to me.[67]

Malcolm frequently observed that King's suffering was an acceptance of white
violence. Rather than the transformation of King's "creative suffering," Malcolm saw black abjection as something that would curb black agency. The
corrective to shame, for Black Power activists, was pride articulated through
a *rejection* of ideal national feelings. As a kind of externalization of shame,
Black Power's articulation of pride demanded a new rhetorical posture (literally, *a new spine*), a new embodied repertoire of behaviors, a new orientation toward both the self, in-group others, and whites. Malcolm understood
nonviolent suffering as a rejection of black pride, which complicated his relationship to nonviolence and to King and prompted him to articulate black
pride as a fundamental goal of his preaching and politics. While Malcolm
described King as a force undermining black dignity through his insistence
on nonviolence, King, too, saw emotional reversal as a potential source of
black pride, regularly telling activists, "You go to jail and turn the dungeon of
shame into a haven of freedom!"[68] Seeing imprisonment as a *source* of black
pride was a nodal point in the midcentury black freedom struggle regardless
of the organizational orientation of black activists.

In contrast, King saw Malcolm and the black Muslims—much as the white
press did—as introducing "bitterness and hatred" into the political conversation, saying in his "Letter from Birmingham Jail" that their rhetoric emerged
from frustrated and faithless adherents who were "perilously close to advocating violence. It is expressed in the various black nationalist groups that
are springing up across the nation, the largest and best known being Elijah
Muhammad's Muslim movement."[69] Pointing to their lack of faith in America—and, by extension, in white people—King described Malcolm and the
Muslims as nonideal citizens as a way of contrasting their emotional fidelity
to the country and its future. This kind of rhetorical work about collective
feelings shaped the kinds of contrasts that were drawn between King and
Malcolm, particularly those that saw King's version of politics, especially in
the early 1960s, as more amenable to *whiteness*, and more accommodating
of *white violence*, than Malcolm's. This, of course, was the point of Malcolm's
critiques, as we will see in the next chapter. Thus did King's mobilization of
moral suasion via shame and indignation invoke complicated feelings among
black Americans, particularly those critical of whites, of political expediency,
and of King himself, let alone his dream for the beloved community.

Beyond '63: Feeling LBJ and Goldwater

The beloved community, as it was forged before and just after Birmingham, began to crumble by 1964 as a result of black separatism, civil rights fatigue from white citizens, frustration over voting rights legislation, white antiwar mobilization (pulling activists away from civil rights work), the emergent women's liberation movement, the student movement, the new conscious-ness emerging from psychedelics and rock 'n' roll, segregationist backlash (especially in white southern churches), and the urban rebellions in America's cities.[70] The brief window of optimism between Birmingham and the March on Washington was destroyed by the white terrorism on September 15, 1963, that killed four little girls in Sunday school at the Sixteenth Street Baptist Church in Birmingham. Black Power activist Julius Lester wrote about this atrocity as retaliatory violence that answered King's call for the beloved com-munity: "Whites could feel morally out-raged, but they couldn't know the futility, despair and anger that swept through The Nation within a nation— Black America. There were limits to how much one people could endure and Birmingham Sunday possibly marked that limit. The enemy was not a system. It was an inhuman fiend who never slept, who never rested and no one would stop him."[71] Lester echoed King's early assessment of Kennedy and charged white America with having a pathological obsession with antiblack vio-lence, and lacking a conscience to which blacks might successfully appeal for respite. Whites produced their own rage in the face of black "futility, despair and anger," suggesting that racial feelings were the actual discursive context through which rhetorical productions were filtered and that produced a ter-rain of racial liberalism where antiblack violence was intrinsic to the national ideal.[72] As the new conservatism circulated through Goldwater's candidacy and writings, and as segregationists mobilized against integration, antiblack violence increased, intensifying the emotional appeals of King's black critics, like Malcolm X, creating a different frame for political hope, especially in the wake of Kennedy's assassination.

In *Why We Can't Wait* (1964), King suggested that Kennedy's political emotions evolved over his brief stint in the White House. King explained that the president "was not given to sentimental expressions of feeling" but that at the time of his death, he was working toward a different version of himself and his presidency.[73] "In 1963, a new Kennedy had emerged. He had found that public opinion was not in a rigid mold. American political thought was not committed to conservatism, nor radicalism, nor moderation. It was above all fluid," wrote King.[74] Characterizations like this cemented Kennedy as a transformational civil rights hero. As King described him, Kennedy "was at his death undergoing a transformation from a hesitant leader with unsure goals to a strong figure with deeply appealing values."[75] King's assessment of this change in Kennedy's relationship to civil rights reflected the president's landmark civil rights speech in 1963, but King's comments also suggest that Kennedy's racial liberalism had appeal, especially after his assassination, and that King held out a black hope that Kennedy's legacy would shape Lyndon Johnson's civil rights policy.

King's early assessment of Lyndon Johnson was quite different from the scathing review he wrote of Kennedy's first year in office. King wrote that Johnson's "emotional and intellectual involvement [in civil rights] were genuine and devoid of adornment. It was conspicuous that he was searching for a solution to a problem he knew to be a major shortcoming in American life."[76] The election of 1964 was, of course, a landslide for Lyndon Johnson, though Barry Goldwater's candidacy "successfully introduce[d] the language of law and order to national politics, with fateful consequences for the Johnson administration, the Democratic Party and liberalism itself."[77] This rhetorical reframing away from *protest* and toward *law and order* undermined the emotional repertoire that King and the SCLC were using to elicit shame and guilt from whites as a way of shifting public culture toward the beloved community, but it *also* undermined Johnson's credibility on civil rights, especially for Black Power interlocutors. Still, Johnson's commitment to civil rights, symbolized in his support for the Civil Rights Act of 1964, was a source of early optimism for King, despite the critiques of men like Malcolm who saw Kennedy's assassination as "chickens coming home to roost" and an inevitable price for the violence that sustained the American Dream even under democratic administrations.

Regardless, Kennedy's assassination shifted the emotional terrain of civil rights and exposed how hope was mobilized *for* civil rights activists while also demonstrating the cruelty contained in the incremental social change that hope demanded. Johnson and King both recognized that "the outpouring of admiration and affection for the late president—along with widespread feelings of grief, remorse, and guilt—had created a compelling opportunity for action."[78] But as van Rijn reminds us, "Ironically, when President Lyndon Johnson pushed through a much tougher act than Kennedy had ever envisioned, he did so in part by packaging it as a fitting memorial to his murdered predecessor. In doing so, Johnson inadvertently reinforced the notion that Kennedy had always been a staunch and indefatigable ally of the black cause, eager for the kind of thoroughgoing civil rights legislation that was enshrined in the 1964 Civil Rights Act."[79] Where Kennedy's optimistic vision was invoked to build support for federal civil rights legislation, the language of law and order was simultaneously undermining its efficacy, exposing hope, Kennedy's rhetorical legacy, as a paradoxical emotion in the face of new conservatism.

Hope, then, was a complicated emotion, particularly as the decade wore on beyond the assassination of its biggest proponent: John F. Kennedy. But the cruelty of hope as a mobilizing political vocabulary is a racial one that has disciplinary functions. As Warren explicates, "The objective of the Political is to keep blacks in a relation to this political object [hope]—in an unending pursuit of it. This pursuit, however, is detrimental because it strengthens the very anti-black system that would pulverize black being."[80] Warren adds, "The politics of hope must actively refuse the possibility that the 'solution' is, in fact, another problem in disguised form; the idea of a 'solution' is nothing more than the repetition and disavowal of the problem itself."[81] James Baldwin, in his assessment of King in those early years, articulated this dilemma in another way:

> King is entirely right when he says that segregation is dead. The real question which faces the Republic is just how long, how violent, and how expensive the funeral is going to be; and this question is up the Republic to resolve, it is not really in King's hands. The sooner the corpse is buried, the sooner we can get around to the far more taxing and rewarding problems of integration, or what King calls community, and what I think of as the achievement of nationhood, or, more simply and cruelly, the growing up of this dangerously adolescent country.[82]

For Warren as for Baldwin, the dangerous adolescence of America is concealed in its racial politics, articulated through an emotional repertoire predicated on social violence masked by political optimism. For both men, the invocation of black hope was a dicey enterprise at best. One the one hand, black hope was an attempt to fortify activists against the violence of white police; on the other, its connection to moral suasion and the politics of (white) shame and guilt was incomplete. And as indignation gave way to rage, the critiques of moral suasion got louder and gained traction, particularly in the face of sustained white pride and expanding scenes of antiblack violence. White backlash, white pride, and law-and-order culture stood next to hope to distort and mystify black suffering even as liberalism itself began to shift.

King elucidates the emotional paradox of liberalism in "The Showdown for Nonviolence," the final essay published before his own assassination in 1968. There he explained, "Black Americans have been patient people, and perhaps they could continue patient with but a modicum of hope; but everywhere, 'time is winding up,' in the words of one of our spirituals, 'corruption in the land, people take your stand; time is winding up.' In spite of years of national progress, the plight of the poor is worsening." Detailing joblessness, a lack of medical care, and starvation, King concludes that the "American people are infected with racism—that is the peril. Paradoxically, they are also infected with democratic ideals—that is the hope. While doing wrong, they have the potential to do right. But they do not have a millennium to make changes. Nor have they a choice of continuing in the old way. The future they are asked to inaugurate is not so unpalatable that it justifies the evils that beset the nation.... All of us are on trial in this troubled hour, but time still permits us to meet the future with a clear conscience."[83]

Juxtaposing black peril and hope while acknowledging both white stasis and state repression, King sees racism as a (dis)ease that undermines black progress as well as the national ideal. But King's last essay describes how white shame and black despair are coterminous. He writes, "America is reaping the harvest of hate and shame planted through generations of educational denial, political disenfranchisement and economic exploitation of its black population. Now, almost a century removed from slavery, we find the heritage of oppression and racism erupting in our cities, with volcanic lava of bitterness and frustration pouring down our avenues."[84] King's essay focuses on how hate and shame are the foundation of white supremacy, and his language echoes the assessments about black despair that concern much of the rest of this book.

King's words at the end of his life detailed how white repression undermined the possibility of the beloved community. After white backlash against the Civil Rights Act of 1964 and the Voting Rights Act of 1965 gave way to the new conservatism and urban rebellion, white stasis and repression prevented racial progress. Rioting, widespread by mid-decade, was incommensurable with the kind of brotherhood King envisioned, and agape was not a compelling affective orientation for urban black youth or for the student leaders of the Black Power movement who saw antiblack violence escalate during the last years of the Johnson administration. As we shall see, they found it impossible to see King's hope through the lens of urban blight and despair. Where King had emphasized an intimate citizenship designed to overcome the interpersonal emotional barriers to racial equality, the structural features of antiblack violence overwhelmed his paradigm especially as formal equality went unenforced across the United States. Even as King marched in Chicago in 1966, though, proclaiming the importance of the beloved community, he acknowledged the affective challenges undermining the possibility of a liberal brotherhood. King used the language of seasons to underscore the chronopolitics of midcentury feelings:

Our people's hopes have been shattered too many times, and an additional disillusionment will only spell catastrophe. Our summers of riots have been caused by our winters of delay. I want to stress the need for implementation and I want to recognize that we have a big job. Because I marched through Gage Park, I saw hatred in the faces of so many, a hatred born of fear, and that fear came because people didn't know each other, and they don't know each other because they are separate from one another.[85]

King was clear that political *delay* produced a racial climate that exacerbated white anxiety and black despair, leading to riots. In this way, King amplified some of the critiques of systematic white repression in America's cities that Malcolm X so vociferously advocated before his own assassination.

Chapter Three

AMERICAN NEGRITUDE
Black Rage and the Restoration of Pride

To be a Negro in this country and to be relatively
conscious is to be in a rage almost all the time.
—James Baldwin

n July 1959, CBS aired a five-part documentary produced by Mike Wallace and Louis Lomax titled *The Hate That Hate Produced*, which investigated the Nation of Islam (NOI) and its leaders. The program portrayed the black Muslims of the NOI as a vengeful response to both racism and integration. The journalist Mike Wallace described the NOI's "gospel of hate" and explained that their preaching would have "set off a federal investigation if it had been preached by southern whites."[1] Wallace recalled that the documentary's title reflected the "hatred and suspicion on both sides," adding that "If indeed the Muslims hated the whites, and they acknowledged that they did, Malcolm was very eloquent about that. Elijah Muhammad was very eloquent about it. They were racists. They were separatists."[2] Wallace's description of the Nation of Islam virtually guaranteed that it would forever be described as a "black supremacist organization" and as a black hate group.

Though the title acknowledged white supremacy as the cause of black separatism, the producers equated rage with hate and promoted the false equivalency between (white) domination and (black) resistance. "Lomax and Wallace's ambiguous condemnation of the NOI was a curious inversion of the rhetoric of American religious freedom. While NOI members were guilty of hatred, it was not exactly their fault. They were so imprisoned by racism that they lacked the freedom to choose hatred," writes Finbarr Curtis.[3] Addi-

tionally, the sensationalism of the documentary produced white fear "by pre-
senting the Nation of Islam as the angry, intractable monster child of white
racism. White Americans assumed that, given black Americans' dehuman-
izing experiences in America, the Nation of Islam labeled whites the devil
because of their suppressed anger against white brutality, and many feared
the unleashing of this rage."[4] The documentary generated such intense curi-
osity and anxiety among viewers about the NOI leader Elijah Muhammad
and minister Malcolm X that CBS rebroadcast it the next week in full.[5]

The misrecognition of black rage propelled white rage; consequently,
despite these white fears—and perhaps because of them—*The Hate That Hate
Produced* drove the popularity of the charismatic minister Malcolm X, whose
speeches were drawing new members to the NOI by the thousands.[6] Actor
Ossie Davis recalled the documentary and "that young man with his flam-
ing—well, it wasn't red—hair, lean and gaunt and quite capable of using language to open wounds. I was amazed at his capacity to communicate and at
the naked honesty with which he expressed his feelings about black people,
about white people. He scared me."[7] These comments point to the importance
of Malcolm's body to his rhetorical resistance as Davis recalls Malcolm's red
hair (inherited from his white grandfather) and his size, but they also speak
to the way that Malcolm styled his messages "to open wounds" with "naked
honesty" as he discussed racism. The recollections center *feelings* and also
pain in shaping perceptions of Malcolm's television debut, and they document how Malcolm's voice and his physicality made viewers *feel*. In this way,
his body functioned as a *gestural refusal* of white nationalism and literally
expressed a new ideological *posture* that refused self-degradation.

While the NOI benefited from the controversy of the series, Malcolm condemned the documentary for downplaying the religious nature of the NOI
in favor of characterizing Elijah Muhammad's followers as a hate group. Malcolm felt that the series intentionally evoked *negative feelings*, what he called a
"kaleidoscope of 'shocker' images" designed to demonize the NOI.[8] Malcolm's
critique emphasized how frequently Wallace and Lomax said the word "hate"
in conjunction with NOI organizing. Malcolm complained, "Hate, hate, hate,
hate. They figured that Negroes would never go near him if they said he taught
hate, because the average Negro don't want nothing to do with hate. He loves
Jesus and he has been taught that Jesus didn't hate nobody, so he wants to be
like Jesus and so he'll end up getting knocked in the head, brutalized, and he
won't fight back because he says Jesus didn't fight back."[9] Malcolm dramatized how the hostility to Islam was rooted in the use of the New Testament
to enforce white supremacy, and he invoked antiblack brutality to highlight
what he saw as the passivity and foolishness of Christian nonviolence. As a

Muslim, Malcolm's paradigm built a Pan-African and global political vision of black identity that did not rely, in Audre Lorde's words, "on the master's tools to dismantle the master's house."[10] Still, by conflating Malcolm's rage and contempt (as both feeling and tone) with *hate*, critics attempted to mobilize antiblackness to undermine his popularity and his political power by creating a false equivalency. They saw Malcolm's attempts to articulate and historicize white wickedness as a kind of reverse racism, since Malcolm was inverting racial generalization against white supremacy. This (intentional) misrecognition of rage as hate operated as a fundamental attribution error of motive.

Malcolm's own speeches and interviews were alternately jarring and fascinating because his articulation of rage had a pedagogical as well as a political function.[11] As sociologist Thomas Scheff has carefully argued, rage is often the product of intense shame and humiliation.[12] Rage is a form of self-preservation and the redefinition of self in the face of perpetual dehumanization; it is a mode of articulating identity in opposition to violence. The process of differentiating feelings "is tied to learning," rather than a biological response to stimuli.[13] Indeed, Agnes Heller's work asks, "What kind of information does feeling communicate?"[14] Malcolm's *tone* provided a rhetorical shock therapy for black listeners (and whites as well) because it was a radical departure from black Christian proselytizing that introduced new political feelings designed to change how they communicated with and about white people. But Malcolm's style was also shocking because he introduced rhetorical techniques and tropes that destabilized racial feelings and habits that insulated white people from criticism while it encouraged black people to access political rage. As we shall see, Malcolm was adept at using slavery as history and metaphor, in analogy and aphorism, in inversion, and in providing trenchant criticism of liberals.

But Malcolm's rhetorical confrontations also *produced trauma* (the "opening of wounds") as a necessary condition of the rage that informed his consciousness-raising. As Scott explains, "Each black person can, through a *traumatic* encounter with the blackness that his societal indoctrination has taught him to hold in contempt, become conscious of the *imposition of blackness* upon him. The black person can identify with the source of his self-division, his internalized self-defeat."[15] Malcolm forced both black and white Americans to confront and recognize the constructedness of blackness (and whiteness) to precipitate new forms of political identification. Although Robert Terrill warns of psychological assessments of Malcolm because they have the danger of reducing the leader to a personality,[16] I argue that Malcolm's circulation over the past fifty years is a result of his successful use of psychological techniques and vocabularies to demystify racial power.

I begin by contextualizing Malcolm's interventions about black feelings in the contemporary psychological literatures that framed and circulated about blackness to understand how new black psychology informed Malcolm's emotional and rhetorical repertoire. Then, in excavating Malcolm's performances of black rage as an easily identifiable feeling and an intended goal of his rhetorical corpus, I argue that Malcolm's psychological strategy articulated what I am calling "American Negritude." Marrying black psychology to the work of African and Caribbean intellectuals theorizing postcolonial black subjectivity, Malcolm's rhetorical skills hinged on his ability to resituate black political and social consciousness around black pride and disidentification from whites. Malcolm's American Negritude, particularly as it embraced rage, was at odds with the affective orientation and the racial liberalism of the integrationists and created both tension and opportunity for a global blackness. Still, while Malcolm reconceptualized feeling and being black, his enactment of black rage was often confused with hatred, which fueled white opposition to Malcolm and the NOI and fed white fragility in the early 1960s. Malcolm's orientation toward American Negritude—or what Keith Miller has called "an alternative literacy" and what Bruce Horner has described as "counter-hegemonic literacy training"—focused on psychic conversion.[17] In Cornel West's words, psychic conversation entails a rejection of white normalization of psychological impulses and "a refusal to measure one's humanity by appealing to any white supremacist standard."[18] West adds that Malcolm's use of psychic conversion "simply rejects Black captivity to white supremacist ideology and practice."[19] Malcolm's critique of black loyalty to white civil religion hinged on his relentless exposure of faulty black identifications, which he saw as a form of modern slavery.

The "Negro Problem," the "Mark of Oppression," and the "Damage Thesis"

The Hate That Hate Produced was a remarkable documentary, in part, for describing the circulation of white feelings pathologizing blackness that framed civil rights at midcentury. White assessments of black separatism offered psychological perspectives on racism and resistance that were incomplete and misread rage as hate as white critics struggled to comprehend how black activism implicated white power. Whereas in previous decades, black political participation had been referred to colloquially as "the Negro Problem," the 1950s marked a new era in describing the obstacles to black freedom. Psychological language, often emerging from the work of black psychologists in Harlem, described the affective and political dynamics of desegregation in midcentury racial productions.[20] For example, in *The Hate That Hate Produced*, Mike Wallace deadpanned to the camera that the title reflected

> the hate that some Negroes are returning for all the hate that all Negroes have
> received in the past 300 years. The burden of being a black man in America has
> proved more than some of them can bear and now they are fighting back with the
> same weapons that were used to subjugate them. They are finding it increasingly
> difficult to identify with America. They have lost faith in the honesty of American
> law enforcement agencies when it comes to protecting individual rights.[21]

Wallace attributed the formation of the NOI to the effects of slavery, segregation, law enforcement, and white religious ideologies; he characterized the NOI as a response to the *psychological toll* of blackness in America; and he saw black rage as a product of *white rage*. Rodolfo Torres and Christopher Kyriakides have termed this kind of assessment "the theory of oppression psychosis" and suggest that despite acknowledging causes of black rage embodied by Malcolm X, the documentary ultimately fixed the NOI as an immediate danger to racial liberalism because of its critique of white behavior and history.[22] They suggest that this (il)logic *created* psychosis in black people, reanimating a new "scientific" racism that pathologized blackness, and, by extension, black people, as permanently damaged.

Black psychologist and Harlemite Kenneth B. Clark's work on the "damage thesis" underwrote much of the midcentury oppression psychosis discourse and influenced Malcolm, whom Clark interviewed frequently.[23] Arguing that segregation caused irreparable harm to both black *and* white Americans, Clark's work heavily influenced the Supreme Court's decision in *Brown v. Board of Education* (1954), the landmark case driving school desegregation, and formally established psychology as a scientific field of study in the United States.[24] But as psychological terminology entered the popular lexicon and informed media framings of civil rights activism as well as the law, new vocabularies delineated the *political feelings* associated with the burdens of inhabiting racialized bodies to explain exclusionary national identification, both *describing* and *prescribing* certain racial feelings within multiple discursive terrains.

Following Clark's early work, Abram Kardiner and Lionel Ovesey published *The Mark of Oppression: Explorations in the Personality of the American Negro* (1951), which investigated the history of black self-hatred. Rather than universalize the trauma of segregation, Kardiner and Ovesey explained that *slavery* created an emotional economy where the "*reciprocity of feeling* between master and slave was destroyed. There was no possibility of emotional interchange. . . . The rage or protest of the slave could be *ignored* or treated with violence. The only really effective form of protest was *flight*."[25] Beyond limiting the free emotional exchange between master and slave, slavery also destroyed "free emotional interaction between slaves."[26] Even after emancipation, the reciprocity of emotional interaction was never restored between former master and former slave, thus guaranteeing a nearly insurmountable inequality that was later codified in Jim Crow laws because "the obstacles toward reciprocal interaction come from the white man."[27] Consequently, they suggested that black Americans face a series of problems stemming from "low self-esteem and aggression, producing anxiety, self-abnegation, ingratiation, [and] denial of aggression with a cover of humour and affability, passivity and general construction of emotions."[28]

In this framework, the psychodynamics of American race politics emerged out of a refusal by *white people* to adapt to the conditions and possibilities of emancipation or to reframe their beliefs and attitudes about black Americans after slavery ended. This inflexibility led to the pathologizing of blackness as both a political project and an emotional regime. The rhetorical and emotional effects of this political regime appeared in "scientific" treatises, educational tomes, and legal rationales that depicted "the Negro" as pathologically weak willed, emotional, intellectually inferior, and insufficiently qualified for citizenship. Thus *white feelings* about emancipation were a *technology* that circumscribed black feelings and behaviors during and after Jim Crow. Unfortunately, the rhetorical articulation of white feelings after slavery used a style that mirrored black critiques of white supremacy, which Mike Wallace evidenced in *The Hate That Hate Produced*. This circulation of white objections to black articulations of racist harm via the same language of trauma and harm served to amplify the white victimology and fragility that undergirds racial liberalism *even when white rhetors acknowledged the harm of slavery or segregation.*

Nonetheless, five years after *The Mark of Oppression*, E. Franklin Frazier published *Black Bourgeoisie*, which echoed Kardiner and Ovesey's findings while also charting how middle-class blacks managed feelings of subordination. Frazier maintained that "since the black bourgeoisie live largely in a world of make-believe, the masks which they wear to play their sorry roles conceal the feelings of inferiority and of insecurity and the frustrations that haunt their inner lives."[29] Frazier chronicled the damaging psychological attachments that middle-class black Americans had as they pathologized the black poor, and his work argued that feelings of insecurity and inferiority predominated their social relations.[30] For Frazier, white *contempt* shaped black feelings about inferiority, and this constitutive process could only be managed through masks that repressed certain feelings, like rage. He expounded:

"Living constantly under the domination and contempt of the white man, the Negro came to believe in his own inferiority, whether he ignored or accepted the values of the white man's world."[31] This internalized oppression shaped black identity and created a black infrapolitics of competition as white contempt and disgust shaped black responses to social violence. But it also offered a form of biological essentialism centered on *feelings* as a mark of blackness.

Frazier's landmark studies mapped an emotional architecture of race politics and echoed Frantz Fanon's *Black Skin, White Masks* (1952). Fanon, a psychiatrist from Martinique working in Algeria, was writing about colonialism's influence on race relations in the African diaspora. *Black Skin, White Masks* was, in Fanon's words, an "attempt to discover the various mental attitudes the black man adopts in the face of white civilization."[32] The masks that Fanon describes (echoed but not cited in Frazier's study) are the adaptations to a culture of exclusion and violence where *whiteness* is the pathology.[33] Fanon argues that the "juxtaposition of the black and white races has resulted in a massive psycho-existential complex. By analyzing it we aim to destroy it."[34] For Fanon, psychology unravels the existential questions and problems of the colonized or the oppressed to develop new strategies of liberation. This was a process of *futurity*; as Fanon explains, "Every human problem cries out to be considered on the basis of time, the idea being the present always serves to build the future. And this future is not that of the cosmos, but very much the future of my century, my country, and my existence."[35] Fanon lays out the "affective disorders" that lock blacks and whites into racial scripts and political stasis.[36] These disorders undermine the possibility of nationalist cooperation or a productive futurity, since Fanon argues that the inferiority process that unfolds as a result emerges first through economic subordination and then through the "internalization or rather epidermalization of this inferiority."[37] Fanon's writings here and later in *The Wretched of the Earth* (1961) describe the psychosocial processes of racial dehumanization that create and maintain the conditions of colonization. Those processes begin with the master-slave relationship and continue to shape the psychology of oppression and resistance intrinsic to relationships between whites and blacks and between colonizers and colonized.

The translation of *Black Skin, White Masks* was tremendously influential on black liberation theorizing because Fanon's writing detailed the *structures* of colonialism alongside the *feelings* it produces to sketch a *psychological history* of antiblackness.[38] Fanon's works offered black rhetors in the United States rhetorical interventions about the relationship between the colonial master and the slave and about the dynamics of intimacy under the conditions of economic servitude. In his famous treatise *Black Power: The Politics of*

Liberation in America (which begins with an epigraph from Kenneth Clark's *Dark Ghetto: Dilemmas of Social Power*), former SNCC chairman and Black Power advocate Stokely Carmichael wrote (with Charles Hamilton) that the "adaptation" strategies of black Americans "deprive[d] the black community of its potential skills and brainpower" because the "integrated people are used to blunt the true feelings and goals of the black masses. They are picked as 'Negro leaders,' and the white power structure proceeds to talk to and deal only with them. Needless to say, no fruitful, meaningful dialogue can take place under such circumstances."[39] Calling it "a classic formula of colonial co-optation," Carmichael argued that black America is an internal colony held hostage by a white colonial superstructure and that black leadership serves at the pleasure of white liberals. Against this domination, Black Power sought "to correct the approach to dependency, to remove that dependency, and to establish a viable psychological, political and social base upon which the black community" could control its communities and "meet its needs."[40]

Citing psychological stability as a top priority in reconceptualizing the relationship between the colonizer and the colonized centered the Fanonian framework in Black Power theorizing. Beginning with Malcolm X, from whom they borrowed much of their early political theory, Black Power leaders embraced a revolutionary telos grounded in the experiences of postcolonial Africa. This articulation of intersubjectivity highlighted the continuous production of black inferiority as a *precondition* of modern American life and offered black pride and Pan-African solidarity as curatives. Malcolm X's rhetorical corpus embodies a Fanoniste radical subjectivity that helps explain his antagonisms with integrationists, particularly given the American turn in the psychology of racial oppression. Fundamentally, Malcolm's interest in the postcolonial perspectives on the psychology of oppression shaped his unique articulation of black feelings in tandem and in opposition to, say, Martin Luther King's formulation of the beloved community, particularly as it included whites and excluded theorization about slavery.

Harlem, Négritude, and Recentering Slavery

Malcolm X's affective politics emerged from a mélange of influences in Harlem as his proto–Black Power theorizing found its affective grounding in psychological terms and frames that harnessed ideas circulating in the African diaspora, where Francophone critics and theorists began writing about Négritude in the 1930s. Fanon's posthistory of colonization used the work of writers, poets, and philosophers like Aimé Césaire of Martinique (Fanon's lycée teacher), Léopold Sédar Senghor (the first president of Senegal), and Léon Damas (French Guinean diplomat and theorist) to help psychologize colonization in ways that created and amplified revolutionary political frames.

Francophone Négritude referred to the recovery of a racial memory, the performance of an authentic racial self, and the engagement with experimental politics encouraging a revolutionary ideology that imagined the death of the West as a foregone conclusion. Négritude was a celebratory discourse of black identity and was rooted in the reversal of shame and the production of pride. Damas elucidated three features of Négritude: "Elle [Négritude] 'est en effet, la prise de conscience d'un état de fait qui se caractérise par trois elements: la colonisation, l'assimilation, une volonté d'intégration humaine'" ("It [Négritude] is indeed 'awareness of a situation which is characterized by three elements: colonization, assimilation, and the desire for human integration'").[41] For Senghor, Négritude also included historicizing whiteness and instructing whites in the history and culture of blackness.[42] In rejecting colonization, assimilation, and integration and in chronicling black history, Négritude writers saw value in black and indigenous history, culture, and identity in the diaspora. While Fanon later offered critiques of Négritude insofar as it attempted to recover what he saw as bourgeois voices of African critical thought, he nonetheless saw it as a useful space for interrogating black subjectivity and fantasizing about new African futures.

Additionally, Négritude writings described black Africans as "both physically and psychologically, at home, but especially in the Diaspora."[43] This feeling of belonging and of being-at-home even while abroad marked a cognitive shift away from feelings of (dis)comfort, self-loathing, inadequacy, and internalized oppression and a shift toward pride, solidarity, and comfort in blackness, despite the pathologizing of it by whites. Rather than succumb to the dehumanization of white colonial culture, Négritude writers explored the consequences of political, spiritual, and social alienation and argued that black civilization was a source of pride, not shame. They wanted to articulate a black ontology invigorated with political promise. Given that Négritude writers corresponded with many of the writers of the Harlem Renaissance (including Claude McKay, Jean Toomer, Countee Cullen, and Langston Hughes),[44] it makes sense that Harlem would animate an affective politics that rebuked assimilationist-integrationist politics while Malcolm was preaching at Harlem's Mosque No. 7. The Back-to-Africa movement and Marcus Garvey's Universal Negro Improvement Association also influenced Négritude writers, garnering sympathy among French-speaking Africans.[45] Négritude discourses heralding African heritage and knowledge and opposition to Western colonial exploitation sharpened American critiques of white domination after emancipation, particularly as Négritude writers rejected the Hegelian dialectic.[46]

Given Malcolm's admiration for Garvey and his political interest in Africa, these influences on him made a strong case for a larger, more cosmopolitan black vision of affect and politics than the cult-of-personality scholarship offers.[47] Despite these dense networks of ideas circulating in Harlem, scholars have never situated Malcolm at the crossroads of the New Negro Movement, the Harlem Renaissance, and the Négritude movement, although he embodied the affective and political postures of all three literatures.[48] This is perhaps in part because, in Goldman's description, Malcolm was a "Fanoniste without having read Fanon: he lived in spirit, if not in literal fact, in the native quarter and understood its vocation for destruction. He did not advocate for the rioting that surprised us so that summer [1964] but he predicted it regularly and was furious when we taxed him with contributing to the atmosphere that produced it."[49]

However, in offering a distinctly *American Negritude*, one rooted in a new pathological economy, Malcolm advanced a black reclamation project firmly rooted in the American experience but with an eye toward Pan-African solidarity and decolonization. By American Negritude, I mean the process by which black American rhetors sought to reverse the psychological toll of white supremacy through an excavation of slavery, the Middle Passage, the shortcomings of racial liberalism, and critiques of the police and prison. Particularly trenchant at the end of his life, after his pilgrimage to Mecca, Malcolm said the following to the representatives of the Organization of African Unity:

> We in America are your long-lost brothers and sisters, and I am here only to remind you that our problems are your problems. As the African-Americans "awaken" today, we find ourselves in a strange land that has rejected us and, like the prodigal son, we are turning to our elder brothers for help. We pray our pleas will not fall upon deaf ears. We were taken forcibly in chains from this mother continent and have now spent over three hundred years in America, suffering the most inhuman forms of physical and psychological tortures imaginable.[50]

In connecting black suffering in the United States to African suffering on the continent, Malcolm acknowledges the history of colonialism and brutality defining black life in the diaspora and marking black psychology through torture. Through these kinds of comparisons, Malcolm's American Negritude created new identifications through an anticolonial critique that sought to reverse degradation with analysis that would broaden and strengthen black agency. Francophone Négritude thinkers "sought to turn the name into an active power that would enable Blacks to see themselves in all their specificity, to discover the deepest springs of life and liberty. A noun turned into a concept, 'Blackness' became the idiom through which people of African origin could announce themselves to the world, show themselves to the world, and draw on their own power and genius to affirm themselves as a world."[51] Thus, in articulating an American Negritude as an *adjacent discourse* to Francophone Négritude writings, Malcolm occupied a distinct political space that promoted American "blackness" as a positive identity asserting *black pride* and rejecting *antiblack shame* through critiques of American slavery and white liberalism.

Malcolm's affective positionality rejected white hope and bypassed shaming whites, whom he did not expect to be transformed by shame. In this way, he understood what Sara Ahmed has argued about shame: "*What is shameful is passed over through the enactment of shame*," leaving the original feelings untouched.[52] Beyond leaving these feelings untouched is the fact that the "recognition of a brutal history is implicitly constructed as the condition for national pride; if we recognise the brutality of that history through shame, then we can be proud."[53] Malcolm's rejection of *American pride* is what helped build a new pedagogy against shame. "The fact that Malcolm ... could reject a white person on any terms caused most of America psychological turmoil. And instill[ed] admiration and pride in black Americans. For the egos of most white Americans are so bloated that they cannot conceive of a black man rejecting them," writes the black historian John Henrik Clarke.[54] Malcolm's position was that national pride was a ridiculous feeling for black Americans because it necessitated a disavowal of the suffering of black people and a belief in white hope despite its articulation through antiblack violence.[55]

Malcolm's rejection of shame as both a black feeling and white appeal hinged on how his American Negritude centered the American slave experience as an interior process of the self and as an external politics of black solidarity.[56] In "Message to the Grassroots," Malcolm exclaims: "You're nothing but an ex-slave. You don't like to be told that. But what else are you? You are ex-slaves. You didn't come here on the 'Mayflower.' You came here on a slave ship. In chains, like a horse, or a cow, or a chicken."[57] Malcolm's assertion here is an *ontological one*: all black Americans are ex-slaves: not humans, not citizens, not free. Their fundamental history and their orientation toward both America and its founding are the slave experience, not freedom. Malcolm's inventive mode, then, is characterized by a mode of "'radical relationality' between political and conceptual activity,"[58] where he unsettled naturalized hierarchies, histories, and relationships to reframe black experience to expand black agency. Malcolm's use of slavery as a master trope formulated an American Negritude bridging past and present to articulate the essential psychological and ontological relationship between racial exploitation and liberalism and to demonstrate that emancipation did not eradicate antiblackness. That is to say, emancipation was a fiction that could not be remedied legally.

Later in "Message to the Grassroots," Malcolm described the relationship between the house Negro and the field Negro (articulated by E. Franklin Frazier and interpreted by Malcolm) as a relationship that has overdetermined black life both during and after slavery. House Negroes "loved the master more than the master loved himself" as they worked alongside and for him in the big house. Describing the physical and psychoemotional labor of the house Negro, Malcolm speaks derisively about the *pride* taken in working so closely to the master and in the displacement of self-concern. Likewise, in defending black separatism, he provides the following critique of the house Negro: "'What do you mean, separate? From America, this good white man? Where you going to get a better job than you get here?' I mean, this is what you say. 'I ain't left nothing in Africa,' that's what you say. Why, you left your mind in Africa."[59] To Malcolm, the house Negro embodied the subservience and internalized oppression that obscured black relationality to the diaspora, and in personifying the United States as a white man, Malcolm dramatized his claim that the Middle Passage destroyed black identification. White supremacy was so mystified that proximity to whiteness (white men, in particular) was the litmus test for a good life. Malcolm suggests that leaving one's mind in Africa facilitates this mystification of black identity as a *tool* of antiblack feeling and as a source of black shame.

But the field Negro, who worked in the fields, had less access to whiteness. Beaten by the master, withstanding the elements, hating the master and his family, s/he hoped for calamity to befall the white household. S/he was critical of white people and white government. S/he dreamed of freedom, of escape. Malcolm says that most of all, the field Negro was skeptical of Uncle Tom house Negroes: "Just as the slavemaster of that day used Tom, the house Negro, to keep the field Negroes in check, the same old slavemaster today has Negroes who are nothing but modern Uncle Toms, twentieth-century Uncle Toms, to keep you and me in check, to keep us under control, keep us passive and peaceful and nonviolent."[60] Comparing nonviolence to novocaine at the dentist, Malcolm suggests that white people numb black leaders to violence and brutality, and black leaders suffer peacefully even though black pain doesn't change the plantation. Malcolm adds that white Christianity functions in the same way: to keep black people passive, suffering, and submissive. Malcolm was prompting listeners to become conscious of historical and contemporary wrongs against black communities, making the case for a new kind of black identification that recognized the permanence of slavery as a disciplinary technology of American life.

Thus did Malcolm articulate how black exploitation provides the foundation for capitalism, suggesting that changing white *feelings* would not change their *economic incentive* to scaffold antiblack inequality. For example, in "The Ballot or the Bullet," he argued that black people needed to be reeducated in how to create and support sustainable black businesses and communities:

> And once you can create some—some employment in the community where you live it will eliminate the necessity of you and me having to act ignorantly and disgracefully, boycotting and picketing some practice some place else trying to beg him for a job. Anytime you have to rely upon your enemy for a job, you're in bad shape.... Let me tell you, you wouldn't be in this country if some enemy hadn't kidnapped you and brought you here. On the other hand, some of you think you came here on the Mayflower.[61]

While highlighting how the kidnapping of Africans fed early American empire, Malcolm attempted to delink American mythology from black identity. And in linking employment discrimination and slavery, Malcolm underscored how black-owned businesses offered a permanent antidote to segregation. Without black businesses, picketing and boycotting would be fixtures of black activism, since protests neither shifted feelings nor displaced white economic control, especially in the South.

While Malcolm insisted on recentering slavery, in his 1963 speech "The Black Revolution," his formulation of American Negritude also described the United States as "a colonial power. She has colonized 22 million Afro-Americans by depriving us of first-class citizenship, by depriving us of civil rights, actually by depriving us of human rights."[62] For Malcolm, the colony dehumanized blacks, just as Mbembe has described it, "as one of the signifying matrices of language on past and present, identity and death. The colony is the body that gives substance and weight to subjectivity, something one not only remembers but continues to experience viscerally long after its formal disappearance. Blacks bestow on the colony the attributes of a founding power in possession of a psyche, that which doubles the living body."[63] The discursive invocation of the colony highlights how deathworlds and lifeworlds are conterminous, but the colonial metaphor also operates "to recall the primordial displacement between the self and the subject," which highlights the role of the psyche or the psychological in the formulation of white supremacy as well as nationalism.[64] The colonial idiom was a notable vernacular shift in 1963 because it opened rhetorical space that was foreclosed for, say, King, because of his fidelity to the Christian vernacular and to integration.

Malcolm's rearticulation of slavery as a contemporary facet of black life rather than a fixed historical point one hundred years earlier is what Mbembe calls "a combination of several temporalities."[65] The exigency of Malcolm's speeches and writings does not hinge on the immediate context of presidential politics and social movement resistance; rather, Malcolm's American Negritude asserts these multiple, simultaneous temporalities to express how black Americans experience time and Being differently as a colonized people. Malcolm's invocations of slavery were a reminder that enslavement had no clear beginning and certainly no end, as well as that slavery was a continuity rather than a past epoch that no longer asserted dominion over blacks or whites. In Mbembe's words, this conceptualization of time is characterized by "an *interlocking* of presents, pasts, and futures that retain their depths of other presents, pasts, and futures, each age bearing, altering, and maintaining the previous one."[66] The descriptive and theoretical utility of offering multiple temporalities simultaneously resides in the ability to harness historical feelings as ingredients of contemporary agitation or in future longing. In this mode of chronopolitical engagement, *feelings* exist continually across space and time.

However, public conversations about the lasting impact of slavery on race relations were not a part of the post-*Brown* civil rights movement discourse writ large. Nonetheless, in *Black Rage*, Grier and Cobbs noted the importance of the slave idiom to reshaping black memory: "The culture of slavery was never undone for either master or slave. The civilization dropped its slaveholding cloak but the inner feelings remained."[67] They argued that this is because "Americans characteristically are unwilling to think about the past," and in their studies of black rage at the end of the 1960s, they demonstrated that the inability to critically reflect on the past brings "white Americans to an impasse when they claim to 'understand' black people. . . . Long association has bred feelings of familiarity which masquerade as knowledge."[68] In creating encounters that undermined racial familiarity, Malcolm created opportunities to dislodge toxic and destructive attachments to racial scripts, black *and* white, that created the norms of segregation. These norms were refined through the generational isolation that "began with slavery and with a rupture of continuity and an annihilation of the past. Many individual blacks feel a desperate aloneness not readily explained."[69] In chronicling this "desperate aloneness," Grier and Cobbs point to the psychic alienation that Fanon so clearly articulated. Malcolm's American Negritude, then, centered the slave experience to demystify white moral psychology and to reveal how the alienation produced by white supremacy has been an essential formation of property rights, the law, surveillance and policing, and the extension of social rights. But he also saw the slave experience as one that alienated black Americans from their African past.[70]

Malcolm's use of psychological tropes was particularly notable not just as a product of new scholarship about consciousness and power as it pertained to blacks in the diaspora but also because his mosque was in Harlem, the most successful space of black bourgeois achievement in the United States. In Harlem, the new racial liberalism emergent after *Brown* was changing the mental health professions to argue for the psychological equality of black and white Americans as a way of undermining stereotypes that pathologized black behaviors.[71] This strategy necessitated rhetorical invention because, as Mbembe so eloquently describes it, "the passage from slavery to liberty required not only a subtle treatment of memory but also a reworking of dispositions and tastes. The reconstruction of oneself at the end of slavery consequently involved a tremendous amount of work on the self. The work consisted of inventing a new interiority."[72] Thus did Malcolm's confrontational rhetorical style create a distinctly American Negritude that used psychology to describe the emotional and political limitations of racial liberalism by (re)asserting slavery tropes in racial discourses. In doing so, Malcolm's American Negritude charted a new black American ontology that reflected and refracted the ideas of black academics and writers in the diaspora and centered *black pride* as a necessity for a new black political identity. Goldman writes eloquently about Malcolm's love for the people of Harlem: "His supreme gift to them was that he loved them; that he believed in their beauty and their possibilities and tried to make them believe, too. He recognized the inner despair of Harlem in its dropouts, its welfare lines, its muscat drunks, its terrifying rates of addiction and crime; he knew that white people made Harlem, but he understand that only black people and black pride could save it."[73] Through his analyses of black sovereignty, racial power, community self-governance, Pan-Africanism, and self-defense, Malcolm articulated an "affirmation of blackness," rooted in city life, that urged the reading and writing of black history in the face of white erasure.[74]

Against Integration, against Assimilation

Malcolm's Negritude offered a philosophy of blackness where the racial present was reanimated by a more critical view of the colonial past, and it often followed Francophone Négritude logics about power. For example, while

Césaire wrote about the "boomerang effect of colonization" in *Discourse on Colonialism*, Malcolm argued that John Kennedy's assassination was an example of the "chickens coming home to roost" (in answering a reporter's question after delivering "God's Judgment of White America"). Both observations highlight the recursive historical structure of state violence while also demonstrating how colonialism's violence does not spare white colonizers, either. Malcolm's early critiques of white liberals mirrored anticolonial language that lampooned colonial rulers and attempted to disidentify black hope with white dominance. Likewise, in "The Black Revolution," Malcolm explains, "America's strategy is the same strategy as was used in the past by the colonial power: divide and conquer."[75] Malcolm saw the United States as a revolutionary situation, especially by 1964, and he saw integration as an absurd answer to colonialism.

As it was for Négritude writers, assimilation (or, in the American parlance, *integration*) was often Malcolm's object of ire. This impulse to reject assimilation via the rejection of integration was consonant with Césaire's writings as early as 1935. Like Francophone Négritude writers, Malcolm encouraged black listeners to refuse imitation as a strategy of assimilation, arguing that both difference and similarity were traps of citizenship that undermine black subjectivity. For example, when E. Franklin Frazier brought Malcolm to Howard University on October 31, 1961, to debate Bayard Rustin on the topic of "Integration or Separation," Malcolm showcased the tone and topoi that would become familiar mainstays of Black Power discourse.[76] Speaking to a packed house of fifteen hundred black students, faculty, and community members in Cramton Auditorium, Malcolm rearticulated Franklin's themes in *Black Bourgeoisie*. These themes of psychological inferiority and self-loathing made their way into Malcolm's speeches frequently afterward and were compelling for college students working to build their adults selves through higher education.

In the debate, Malcolm supported separation and opined that the black man "will never be equal to the white man as long as he attempts to force himself into his house. The real problem," he continued, "is that the anemic Negro leader, who survives and sometimes thrives off of gifts from white people, is dependent upon the white man whom he gives false information about the masses of black people." Rustin replied, to thunderous applause: "You say America as presently constituted is a sinking ship, and Negroes should abandon this ship for another called 'Separation' or another state. If this ship sinks what possible chance did you think your 'separate' state would have?"[77] At stake in this back-and-forth is the utility of the confrontational rhetoric in creating space for the production of more radical black political space, where the stakes of separatism are clearer, particularly as liberalism persistently fails to secure an integrated nation. Malcolm's delivery was particularly important to this crowd because debates allowed him to showcase the refutational skills he learned on the prison debate team, which modeled oppositional black reasoning.[78] Malcolm's advocacy of separatism as a critique of integration and as the major rhetorical intervention of American Negritude hinged on the recognition that *blackness* and the *fear of it* undermined state and federal attempts at integration.

Thus Malcolm's *living body* existed as embodied resistance to integration. His body was *black*. His attitude was *black*. His knowledge was *black*. Malcolm, of course, used to joke that the "only thing he liked integrated was his coffee," which is interesting given that he was biracial. Nonetheless Malcolm redefined "doing blackness" as a public, consumable, didactic critical positionality. Malcolm's body was a site of resistance to integration, particularly as Malcolm's Negritude centered on both slavery and economic discrimination. For Foucault, the body becomes political as it operates within "complex reciprocal relations, with its economic usage; it is largely as a force of production that the body is invested with relations of power and domination; but, on the other hand, its constitution as labour power is possible only if it is caught up in a system of subjection.... The body becomes a useful force only if it is both a productive body and a subjugated body."[79] Malcolm's proto–Black Power evidenced his investment in a black male standpoint that sought autonomy over his own body precisely because he understood slavery and coloniality as hegemonic influences on race relations. Malcolm was no man's Negro, and he certainly wasn't a slave.

Malcolm's appeal was rhetorical, but it was also extradiscursive as it was embodied by the controversial leader. Much of Malcolm's rhetorical posture was invested in restoring black dignity and black manhood, tropes that reappeared prominently in Ossie Davis's eulogy of Malcolm as he proclaimed Malcolm "our manhood, our living black manhood."[80] As James Tyner has argued, "The struggle for liberation was imagined as one of a proud black man, with head held high and chest thrust forward. In doing so, Malcolm X replaced the subservient slave image with a positive image of a powerful black man standing up against the oppression of a white power structure."[81] Ossie Davis confirms this perception, writing, "Malcolm kept snatching our lies away. He kept shouting the painful truths we whites and blacks did not want to hear."[82] This embodiment of resistance was appealing, particularly for northern black men, whose own bodies were in constant tension with white people and white power. Thus Malcolm's body stood as evidence of his radical individualism and as an assertion of black *pride*. Just by living, Malcolm disrupted space, both black and white space, and provided an embodied example of why integration would fail.

But Malcolm also wanted independence from white feelings, white money, and white direction. In the NOI years, he saw black separatism as the only way to control black futurity. In a 1963 interview, Malcolm explained:

> *White* people follow King. *White* people pay King. *White* people subsidize King. *White* people support King. But the masses of black people don't support Martin Luther King. King is the best weapon that the white man, who wants to brutalize Negroes, has ever gotten in this country, because he is setting up a situation where, when the white man wants to attack Negroes, they can't defend themselves, because King has put this foolish philosophy out—you're not supposed to fight or you're not supposed to defend yourself.[83]

He adds, "Any Negro who teaches other Negroes to turn the other cheek is disarming that Negro."[84] Critical of the body politics of Birmingham, where black children were beaten, nearly drowned with water hoses, and attacked by dogs, Malcolm's body offered another vision of black pride that would not succumb to white violence as a precondition of citizenship. Malcolm did not share King's optimism that moral suasion would influence white people to divest from white supremacy, and he persistently expressed skepticism about white liberals, particularly before he created the Organization of Afro-American Unity (OAAU) in 1964 after his ouster from the NOI.

Replacing Hope with Disgust and Rage

Malcolm's Negritude project demystified racial assemblages like *hope* as they pertained to both segregation and integration, what Cornel West has called "hope on a tightrope."[85] Malcolm was producing an archive of thoughts on the biopolitics of race and racism, using what Alexander G. Weheliye calls "lexicons of resistance and agency" to create "modes of analyzing and imagining the practices of the oppressed in the face of extreme violence."[86] Malcolm denied black people the fantasy of political hope in the face of the era's racial liberalism while holding out the possibility of a new radical black politics. For example, talking to George Plimpton, Malcolm impugned the hope of integration, saying: "Integration is ridiculous, a dream. I am not interested in dreams, but in the nightmare. Martin Luther King, the rest of them, they are thinking about dreams. But then really King and I have nothing to debate about. We are both indicting. I would say to him: 'You indict and give them hope. I indict and give them no hope."[87] While Malcolm regularly disavowed liberalism's hope project, his existence was and is imbued with black hope. Hans-Jürgen Massaquoi waxed eloquent in a 1964 essay about how Malcolm "triggers mixed emotions, but among the dispossessed masses of Harlem, it inspires devotion and hope."[88] Malcolm's (black) hope existed in opposition to the nightmare of American segregation, which is why separatism was so necessary to his project: it disabused black listeners of their hope in liberalism and invigorated in them an interest in black nationalism as an alternative site to imagine political agency.

To undermine the white liberal as a national ideal, Malcolm's Negritude *mobilized disgust of whiteness as a black feeling.* "Disgust does something, certainly: through disgust, bodies 'recoil' from their proximity, as a proximity that is felt as nakedness or as an exposure on the skin surface."[89] Disgust, as a feeling, is an index of "corporeal intensities," in this case directed at the hunger for white attention. Speech acts can shape disgust as a corporeal feeling around objects of contempt.[90] These speech acts orient listeners to an object of disgust where they can attach both disgust and contempt as lingering negative affects.[91] Disgust is especially sticky as a political feeling: it attaches and is hard to dislodge, which makes it an emotion that has more longevity than, say, shame, which has a shorter temporality. "Disgust is clearly dependent upon contact: it involves a relationship of touch and proximity between the surfaces of bodies and objects. That contact is felt as an unpleasant intensity: it is not that the object, apart from the body, has the quality of 'being offensive,' but the proximity of the object to the body is felt as offensive. . . . As a result, while disgust *over takes* the body, it also *takes over* the object that apparently gives rise to it."[92] The mobilization of disgust toward integration, hope, white supremacy, slavery, and hypocrisy helped black auditors to disidentify with white norms and white ideals.

If disgust amplified the impulse to separate ideologically from whites, rage provided an affective backdrop for political and ontological theorizing that easily contrasted with integrationists. Malcolm's use of black rage emerged as a central vector of political consciousness for Black Power because it offered a radical pathway for feelings of black disenfranchisement. As Barbara Ritchie wrote in the 1969 *Riot Report*, Malcolm X "more than another other" "became the spokesman for [black] anger. . . . He perhaps best embodied the belief that racism was so deeply ingrained in white America that appeals to conscience would bring no fundamental change."[93] Likewise, Michael Eric Dyson describes the "ingenious aggression and edifying rage" of Malcolm as his major contribution to black nationalist rhetorical inventions.[94] Cornel West describes Malcolm's unprecedented articulation of black rage, which "bespoke an urgency and an audacious sincerity; the substance of what he said highlighted the chronic refusal of most Americans to acknowledge the sheer absurdity that confronts human beings of African descent in this country—the incessant assaults on Black intelligence, beauty, character, and possibility. His profound commitment to affirm Black humanity at any cost and his tremendous courage to accent the hypocrisy of American society made Malcolm X the prophet of Black rage—then and now."[95] West explains that Malcolm's rage came from a place of deep love for black people, and both rage and love helped Malcolm forge "a concrete connection with a degraded and devalued people in need of *psychic conversion.*"[96] Malcolm's Negritude taught black people to convert their self-loathing into self-love, their disgust into rage. But as West notes, especially during the years of Malcolm's life, "such a psychic conversation could easily result in death."[97] Still, Malcolm "knew that the electoral political system could never address the existential dimension of Black rage—hence he, like Elijah [Muhammad], shunned it."[98] This led him to a "deep pessimism about America's will to justice."[99]

This awareness of the necessity of a new black ontology drove Malcolm's rhetorical interventions around disgust and rage and his political inventions around pessimism about America's commitment to black equality toward a politics of American Negritude. But as West argues, critics need to distinguish "effectively between a politics of hate and a politics of anger."[100] Critical of a lack of ability to see emotional granularity and to distinguish black feelings owing to an impoverished emotional vocabulary, West's comments expose how negative affects are often lumped together in the political realm, particularly when doing so is expedient for white interlocutors (as in *The Hate That Hate Produced*). Anger and its more intense cousin rage are different from hatred because hatred is so tied to fantasies of love. Narratives about hatred produce a precarious

> subject that is endangered by imagined others whose proximity threatens not only to take something away from the subject (jobs, security, wealth), but to take the place of the subject. The presence of this other is imagined as a threat to the object of love. This narrative involves a rewriting of history, in which the labour of others (immigrants, slaves) is concealed in a fantasy that it is the white subject who "built this land." The white subjects claim the place of hosts . . . at the same time as they claim the position of the victim.[101]

Thus it makes sense that people invested in the fantasy of liberalism as an egalitarian discourse would see black nationalism as a threat precisely because it is a discursive unmasking of the affective and racial labor of nation and empire. Here, "reading of others as hateful aligns the imagined subject with rights and the imagined nation with ground."[102] White rhetors describe rights they have "earned," and the "hateful others" are stuck with epithets that highlight the passionate negativity that both solidifies whiteness as normative and ideal and blackness as revolting and antination.

The fantasy of displacement drives rhetorical substitution as *white hate* is displaced onto black rage *as black hate*. This move is evidenced in a memo on Malcolm X dated December 6, 1963, where FBI director J. Edgar Hoover describes how the NOI "teaches the extreme hatred of all white men."[103] This provides the warrant for FBI surveillance, harassment, and targeting of Malcolm and the rest of the NOI because it intentionally reads black contempt and rage as permanent threats to whiteness through the language of black hate. The logic works like this: where hate solidifies whiteness, mustn't the same be true of blackness? And yet Malcolm's discourse expresses rage but not hatred, as he explains in response to *The Hate That Hate Produced*. Discourses of white supremacy and discourses of black separatism are different precisely because they have different rhetorical strategies and political ends. Discourses that deliberately read rage as hate cast the white citizen as the aggrieved party who is hurt by the speech acts of the oppressed group despite centuries of antiblack structural violence. Antimiscegenation language and policy arise from this language of feelings because the mere proximity to blackness or black radicalness is seen to somehow "dilute" or "pollute" white feelings of love for the nation. Thus when racism itself is a politics of hatred, the urge to read rage as reverse racism is strong among white interlocutors, a move the psychoanalysts would call projection.[104] Indeed, the language of hate here is what makes the false equivalency between the KKK and the Black Muslims function as a rhetorical erasure of political motivation. *The Hate That Hate Produced* collapsed any distinction between hate and anger and undermined arguments about the political necessity of rage for black Americans and, by extension, likened Black Muslim organizing with Klan lynchings although the NOI was a nonviolent religious organization. A preacher like Malcolm, however, resisted the erasure of black rage by channeling it in the service of global blackness. Malcolm's pessimism about racial justice emerged because he found racial liberalism to be legible as a discursive structure that animated the idea of black hatred to unify white hatred even by liberals. As I have written elsewhere, Malcolm's "critique was an ever-present accusation about the limits of liberalism as it pertained to the Black freedom struggle."[105]

But rage only emerges after black Americans (or other subaltern groups) transform abjection. In fact, one of Malcolm's most important contributions to American Negritude, as a rhetorical style, was his insistence that black people conceptualize themselves as moral and political agents, *rather than victims*. Malcolm's admonishments served to underscore the importance of black rage as a political tool, especially powerful in exposing hypocrisy and duplicity. bell hooks explains, "Internalization of victimization renders black folks powerless, unable to assert agency on our behalf. When we embrace victimization, we surrender our rage."[106] Thus is *victimage the opposite of rage*. Indeed, the pursuit of justice as a political goal should be enough to disaggregate rage from hate. hooks adds: "Malcolm X's passionate ethical commitment to justice served as the catalyst for his rage. That rage was not altered by shifts in his thinking about white folks, racial integration, etc. It is the clear defiant articulation of that rage that continues to set Malcolm X apart from contemporary black thinkers and leaders who feel that 'rage' has no place in anti-racist struggle. These leaders are often more concerned about their dialogues with white folks."[107] hooks contends that a large part of the colonization of black Americans by whites has been the insistence that black people repress rage rather than channeling it against structural racism.[108] Like West, hooks explains that she "felt Malcolm X dared black folks to claim our emotional subjectivity and we could do this only by claiming our rage."[109]

The rage that Malcolm's Negritude modeled had a precision and intelligibility that transformed black emotional subjectivity and political agency. Within this paradigm, hooks explains, "My rage intensifies because I am not a victim. It burns in my psyche with an intensity that creates clarity."[110] There is a sense, too, that black rage provides emotional fortification and grounding in response to systemic antiblack urban violence in an opposite way to King's hope for the beloved community. hooks explains that rage is an important vector of the more militant response to white supremacy and argues that censoring it "ensures that there will be no revolutionary effort to gather that rage and use it for constructive social change. The young Black generation is up against forces of death, destruction, and disease unprecedented in the everyday life of Black urban people."[111] West bemoans the fact that Malcolm did not live long enough to create new constructive channels for black rage, but it remains the case that his use of rage created an innovative emotional template for a new black consciousness.

Malcolm's body was a battleground, communicating new forms of black agency. Amiri Baraka praised how Malcolm spoke "of another black consciousness that proposed politics as its moving energy."[112] Baraka urged readers to take up "the teachings of Garvey, Elijah Muhammad and Malcolm X (as well as Frazier, Du Bois, and Fanon)" to help accelerate the path to black national consciousness to which Malcolm contributed so greatly. Baraka added, "If we *feel* differently, we have different *ideas*. Race is feeling. Where the body, and the organs come in. Culture in the preservation of these feelings in superrational to rational form."[113] Baraka's assertions demonstrate the way in which race itself is fundamentally an assemblage of black feelings, connecting Malcolm to a radical legacy that more closely reflected an embodied nationalist perspective; even news accounts (as we shall see) hyperfocused on his *body* and, by extension, his manhood.

American Negritude as Rhetorical Style

Malcolm's American Negritude focused on reframing slavery, deploying the colonial idiom, and honing disgust and rage as resources for a new emotional and political repertoire that demystified the psychology of racial domination and submission and advanced a radical praxis targeting black audiences. In addressing the psychology of race relations in the United States through these new frames, Malcolm was able to shift public discourse to emphasize black identity, black pride, and a more radical understanding of localism in black politics that created the context for the rise of revolutionary Black Power rhetoric. Calling Malcolm "the most original and most important theorist of whiteness," Keith Miller suggests that his pedagogical interventions remain persistently undertheorized.[114] I would argue that the lack of scholarly attention continues to hinge on the deliberate misreading of black rage. I agree with James Baldwin's assessment of Malcolm's racial politics: "If [Malcolm] had been a racist, not many in this racist country would have considered him dangerous. He would have sounded familiar and even comforting, his familiar rage confirming the reality of white power and sensuously inflaming a bizarre species of guilty eroticism without which, I am beginning to believe, most white Americans of the more or less liberal persuasion cannot draw a single breath."[115]

Baldwin acknowledges that Malcolm's danger came from his refusal to participate in violence or vengeance, making his rhetorical power illegible for many whites and leading them to misconstrue him for their own self-protection from his critiques. In doing so, white critics read *rage* as *hate*. Nonetheless Baldwin saw Malcolm as "a *genuine revolutionary*, a virile impulse long since fled from the American way of life." Malcolm himself was "a kind of revolution, both in the sense of a return to a former principle, and in the sense of an upheaval.... In some church someday, so far unimagined and unimaginable, he will be hailed as a saint."[116] Malcolm's orations and performances helped him harness emotions to, in the words of Berlant, create "discourses of possibility and contestatory experimentation, seen here as modes of *practi-*

cal politics."[117] That his American Negritude was so confrontational and used a rhetorical style rooted in argumentative proofs and forms adapted from postcolonial contexts created a different rhetorical texture to his arguments, making his embodied resistance to white supremacy extremely appealing, especially for young black urban youth.

Malcolm is rightly identified as a proto–Black Power intellectual *precisely* because he reframed black life and experience to build emotional and political identification that could sustain practical community activism. He was able to accomplish this feat by overcoming white political defensiveness, black accommodationism, and the atomization of American individualism. Instead he performed a kind of radical openness, where the goal was not a specific political program per se but the collective black imagining of new futures by interrogating the (anti)black past and reassessing the gestures of refusal possible in the present. Simply put, Malcolm was hypothesis-testing alternative explanations that had no space for consideration in American public life, given its chronopolitics during the Kennedy and Johnson administrations. His American Negritude bridged the failures of white liberalism, its insistence on political hope, and civil rights organizing to offer a liminal third way. His was a partial excavation of black politics; a thought experiment without a legislative goal; an incomplete assessment of politics that demanded a playfulness, a mobility that only subaltern, minority figures can really harness. Malcolm was what we might now call an Afrofuturist, and his discursive impact can be seen in dozens of ways in Black Power's political and aesthetic interventions as they have manifested since the 1960s. Malcolm's evocation of black feelings, especially in the context of slavery and colonialism, moved beyond the incrementalism of the civil rights movement and its early focus on changing laws through public action and legal suits and on changing minds through moral suasion. Malcolm's orations and writings engaged time and being through a colonial framework that saw slavery as a never-ending condition of black life and as one that overdetermined race relations and power dynamics. His articulation of simultaneous temporalities encouraged critical thought about the role of blackness in defining Americanism.

Malcolm was a master of bodily discipline, which helped to shape his pedagogy of embodied feelings. His body both within and outside of the Nation of Islam offered a prime example of how black American men could restyle their bodies to discipline new emotions, and new political attachments and detachments. Nonetheless Malcolm's death marked a turning point for the black freedom movement because it created a kind of cultural insistence on the continuation of his radical, embodied resistance. Malcolm's death was important precisely because of his aliveness while he lived. Malcolm was nobody's Negro. His body was the example of the radical individual whose body was a living example of anti-assimilationism. His living body stood as perpetual evidence of his radical individualism. Just by living, Malcolm disrupted both black and white space. Thus was Malcolm the quintessential American Negritude intellectual. As Goldman asserts: "He had been our Frantz Fanon; the natives in America have neither the numbers nor the guns to do whites that gratifying violence that Fanon identified at the heart of the Algerian terror. . . . It was Malcolm, really, who discovered this—discovered how close the specter of black revenge lies to the surface of white American consciousness—and, having discovered it, he could rarely resist its pleasures."[118] The specter of black revenge was, of course, mobilized against Malcolm, but not before he harnessed its radical potential to animate new black discourses around political and social agency. Scholars have long argued that Black Power's largest contribution to black political theory has been its circulation and augmentation of postcolonial impulses. If so, those impulses do not begin with Malcolm (they begin with Garvey, Du Bois, and Robert F. Williams, among others), but they do consolidate with him in ways that make it into popular culture and the public imagination.

Malcolm's orientation as a provocateur and his harnessing of black rage certainly amplified this aspect of black political theorizing in ways that transcended his life. Julius Lester explains that Malcolm was singularly responsible for the black militancy in 1965:

> Malcolm X said aloud those things which Negroes had been saying among themselves. He even said those things Negroes had been afraid to say to each other. His clear, uncomplicated words cut through the chains on black minds like a giant blowtorch. His words were not spoken for the benefit of the press. He was not concerned with stirring the moral conscience of America, because he knew—America had no moral conscience.[119]

The rhetorical appeal of Malcolm's American Negritude hinged on how he clearly reframed black pride through disgust and rage, describing the harms of white norms and performing the affect that the harms evoked. Evocation is an important rhetorical tool of any minister, but especially a black Muslim minister chronicling the negative feelings produced by antiblack exploitation. As Van Deburg explains, "Frustrations and disappointment with the performance of federal officials, black moderates, and white liberals could be found in most black communities at mid-decade. But it was not disillusionment alone that stoked the fire of Black Power. . . . Black Power was [a] psychological antidote to despair that spread a sense of pride throughout black

America."[120] Malcolm's American Negritude invited urban blacks "to express negative feelings, to excoriate those individuals and institutions seen as promoters of despair."[121] In Van Deburg's assessment, in promoting the sharing and circulation of negative black feelings, Black Power activists followed and augmented Malcolm's affective template to create the conditions for positive black group identification.

Malcolm X's orations and writings encouraged modes of political engagement that centered on transforming rage and disgust from reactive feelings to emotional resources. In doing so, Malcolm's rhetorical inventions created a new sense of intimacy with black urban communities that was bolstered by his articulation of black pride as well as his presentism of the master-slave relationship. Malcolm's own interest in psychology helped him to articulate a politics of feelings that really challenged the orientation and mood of the southern civil rights movement, particularly after Birmingham.[122] In this way, Malcolm's rhetorical production had an intensely pedagogical function that centered feelings like disgust and rage as conduits for a new political awakening. He taught black audiences how to label and differentiate feelings as a mode of political engagement. He taught black auditors how to associate political performances with feelings. Without Malcolm's orations and writings, Black Power would have been an incomprehensible phase of the black freedom struggle because there would have been no rhetorical centering of rage or contempt as permissible and desirable political feelings. Malcolm's pedagogical engagement with racial history presented an account of intersubjectivity that asserted that black freedom emerges from collective black identity and action. Malcolm was hardly the first black orator to make such claims of intersubjectivity in black political circles, but his writings and speeches pursued a line of argumentation that highlighted freedom's relationality and created permanent lines of thought within black political philosophy about black feelings and their relationship to modes of pressure and coercion. In fact, it is this last paradox of political action that Malcolm was perhaps most maligned for producing and promoting. His rhetorical use of coercion highlighted how black orators could turn the tables on white power and mobilize resistance to political subjugation. It is interesting to note that he paired this approach with restraint, creating space for silence and speech to commingle.

As we will see in Chapter Five, Malcolm was not the only Black Power intellectual to use Fanon and other Négritude thinkers to develop new repertoires of engagement with power and resistance; Huey Newton's *Revolutionary Suicide* was also a meditation on Fanon's claim that black identity is preoccupied with "a feeling of not existing."[123] The existential crisis of blackness is one of perpetual abjection as well as dislocation. Fanon argued, "Without a black past, without a black future, it was impossible for me to live my blackness."[124] For speakers like Malcolm, this psycho-existential crisis had to be articulated and attended to through speech acts that dramatized their tremendous impact on black people and communities. Black Power shaped the vernacular space where black ontology became a radical process of individuation and collective identity. "Malcolm X crystallized sharply the relation of Black affirmation of self, Black desire for freedom, Black rage against American society, and the likelihood of early Black death."[125]

While Chapter Five will take up ways that these ideas circulated beyond Malcolm's life, particularly in the case of the Black Panther Party, it remains that his articulation of black feelings (affirmation, desire for freedom, and rage) propelled a new relationality among black people. Likewise, Malcolm's assertion of the "American nightmare" as opposed to Martin Luther King's "dream," for example, entailed a fundamental rejection of (colorblind) humanism by recognizing that antiblackness precludes black humanity and black Being.[126] For Malcolm, nonviolence is *not* the antidote to antiblackness because the entire state apparatus in the United States is predicated on scaffolding antiblackness. Nonetheless many critics saw Malcolm "as an example of the pathological personalities thrown up out of the dispossessed urban ghetto."[127] But as we shall see in the next chapter, the urban rebellions across America's cities at midcentury also mobilized "damage thesis" proclamations that depicted rioting as irrational mob behavior, driven by reverse racism and uncontainable feelings.

Chapter Four

FEELING RIOTS
The Emotional Language of Urban Rebellion

The photo-editorial in *Ebony* magazine's September 1964 issue provided a sober assessment of the Harlem riot that lasted from July 15 to July 22 after James Powell, a fifteen-year-old black student, was shot and killed in front of his friends by a white police lieutenant named Thomas Gilligan.[1] Coming as it did two weeks after President Lyndon Johnson signed the Civil Rights Act of 1964 into law, the riot captivated the country. The editorial explained that the racial inequality of urban life in America was undeniable: "No one was surprised when the violence came. Almost every one knew that the ghettos of the North had no strong leader like the Rev. Martin Luther King Jr. Almost everyone knew that Rev. King's philosophy of non-violence was not the philosophy of the black youth of ghettos like New York's Harlem or Jersey City's Ward F. Almost everyone knew that the stifling, smelly tenements were like bombs waiting for the fuse to be touched off."[2]

Blaming inaction on urban infrastructure and citing a lack of black leaders willing to tackle structural racism, the editorial saw black youth succumbing to the relentless poverty of the inner city, unable to speak about their plight. The essay sketched the ontological trauma of being young, poor, and black in places like Harlem, where violence destroys black futures. It described "the hopeless life in the ghetto," where black youth are "trapped by their environment" and "restlessly try every trick they know to escape. Not content with being a black cipher in a white numbered world, they seek to make themselves known in any possible way. Joining a gang, defying a policeman, fighting a teacher, refusing to obey a parent—all of these acts help define them as individuals, help prove they really exist."[3] The editorial described how this existential crisis of black selfhood—beginning in black youth—was defined by both physical and emotional *containment*. Like Malcolm X's speeches, it suggested a colonial relationality that provoked black feelings of frustration and alienation.[4] As we saw in the last chapter, Harlem functioned as a synecdoche for all urban centers, signaling an affective and political shift even before it was felt or seen in Watts, Detroit, Newark, or Chicago. Calling Harlem residents "bombs waiting for the fuse to be touched off," the editors liken black city inhabitants to explosives: unpredictable, volatile, and destructive, easily incited to rebellion. In this way, the idiom of explosives elaborated on the ontological traumas of black urban life.

The *Ebony* editors punctuated their account of urban poverty and despair with an agonizing encounter with a Harlem rioter, bleeding and hysterical, who begged to be shot by the police. When no one would kill him, he shouted: "They won't even kill me. I'm not even good enough to kill."[5] The editorial muses: "Seeking recognition as a human, if only as an enemy to be destroyed, this man symbolizes the desperation of many Negroes today. If necessary, he would pay the price of his life to prove that he existed."[6] This assessment highlights the intense, perpetual dehumanization of black Americans, particularly in the cities, as well as how the crisis of being black in America is internalized through a recognition that black people exist in neither life nor death. Cornel West explains that black nihilism, as a response to a politics of neglect and an antiblack culture, sketches "the lived experience of coping with a life of *horrifying meaningless, hopelessness, and (most important) lovelessness.*"[7] This is precisely the dynamic that the *Ebony* essay explores, and it reflects what Lauren Berlant has termed "slow death" to describe "the physical wearing out of a population and the deterioration of that population that is very nearly a defining condition of their experience and historical existence."[8] In cities with egregious residential segregation and tremendous police violence, riots were one response to slow death.[9]

I return to the issues of despair and (slow) death at length in Chapter Six, but here the *Ebony* editorial illustrates not just the precarity of black urban youth but also the *materiality of rioting as a discourse* where black residents and youth saw themselves through a kind of colonial lens, in Mbembe's words, as "*thing(s) of power*" belonging "to the *sphere of objects.*"[10] The colonized becomes this "body-thing" as a result of colliding forms of social violence; here "the colonized was neither the substratum nor the affirmation of any spirit. As for his/her death, it mattered little if this occurred by suicide, resulted from murder, or was inflicted by power; it had no connection whatever with any work he/she had performed for the universal. His or her corpse remained on the ground in unshakeable rigidity, a material mass and mere inert object, consigned to the role of that which is there for nothing."[11] The recognition of black nothingness, of the absence of black Being, dominates rioting as the specter of unfulfilled liberal promises about equality and the reality of urban culture built on antiblack resource management. Rioting is a confrontation with the undulating horrors of black slow death, what Hubert Locke has called "hope disappointed."[12]

Alongside this harrowing story is a discussion of the role television plays in mediating the movement and in transporting black people and feelings beyond their neighborhoods and into the antiblack state violence that civil rights direct actions both confronted and prompted. The editorial emphasized how *hopelessness* functioned as *technologized feeling* amplified by the direct action confrontations with whiteness. But it also worked in opposition to the hope circulating in the early years of the Kennedy administration, suggesting that the affective shift would undoubtedly influence the *politics* of the Johnson administration. There they could see "the crowning of kings, the burial of presidents, the launching of satellites to orbit the earth, the homes of movie stars, the coming of independence to African nations, [and] Willie Mays hitting a home run in Candlestick Park," but the black kids in Harlem saw other things through their TV sets. They saw, for example, "the story of the civil rights struggle, Martin Luther King speaking, dogs chasing Negroes in Birmingham and sailors dragging swamps in search of the bodies of three civil rights workers murdered" during Mississippi Freedom Summer.[13] Linking the violent repression of the civil rights movement to the urban despair propelling rebellions in places like Harlem, the editorial connects the images of police power in the South with conclusions about black feelings in the North, creating a material and affective continuity for black America. The writers conclude that black kids in America's ghettos "only know that their lives are so miserable, so completely hopeless and so ignored that, perhaps, even death would be better."[14] This feeling of *hopelessness* was overwhelmingly cited in official reports and journalistic accounts as *the cause* for rioting in urban American during the mid-1960s. It was this feeling that hope was unattainable and foreign that propelled black Americans into urban rebellion.

This chapter reflects on the multiple interpretations of major urban rebellions in the United States between 1964 and 1969 to understand how descriptions of the major race riots, especially the metaphor of the powder keg, created and reflected racialized political feelings where *hopelessness replaced hope* as the emotional framework for racial liberalism as the possibility of integration ebbed.[15] The assassinations of John Kennedy and, later, Malcolm X, along with the passage of the Civil Rights Act of 1964 and the Voting Rights Act of 1965, evacuated black hope from political liberalism and replaced it with different political emotions, including rage, frustration, and fear. Blacks feared white terrorism, and whites feared blacks. This impasse augmented the hopelessness and anger that undergirded the riots. It prompted the passage of the 1967 DC Crime Bill and helped undermine the 1968 Civil Rights Bill as *protest* was elided with *crime* in news accounts and in public policy, effectively mystifying the context and content of urban rebellion. As the war on poverty transformed into the war on crime, *feelings* became a major rhetorical vector of policy discussions about urban rebellion. Law-and-order rhetoric reasserted white statism as the only permissible loyalty and effectively harnessed white anxiety and anger toward ending any possibility of black equality *through the law*. Riot commissions, *as official discourses of racial feelings*, often described the structural inequalities that propelled black despair and hopelessness, while also blaming the victims of structural inequality. Even when the commissions had earnest, concerned civil servants producing their reports, the political will to transform racial psychodynamics and material segregation never emerged. Thus did riots highlight the continuities of slavery in contemporary life throughout the long sixties.

Riots and the Materiality of (Post?)colonial Feelings

In his 1944 masterpiece *An American Dilemma: The Negro Problem and Modern Democracy*, Gunnar Myrdal explained that riots emerge from structural violence that precipitates *political feelings* about antiblack public policy:

> The causation of riots would seem to be much like that of lynching. There is a background of mounting tension, caused by economic insecurity of whites, belief that the Negro is rising, sex jealousy, boredom on the part of the lower strata of the white population. The local police are often known to be on the side of the whites. The breaking point is caused by a crime or rumor of crime by a Negro against a white person, or by the attempt of a Negro to claim a legal right. The effects of riots may be even more harmful to amicable race relations than are those of lynching. Whites do not feel the twinge of bad conscience which they have when they have lynched helpless and unresisting Negroes.[16]

Myrdal's reflections on rioting point to *white feelings* (insecurity, jealousy, boredom) in creating the terror and police violence to which rioting responds, invoking *lynching* as a postemancipation disciplinary practice used to reinscribe what Négritude writers would characterize as "the colonial." As rumors spread about police violence, urban rebellions begin, and white people use the disruption to escalate repression and justify antiblack feelings via antiblack violence.

Importantly, Myrdal's observations use a psychological schema to center *tension* as a negative feeling in the *white body* as a way of orienting whites toward and away from particular political feelings, in this case toward whiteness and away from civil rights.[17] Myrdal anticipates arguments made a decade later in *A Dying Colonialism* when Frantz Fanon characterized this kind of muscular tension as bearing "the signs of disturbance to which the phenomenology of encounters has accustomed us."[18] Fanon elaborates on this phenomenological encounter between colonizer and colonized, white and black, in *The Wretched of the Earth*, writing, "Every time the issue of Western values crops up, the colonized grow tense and their muscles seize up. During the period of decolonization the colonized are called upon to be reasonable. They are offered rock-solid values, they are told in great detail that decolonization should not mean regression, and that they must rely on values which have proved to be reliable and worthwhile."[19] Fanon elucidates how conservative appeals to labor and civility frame debates over racial domination in the polis even as they amplify frustration and fear, adding: "The colonist is an exhibitionist. His safety concerns lead him to remind the colonized out loud: 'Here I am the master.' The colonist keeps the colonized in a state of rage, which he prevents from boiling over. . . . The muscular tension of the colonized periodically erupts into bloody fighting between tribes, clans, and individuals."[20] In Fanon's schema, rage, tension, and internecine strife are all precipitated by *white colonizer feelings* that are presented as *normative values*. The bloody fighting—in the American context, rioting—is a *product* of those white feelings that overcode the colonizer-colonized or slave master-slave relationship, as we saw in the previous chapter.

The production and overproduction of political feelings through persistent rhetorical forms intrinsically shape black emotional responses to colonization and violence. As increasingly desperate black residents are met with pleas to "be reasonable" and "have faith" in white America or in the very governance that is often used against them, they embrace strategies of resistance that break the tension preserving antiblack stasis. Fanon's observations about the circulation of racial "tensions" demonstrate how the political feelings that fed whites a steady diet of antiblack social panic functioned to undercut evidence about widespread social injustice for nonsympathetic white auditors. Paula Ioanide observes that groups "targeted by hegemonic economies of emotion" are "overdetermined through cultural and political processes of circulation, repetition, and association."[21] The repetition of certain depictions of political action, particularly when it is a response to racial injustice, creates economies of emotion that become predictable circuits, such that observers of urban rebellion use the same language of explosives to underscore the *certainty* of particular emotions and responses. This certainty, then, might lead us to understand riots as *intrinsic* to postemancipation public life.

In connecting the emotional and structural causes of urban rebellion to lynching, Myrdal defined riots as a northern phenomenon. In the North, "when Negroes think they might have something to gain," they will weigh the "risk of fighting back, and in the North they know that some portion of the white population is on their side and that the police will ultimately restore order."[22] Myrdal saw riots as *calculated risk* designed to create immense political pressure in moments of precarity. While Myrdal's comments were penned well before the modern civil rights era, they speak to the kinds of *predictable emotional dynamics* that precipitate black mass resistance. Psychologist Price Cobbs echoed this view in a July 1967 essay in *Negro Digest*, where he argued: "Watts was rejected because most people were unable to separate the wanton lawlessness from the more significant evidence of a large group of men attempting to establish themselves psychologically."[23] Cobbs argued that black modernity was intensely preoccupied with building and sustaining spaces for psychological transformation (what Fanon called "psychic conversion") and grounding. But as we saw in Chapter Three, Grier and Cobbs described urban rebellion as a fundamental product of *slavery*. They saw the street corner in Harlem, for example, as "a direct remnant of slavery. Move back in time and this could be an auction block."[24] Noting that the psychic structures of blacks and whites remained unchanged after slavery, they lamented how "cruelty remained unabated in thoughts, feelings, intimidation and occasional lynching."[25]

Take, for example, the 1967 Detroit riots, which would be illegible without histories of Detroit's fugitive slave riots between 1815 and 1865. Designed to protest runaway slaves in the city, these riots shaped the psychological and emotional landscape in antebellum and postbellum Detroit, marking the city's psycho-emotional landscape even today.[26] Nonetheless the importance of slavery to Detroit's history "is belied by its almost complete absence in the collective memory of Detroiters," making it difficult to reckon with the contemporary vestiges of slavery in the city.[27] Thus have the psychological dispositions of white and black people remained relatively unchanged in the United States as a continuation of the *feelings engendered by slavery*, as Malcolm X (a former Detroit resident) made plain. In writing about the riots of 1967, however, even contemporary historians who do not invoke the city's history of slavery as context for the riots nonetheless use the language of *feelings* to describe the riots as "hope disappointed" and as the result of "a mood of apprehension" that spread across the country after the Harlem riots.[28]

In the case of the Watts riot in 1965, slavery was not the omnipresent historical force shaping riot discourse; migration and labor rights were. The Watts riot, begun in response to perceived harassment by a white California state highway patrolman who stopped a black motorist, caused $35 million in damage from looting and arson and left thirty-four people dead. During and after the five-day riot, Watts was illegible to whites because it *did not* share the same racial history as, say, Harlem or Detroit. Watts complicated the political field of civil rights during the Johnson administration because it was a *product* of migration, economic inequality, and unfulfilled liberal promises. In *Fire This Time*, Gerald Horne writes that Los Angles was different sociologically because "it had been subjected to enormous strain as a result of massive migration; this combined with unique racial tensions . . . produced an explosion." Migrants expected Hollywood's California, he adds, but "when they were confronted with the grim reality, they were as disillusioned as the others, except their disillusionment was leavened with an anger about racism and a history of militance."[29] Robert Dalleck elaborates that Watts seemed like an unlikely place for riots except that it "was full of joblessness, crime, suffering, and hopelessness about escaping the miseries of black urban life as any other ghetto in America."[30]

This crucible of black hopelessness and white anxiety and jealousy underscores how antiblack exclusionary economic policies after emancipation have structurally defined permissible political participation. Black Power activist Julius Lester saw these midcentury emotional dynamics turning on the paradox—and impossibility—of integration. In his influential essay "The Angry Children of Malcolm X," Lester described the paradox thus: "Feeling most comfortable when the black man emulates the ways and manners of white Americans, America has, at the same time, been stolidly unwilling to let the black man be assimilated into the mainstream."[31] Lester pointed to the impossibility of black equality given perpetual white *dis-comfort* with black autonomy. This feeling of racial *tension* (evidenced by *dis-comfort*) produces antiblack public policy as white comfort ebbs and flows relative to black protest, suggesting that riots—as a product of racial feelings—are a language that shapes the polis. Riots, then, function as embodied discourse, as the material consequence of language made real and anchored in a critique of the ways that white supremacist resource distribution mimics colonial habitus.

Riots as Language of Feeling

In a 1966 interview with Mike Wallace of CBS News, Martin Luther King Jr. was asked to reflect on that summer's urban rebellions in Omaha, Chicago, and Cleveland. Perhaps anticipating Spivak's question "Can the subaltern speak?," King answered, "[A] riot is the language of the unheard." He continued, "And what is it that America has failed to hear? It has failed to hear that the economic plight of the Negro poor has worsened over the last few years." He added that the "mood of the Negro community now is one of urgency. One of saying that we aren't going to wait, that we've got to have our freedom, we've waited too long." While King characterized riots as "self-defeating and socially destructive" in this interview, he was clear about the "militant" and "determined" commitment of black America to pressure federal, state, and municipal governments for social change. Wallace asked how long the rebellions would continue, and King explained that the duration as well as the scope of black protest depended on how white America decided to answer the call for equality.[32]

This oft-quoted exchange is remarkable for several reasons. First, King suggests that riots are a *language*. That is, they are a method of communication employed by a particular community, in this case, "the unheard," through the use of symbolic action. As a speech act, riots are like any other language; they contain symbols that mark identity and emotions. Second, King's quote characterizes the exchange as a *refusal* of politics as usual that has come after other options have failed; riots are a last resort. Third, King's characterization notes *failure* on the part of the auditor(s) to understand the language of riots, rather than a failure of the speaker(s) or the speech itself, suggesting that the communication barrier is one that can be ameliorated with an attention to *listening* both better and differently. Fourth, he suggests that riots are an expression of a "mood" that is characterized by urgency, militancy, and determination, nodding to the birth of Black Power as a new rhetorical arena. Fifth, King articulates riots as a chronopolitical expression of black time, since he explains that black Americans have waited far too long for their natural rights—an argument he made throughout his career, as we saw in Chapter Two. Sixth, this passage demonstrates that *feelings have political consequences*, and these feelings are linked to economic factors as well as a lack of social equality. Finally, King's words provided a temporal interpretation of riots that was structural and not immediate. Even when an instance of police brutality (reported or rumored) sparked a rebellion, King's comments point to the existence of an oppositional and embodied language that historically functions as a means of redress for long-standing social violence.

Riots, then, have a temporality that we can understand only from a postcolonial perspective that acknowledges the circularity of antiblack violence and the prevention of black Being as central features of black time. Riots and urban rebellions expose multiple temporalities within the space of the political because they disrupt white time by demonstrating the urgency of political change and expose the racialization of history and policy. King's observations continue to circulate because he interpreted the motivations of riots for white listeners from a dual positionality: he was both *of* the community rioting but also *separate* from them, commenting on what Michael Herzfeld has called "the social production of indifference."[33] Thus do we see how causality is mystified by racial relationality: whites cannot read riots as a political expression because they see riots as asymmetrical responses to immediate, hyperpresent events rather than as symptoms of long-standing repression. King's observations, then, acknowledge what we might describe as the colonial hardships that emerge from "being a subject in contexts of instability and crisis."[34] But they also demonstrate that increasingly urgent calls for political intervention to ameliorate suffering are met with staggering rejection of the notion of common humanity and the denial of black selfhood.

King's 1967 text *Where Do We Go from Here? Community or Chaos* elaborated on this exchange and addressed the production of *white* indifference to describe the feelings that are both the *affect* and the *effect* of a riot. Looking back on the long, hot summer of 1967, when dozens of riots erupted across the country, he wrote: "There is something painfully sad about a riot. One sees screaming youngsters and angry adults fighting hopelessly and aimlessly against impossible odds. Deep down within them you perceive a desire for self-destruction, a suicidal longing."[35] I return to the idea of "suicidal longing" at length in Chapter Six, but this passage seems noteworthy given its reliance on feelings to describe what propels riots alongside King's notion of how auditors and viewers make sense of riots. King notes how *hopelessness* permeated black communities in this period, and he performs *pity* in response to riots. I say pity rather than empathy because King articulates himself as an ideal national subject (one separate from the rioters) who understands the political context more completely than the rioters do, and who would never participate in any action that would undermine the credibility of his fidelity to the nation. King positions himself as a credible outsider who can interpret black feelings for white audiences, but his comments also underscore the premium that nonviolent civil rights activism placed on social cohesion.

While hopelessness characterizes so many accounts attempting to humanize the motives of rioters, the rebellions of the 1960s in cities like Harlem, Watts, Newark, and Detroit were also labeled "bursts of rage," suggesting that these rebellions resulted from short-lived feelings that bubbled up in response to untenable economic and social conditions.[36] Additionally, in many descriptions of the period, riots are described *pathologically* and are compared to fire, suggesting their danger, mutability, and contagion. Riots are read as a dis-ease that can spread through the body politic, ultimately undermining its stability and legibility. These psychological accounts of riots privileged readings that relied on the *mob* and the *demagogue* as the agents in the scene and the only lenses through which to understand urban rebellion. They offered descriptions that connoted short, intense, fiery conflict to describe rioting. For example, in a 1966 interview, King described riots as "unplanned, uncontrollable temper tantrums brought on by long neglected poverty, humiliation, oppression and exploitation."[37] This description likens rioters to children: emotionally immature and unable to navigate urban desperation, they throw a tantrum. And though King does name structural inequality as the cause of rioting, his descriptions of the rioters displace the causality onto the victims as a kind of developmental problem, echoing the kinds of pronouncements seen in the "oppression psychosis" literature, as we saw in the last chapter. These readings demand *containment* as the only legitimate response because contagion amplifies fears of blackness. From the Latin *contagio* (a touching, contact, or contagion) and *contingo* (to touch closely), contagion as applied to riots speaks to fears of miscegenation and to contact with blackness and demands the eradication of black Being as a prophylactic against contact with blackness.[38] This is, in part, because blackness itself carries what Bryan McCann calls "the mark of criminality."[39] But King rightly points to the cause of riots even as he walks a tightrope of denouncing urban rebellion as a black political tactic. He says, "So far, only the police have goaded our people to riot." But, he adds, "All the sound and fury seems but the posturing of cowards whose bold talk produces no action and signifies nothing."[40] Calling out white liberals for using police power to quell black responses to white political inaction, King squarely locates blame for riots on inadequate support for black communities combined with police brutality, highlighting how repressing black political action exposes white liberal protections as a fraud.

For their part, communication scholars have tended to see riots as rhetorical confrontations, which of course they are.[41] But riots are also rhetorical scripts of refusal. Riots are a refusal to wait any longer for conditions to change. They are both call and response. They are a refusal to continue with politics-as-usual. They are a rejection of hope as a major affective discourse of blackness. They are a refusal to play nice or be quiet. They are rhetorical maneuvers that take up space. You can't ignore riots. They are visceral. They are also costly and destructive. But they command a nation's undivided attention. Riots wrench the public away from their banal habits and into a space that questions the arrangements of racialized power. Riots are met with troops, which dramatizes the colonial situation as black communities are occupied.

Undoubtedly, the powder keg was the controlling metaphor of riot discourse in the 1960s as observers described the explosive nature of riots, as we saw in the *Ebony* editorial about the Harlem riot. The persistent use of the powder keg metaphor exposed how governance was deployed *against* poor black Americans when they assumed that the civil rights struggle would help governance target white excess. As a metaphor, though, the powder keg has several important elements. First, it demonstrates the temporality of riots.[42] The powder keg functions discursively as an anticipation, as an *anxiety* about potential future violence. This means that the metaphor helps people linger in an imaginary place that may or may not emerge as a rationale for anti-black action. It also means that the metaphor has a temporal dimension that is about political and emotional thresholds that, once crossed, will trigger riots. Second, the powder keg is a receptacle, a repository of *feelings* about antiblackness in America. It holds black feelings about disenfranchisement, poverty, discrimination, segregation, and violence just as it also holds white feelings about fragility, change, confrontation, and accountability. Third, as a container, the powder keg provokes fear because it visually suggests miscegenation; it is the fear of *mixing these feelings* or *tensions* that creates the anticipation of the explosion, which also implies *white purity* in a social as well as an emotional sense. Fourth, while the explosiveness of the powder keg would seem to be the essence of the metaphor, when employed *by white rhetors*, it works to create fear *among whites*. So the powder keg, as an *anticipatory discursive form*, is about *creating racial feelings*, too. It's a race to create more fear in whites before blacks actually get social power as a preventative to black nationalist organizing or what eventually became Black Power. Thus the powder keg metaphor's ability to manufacture political feelings fundamentally undercuts efforts to enfranchise racial minorities. Likewise, when paired with "explosive" as a modifier of race relations, as was often the case, the powder keg metaphor suggested that it was *black* dissatisfaction that was destabilizing the country, scapegoating black Americans for problems that were ultimately the intentional rhetorical and political product of white policy makers.

The powder keg metaphor is prevalent in the discourse of movement leaders and activists, where it functions as an acknowledgment of the threshold where black frustration meets the failure of white liberal promises. For example, King's use of the powder keg metaphor peppered his criticisms of federal inaction on poverty and his critiques of the police. He rails that "our

government declared a war against poverty and yet it only financed a skir-
mish against poverty," and he describes the feeling this inadequate resource
management engendered: "And this led to great despair. It led to great cynicism and discontent throughout the Negro Community. I had lived in the
ghettos of Chicago and Cleveland, and I knew the hurt and the cynicism and
the discontent. And the fact was that every city in our country was sitting on
a potential powderkeg."[43] Framing *despair, cynicism,* and *discontent* as black
responses to white failure, King exposes how poverty policy amplified black
misery, aligning King's observations with those of Malcolm X and James
Baldwin, demonstrating a point of consensus among black intellectuals.

Like King, Malcolm understood the utility of the powder keg as a metaphor
invoking white feelings and augmenting antiblack racism, and he frequently
used it to describe the precariousness of race relations in Harlem resulting
from pernicious police brutality. In one representative sample, Malcolm
explains that white people support nonviolence "because they're so guilty,"
but he suggests that when whites "fool themselves into thinking that Negroes
are really nonviolent and patient, and long suffering, they've got a powder
keg in their house. And instead of them trying to do something to defuse the
powder keg, they're putting a blanket over it, trying to make believe that this
is not a powder keg; that it is a couch we can lay on and enjoy."[44] Malcolm
emphasized how white people want to feel *powerful* rather than *responsible,*
so they see black hopelessness and rage as aberrations. Rather than ameliorate the conditions that create these feelings, white people invest in narratives that make them feel superior rather than culpable. In his famous 1964
speech "The Ballot or the Bullet," Malcolm describes the false promises of
white liberalism and the response of black Americans, who have become "fed
up," "disenchanted," "disillusioned," "dissatisfied," and "frustrate[ed],"" making

> the black community throughout America today more explosive than all of the
> atomic bombs the Russians can ever invent. Whenever you got a racial powder
> keg sitting in your lap, you're in more trouble than if you had an atomic powder
> keg sitting in your lap. When a racial powder keg goes off, it doesn't care who it
> knocks out the way. Understand this, it's dangerous.

Malcolm's invocation of the racial powder keg hinges on negative black *feelings* about the *inadequacies of racial liberalism.* These black feelings emerge
in response to *white failure* within the regime of racial liberalism, creating
a cycle of unkept promises that fundamentally undermined the civil rights
project as whites saw it in 1964. But given that this speech occurred almost
exactly three months before the passage of the Civil Rights Act of 1964, it

is also possible to read this kind of rhetorical posture as political pressure on Johnson to act. And while Malcolm wasn't pushing for the civil rights bill per se, his rhetorical interventions *did* create an oppositional space that justified the bill's passage, at least in the short term, although enforcement would be difficult given that states' rights continued to be the political cover for segregationists in the South, and given that the Johnson administration could not see that the terrain of struggle over civil rights was vastly different in the North.

For his part, James Baldwin was dismissive about white politicians who claimed not to understand the causes of riots, suggesting that such disavowals were disingenuous, since riots are an *anticipated consequence* of white political inaction. Like the *Ebony* editors at the beginning of the chapter, Baldwin dramatized white shock at urban riots: "One day, to everyone's astonishment, someone drops a match in the powder keg and everything blows up. Before the dust has settled or the blood congealed, editorials, speeches, and civil rights commissions are loud in the land, demanding to know what happened. What happened is that the Negroes wanted to be treated like men."[45] Baldwin argued that there is no political deniability about riots, suggesting that liberal anxiety was not about rioting per se but about refusing black mass politics of any kind. His assertion of "manhood" here is much like Ossie Davis's about Malcolm X in that both articulated a new form of black (masculine) subjectivity that was emergent in and through responses to police violence. Baldwin elaborates to describe how white people

> live in a state of carefully repressed terror in relation to blacks. There is something curious and paradoxical about this terror, which is involved not only with the common fear of death, but with a sense of its being considered utterly irrelevant whether one is breathing or not. I think this has something to do with the fact that, whereas white men have killed black men for sport, or out of terror or out of the intolerable excess of terror called hatred, or out of the necessity of affirming their identity as white men, none of these motives appear necessarily to obtain for black men: it is not necessary for a black man to hate a white man, or to have any particular feelings about him at all, in order to realize that he must kill him.[46]

In cultivating this antiblack terror, Baldwin articulates the (white) ego-function of these political feelings that contain black life in America, concluding that white men must kill black men to convince themselves that they exist. Black men must resist even on pain of death, since the terror is the all-encompassing rationale for antiblack policy.

King's description of riots as a *language* of rage, despair, and hopelessness, paired with the articulation of riots as the *response to terror*, demonstrates how riots were a primary discursive terrain of social violence and systemic trauma. Because riots are a response to trauma and also a trauma in and of themselves, it is also useful to think about riots as wounds as well as responses to wounds. This is why, for King, riots are so sad. They are imbued with melancholy because pain is omnipresent. "I think we have come to the point where there is no longer a choice now between nonviolence and riots," said King in that famous 1966 interview with Mike Wallace. King was clear:

> It must be militant, massive nonviolence, or riots. The discontent is so deep, the anger so ingrained, the despair, the restlessness so wide, that something has to be brought into being to serve as a channel through which these *deep emotional feelings*, these *deep angry feelings* can be funneled. There has to be an outlet, and I see this campaign as a way to transmute the *inchoate rage* of the ghetto into a constructive and creative channel. It becomes an *outlet for anger*.[47]

By 1966, as Black Power began to circulate as a *mood*, riots become a foregone conclusion even for King as a result of discontent and anger about unfulfilled promises and disappointment with the progress of civil rights initiatives and the failure of moral suasion. King's language clearly demarcates *feelings* as the terrain of black action and reaction and as the authorizing discourse of riots.

But King is also clear about the importance of teaching whites to read black feelings about white repression and inaction as a way of conceptualizing riots as *inevitable* without nonviolent black activism curbing black rage and despair. In a 1965 *Playboy* interview, King described this emotional dynamism of black discontent, saying, "White Americans must be made to understand the basic motives underlying Negro demonstrations. Many pent-up resentments and latent frustrations are boiling inside the Negro, and he must release them. It is not a threat but a fact of history that if an oppressed people's pent-up emotions are not nonviolently released, they will be violently released. . . . For if his frustration and despair are allowed to continue piling up, millions of Negroes will seek solace and security in black-nationalist ideologies. And this, inevitably, would lead to a frightening racial nightmare."[48] Rhetorically, asserting that urban centers are a powder keg, for example, works to undercut conversation about the underlying causes of riots as legitimate political concerns. And while I do not have space here to provide a detailed analysis of all the major rebellions as they unfolded after Harlem's uprisings in 1964, the rhetorical framing of the riots is tremendously consistent and is then echoed in the governmental discourses of the riot commissions set up to study and analyze the causes of the riots. Still, if there were any official spaces to *teach whites* about the causes of riots, riot commissions were clearly that space. The language of the powder keg and its explosion can be found in congressional hearings, in presidential statements (official and off the record), and in the findings of the riot commissions, demonstrating the ubiquity of this rhetorical frame.

Feeling Watts, Teaching Black Feelings

The riots sweeping across the country after the Harlem riot were discon-certing, but the size and scope of the Watts riots forced President Johnson to address the urban rebellions overtaking many of America's cities. Before Watts, the images of antiblack brutality from Birmingham and the early sit-ins circulated to frame black protest. "After Watts, Americans were instead witness to pictures of mobs of young city blacks, hurling bricks at police cars, torching their own neighborhoods, and looting stores of all they could carry. Such pictures invited the conclusion from whites that after all that had been done for blacks, after all that had been given to them, it was not enough. Blacks wanted more, demanded more—and they took it."[49] Whites internalized the early riots of the period as a lack of *gratitude* combined with wanton *lawless-ness*. Randall Woods describes LBJ's thinking: "LBJ was tempted to buy into the notion that the riots were communist inspired. King's apostasy and the black power movement, with its apocalyptic anti-liberal rhetoric and advo-cacy for violence in the nation's inner cities continued to distress him. How could blacks, for whom he had done so much, be so ungrateful?"[50] This insis-tence on the performance of black gratitude as a public feeling in response to marginal civil rights gains demonstrates the pathological economy at work, especially after Watts, in terms of both expectations and political judgment.

But Watts also exposed the ineffectiveness of black organizing without clear attention to class politics, particularly as they emerged in urban centers with different histories. Gary Orfield's work on racial liberalism makes the case that midcentury race riots undermined racial liberals' ability to defend racial equality as a moral stance. Despite the legal gains of the civil rights movement, black Americans were worse off financially and socially by the mid-1960s, and combined with urban unrest, it seemed that black America wasn't ready for, or was undeserving of, equality. Orfield writes, "The lib-eral view seemed weak and defensive in contrast to the clear and aggressive conservative defense of law and order, and of firm action against violence."[51] Consequently, law-and-order discourses painted a clearer, if totally inaccurate, picture of riots as the consequence of black Americans being nonideal citizens. Lyndon Johnson used this language as early as 1964 in his response to the Harlem riot, saying that the "overriding issue in New York City is the preservation of law and order."[52] And the larger, structural causes and consequences of black inequality were articulated mostly in official discourses that were too big and too nuanced to be messaged effectively to a white public turned off to black organizing, let alone to the public display of black feelings.

After Watts, administration officials attempted to define the conditions that produce riots. President Johnson acknowledged as much as he courted former CIA director John A. McCone to lead a riot commission on Watts that would establish a chronology of the riot, investigate the causes, and make recommendations for action.[53] Invoking the dominant idiom, Johnson described America's urban race issue as a "powder keg," explaining: "You just have no idea [of] the depth of feeling of these people. I see some of the boys that have worked for me, have 2,000 years of persecution, now they suffer from it. They [the ghetto dwellers] have absolutely nothing to live for, 40 percent of them are unemployed, these youngsters live with rats and have no place to sleep, and they all start from broken homes and illegitimate families and all the narcotics circulating around. . . . We have just got to find some way to wipe out these ghettos and find some housing and put them to work."[54] Empathizing with black urban residents, Johnson saw housing and jobs as the curative to hopelessness. This private exchange is remarkable because Johnson conceded that riots are an expression of *deep, historical feelings* grounded in economic and social disenfranchisement designed by public policies pertaining to housing and employment discrimination to intentionally destroy black futures. Likewise, former attorney general Nicholas Katzenbach explained that "the most dangerous agitators in the ghettoes are disease and desperation, joblessness and hopelessness," and thus "the program of the extreme 'militants' will of necessity find favor."[55] Even big labor weighed in: "The lesson of the Watts riots, as has been made clear to all, is that the disappointment, frustration and bitterness bred by discrimination in housing, employment and education cannot be contained forever."[56] And especially given migration to Los Angeles and "the decline of progressive trade unionism, there was no other channel for this rage."[57]

In accounts like these, politicians described the *structural barriers* to black equality as *causes* of the *feelings* propelling urban rebellion. Kilpatrick supplements these narratives by adding that in Los Angeles "the unemployed and dispossessed were not actually committing more crime. But with deindustrialization, public fears of a lumpen underclass threatening the majority escalated, partly because politicians stoked these fears for electoral reasons.

This fueled the tough-on-crime stance—which became tough on African Americans in particular, thanks to the longstanding history of the racialization of crime in the United States for political purposes."[58] In California, then, law-and-order responses to black hopelessness fueled Barry Goldwater's new conservatism, which was successfully weaponized in the gubernatorial election of Ronald Reagan in 1966, just as Black Power began to emerge in the Bay Area.

From his perspective, Black Panther Party chairman Huey Newton saw Watts as an expression of discontent with racial politics in California that propelled a tremendous break in the community, with rebellion focused on bringing attention to the blight of segregation and poverty in urban America. Newton elucidates how Watts propelled the disidentification of urban blacks from the integrationist "Dream" of the southern civil rights movement: "I'm sure the people of Detroit were educated by what happened in Watts. Perhaps this was wrong education. It sort of missed the mark . . . but the people were educated through the activity. The people of Detroit followed the example of the people in Watts, only they added a little scrutiny to it."[59] Oddly enough, Newton echoed both King and Johnson in his description of the pedagogical function of Watts in teaching blacks about riots as a language of dispossession.

But mainstream civil rights leaders disagreed with this approach, deciding to take a hard-line oppositional stance to rioting without elucidating any of the structural causes of urban despair. In a striking denunciation of rioting on October 14, 1966, the civil rights leaders Roy Wilkins, Whitney Young, A. Philip Randolph, Dorothy Height, Bayard Rustin, Amos T. Hall, and Hobson Reynolds published a manifesto titled "Crisis and Commitment" in the New York Times to repudiate Black Power. Their statement "condemn[ed] both rioting and the demagoguery that feeds it" and recommitted the leaders to "integration, by which we mean an end to every barrier which segregation and other forms of discrimination have raised against the enjoyment by Negro Americans of their human and constitutional rights." The statement also notes the inconsistency of the white perspectives on Black Power, asking if the nation has selective amnesia and has forgotten "that for every Negro youth who throws a brick, there are a hundred thousand suffering the same disadvantages who do not? That for every Negro who tosses a Molotov cocktail, there are a thousand fighting and dying on the battlefields of Vietnam?"[60] While this statement does not play a huge role in the rhetorical historiography of 1966, it probably should, because it shows how, at midcentury, Black Power exposed the ideological conservatism of integration as civil rights leaders sought common ground with the "law and order" crowd demonizing the popular and magnetic personalities that were shouting Black Power for the cameras. In positioning riots as the refuge of the black nationalists, civil rights activists (including King on some occasions) helped facilitate white backlash against all black mass action.

Still, King's signature was notably absent from this manifesto. Strategically, King occupied a different positionality, where he held rhetorical space for Black Power activists *to continue to occupy rhetorical space.* This ambivalence about Black Power helped facilitate the white misreading of riots. In his response to the manifesto, King explained: "It is a false assumption that the so-called white backlash is caused by the slogan, 'black power.'. . . Actually, the black power slogan has been exploited by the decision makers to justify resistance to change."[61] Couching his critique of the mainstream civil rights leaders in the language of accommodationism, King lampooned their read on Black Power by suggesting that their convergence with law and order clouded their judgment. Glossing King but elaborating on his comments, the *Times* echoed this logic, writing that in "the view of some civil rights leaders, however, other whites . . . have found the black power cry a useful excuse for stiffening their resistance to civil rights pressures without feeling guilty about it. For some time, a number of the more moderate leaders have contemplated combatting this trend by taking a strong and united stand against black power and its advocates."[62] In this view, whites shut down Black Power organizing to avoid the guilt precipitated by King's attempt to build the beloved community. But even with these accounts demonstrating the relationality of feeling and riots, the commissions established to study riots were even more articulate about the causes for riots, even as they were instrumental in forestalling solutions to structural inequality in the cities.

Riot Commissions and (Emotional) Governmentality

In her outstanding history of riot commissions, Lindsey Lupo writes that riot commissions have a politics centered on political feelings that seek to restore a kind of emotional stasis for both rioters and the public. Lupo explains that riot commissions "evoke emotions" as "feelings of safety are conjured up for the non-rioting public and feelings of power are invoked for the rioters. In other words, both feel as though they have 'won' in some way."[63] While anomie drives riots, the language of safety dominates their containment. And just as the containment language imbues the riot with a political context, so too does it drive the political response to the racial elements of riots. Lupo explains that Nixon's 1968 election demonstrates how the "southern strategy" "quietly drew on race and feelings of white resentment regarding policy programs that appeared to leave whites on the sidelines, thus ushering a new era of antagonism towards preferential programs."[64] This antagonism harnessed resentment about the possibility of black equality and directed it at undermining black Being.

The McCone Commission elaborated at length on the causes of the Watts riot, linking the rebellion to white resentment and black despair. "What happened," the commission's report concluded, "was an explosion—a formless, quite senseless, all but hopeless violent protest—engaged in by a few but bringing great distress to all."[65] Using the metaphor of the explosion, the report interpreted Watts through the lens of black childhood and through the language of pathology: "In examining the sickness in the center of the city, what has depressed and stunned us most is the dull, devastating spiral of failure that awaits the average disadvantaged child in the urban core." Portraying black home life as an impediment to early childhood learning and anemic public policy as an urban *sickness*, the report describes black children as unprepared for school and as susceptible to illiteracy despite having good teachers. "Frustrated and disillusioned, the child becomes a discipline problem" until, at the end of this "spiral of frustration," the teenager runs into "unemployment two to three times the country's average."[66] In choosing to focus on black childhood, the McCone Commission engaged in an interesting project of futurity, where rescuing black childhood from political pessimism seems like a project on the horizon. But it also trades in the oppression psychosis discourses examined in Chapter Three. As an attempt to resuscitate social innocence for black children, the McCone report seems like a surprising space to find such a searing report of black childhood poverty because it depicts systemic problems that affect the entire black life cycle in America's cities. Nonetheless, as Kathryn Bond Stockton observes, "Children, as an *idea*, are likely to be both white and middle-class. It is a privilege to be protected—and sheltered—and thus to have a childhood."[67] And while the report stops short of proposing interventions that would respond to the crushing despair felt keenly by all black people, but especially black children, it evidences the incompleteness of equality under a regime of racial liberalism, where the harms can be described but the solutions (beyond more police) are not forthcoming. Given President Johnson's desire to distance himself from the report's conclusions about the Watts riots, one can make a compelling case that Watts is where Johnson's commitment to racial justice ended and where law and order became a foregone conclusion.

Still, the McCone Commission's report was replicated for the public by Kimex and included a sixty-four-page magazine insert leading with a sensationalist tagline promising "One Hundred Four Shocking Photos of the Most Terrifying Riot in History" that "show infinitely better than words possibly could the utter, horrible chaos that existed" during the riot, which the publisher termed "a holocaust."[68] So even if the actual contents of the report highlighted the cycle of poverty in urban America, the report was hawked to the American public as an exceptional moment in history, rather than the culmination of hundreds of years of banal horrors.

The National Advisory Commission on Civil Disorders (also called the Kerner Commission) was led by Illinois governor Otto Kerner in 1968 to investigate the 1967 race riots and followed on the heels of the McCone Commission. "White society," the commission opined, "is deeply implicated in the ghetto. White institutions created it, white institutions maintain it, and white society condones it."[69] The 1967 riots killed forty-three in Detroit and twenty-six in Newark, though riots in twenty-three other cities that year had fewer casualties. Still, the NACD was the result of white panic about black mass politics. But though it was propelled by "a combination of scholarly examination, congressional documents, public testimony, and the moral outrage of political officials and civic leaders, the Kerner Commission Report was the last thing that Lyndon Johnson wanted to hear. The man whose signature domestic policy sought to wage an unconditional war against poverty as a way of building the Great Society refused to meet with the commission he appointed."[70] While Johnson publicly praised the commission's findings, "privately, the President was seething. Feeing betrayed by the commission he himself instituted, President Johnson and his administration began a discreet campaign to undermine the Kerner Commission and its recommendations."[71]

The historiography of the NACD is important because it shows the ambivalence that even Johnson had about civil disorders as a language of redress, and demonstrates *why* law and order became the white liberal establishment's reaction to black mass politics near the end of the decade. Even with his support for the war on poverty, Johnson didn't want to hear the commission's enumeration of the causes of the riots, but his inability to *hear* riots as a *language* of black political feeling was exacerbated by the popularity of the new conservatism. Where the McCone Commission took a hard-line stance against rioting, the Kerner Commission offered a liberal rebuttal that blamed riots on structural racism, but its findings were lost as the nation plunged into law and order.[72] Legitimation became the goal of the Johnson administration, even as the president elected not to seek reelection.

New Conservatism, White Backlash, and White Rage

Although Barry Goldwater was the standard-bearer of law-and-order rhetoric with the publication of *The Conscience of a Conservative* (1964), his message

was premature; people found him to be angry, and they found his pronouncements unfounded. While this was true in 1964, by 1968, the conditions that
Goldwater described had, in some ways, come to be. Law and order became
an important rhetorical frame for white backlash because it combined political concern about traditional crimes (robberies, muggings, murder, and rape)
with white resistance to civil rights, civil liberties, and civil disobedience.
The hippie movement, the use of recreational drugs, and the sexual revolution only added to the conservative response to urban rebellion in ways
that amplified the anxieties about the movement for black equality. Flamm
and Steigerwald write, "In 1966, a rising tide of public anxiety over law and
order helped sweep incumbent liberals from power and presented insurgent
conservatives with new opportunities. The issue enabled conservative leaders to mobilize grassroots conservatives, who in turn received a language of
protest and a vocabulary of ideas in which to link troubling changes in their
communities to broader developments in American society and culture."[73]
Anxiety mobilized law-and-order culture to undermine liberal humanism by
reasserting static whiteness as the precondition for citizenship.

Law-and-order culture is fundamentally a temporal discourse that stops
progressive time and reverts to colonial time through nostalgia and a fetishizing of colonial relationality. Law and order is a call hastening the destruction
of black people and the removal of black people from public life. Likewise,
law-and-order culture provides the rationale for the modern regime of terror,
one that suspends black political participation through a reassertion of antiblack Being. It is a compulsion to obeisance, a call to genuflection, to bowing
and scraping, to the Law of (White) Being. As Calvin Warren reminds us, the
"law is an ontological instrument" that functions as the ultimate assertion of
white statism over black Being.[74] But beyond the shifting political landscape in
Washington was the fact that racial liberalism was consolidated through the
conflation of *crime* and *protest*. Vesla Weaver explains that "crime is a symbol
for other societal anxieties," particularly racial anxieties, and in this case the
anxiety focused on black protest.[75] As Weaver explains, from "1965 to 1969,
nearly 100 pieces of legislation made participating in a riot a federal offense
with stiff penalties," including the "1968 Omnibus Crime Control and Safe
Streets Act, which made it a felony to cross state lines with the intent of incit-
ing or taking part in a riot," and the 1968 Civil Rights Bill, which contained an
antiriot bill known as the "H. Rap Brown bill" after the Black Power leader.[76]

As I mentioned in the introduction, the *Riot Report* characterized Black
Power as a mood, as a set of feelings that predominated the politics of the
moment. But the *Riot Report* is rife with assessments about the political feelings that give rise to urban riots. For example, Barbara Ritchie describes how

"feelings of desperation and anger" "breed civil disorders."[77] But Ritchie also describes the Black Power movement as a fantasy motivated by the decline of the civil rights movement and changing ideology that was met with popular and political resistance to its changing goals, particularly as law-and-order language consolidated white political power in both parties. Ritchie adds, "This combination of circumstances provoked anger deepened by impotence. Powerless to make any fundamental changes—powerless, that is, to compel white America to make those changes—many advocates of Black Power have retreated into an unreal world, where they see an outnumbered and poverty-stricken minority organizing itself independently of whites and creating sufficient power to force white American to grant its demands."[78]

The riots after King's assassination (which I take up in earnest in the next chapter) spoke to the kinds of feelings that were a permanent feature of American political life by the end of the 1960s and to the kinds of fantasies that shaped Black Power activism. With riots in 110 cities, including the District of Columbia, the urban rebellion after King's murder led Johnson to dispatch more than thirteen thousand federal troops to try to contain the rebellions. Grier and Cobbs wrote extensively about the trauma of King's assassination, explaining, "No more dreams to fix on. No more opiates to dull the pain. No more patience. No more thought. No more reason. Only a welling tide risen out of all those terrible years of grief, now a tidal wave of fury and rage, and all black, black as night" (213). If there is any moment in the twentieth century where black emotional contagion could be charted, it was in the riots that spanned the end of the 1960s, especially those that followed King's assassination. In the art (particularly the poetry) of the period, Aida Hussen explains, "the psychic discomfort of ambivalent mourning is overwritten by black nationalists' claim to a fully conscious politics of grief, and King's assassination is refigured as the martyrdom that produces and legitimates the vengefully heroic black subject."[79] And after the assassination of the most prominent activist supporting nonviolence, the heroic black subject could only emerge in opposition to liberalism's claims to meritocracy, integration, and colorblindness, as we shall see in the next chapter.

Still, after his landslide victory in 1970, Richard Nixon provided a rebuttal to King's claims about the role of poverty in the emergence of riots. In his "Freedom from Fear" campaign speech in 1968, Nixon decried any analysis that demonstrated how poverty contributed to crime, saying: "We cannot explain away crime in this country by charging it off to poverty—and we would not rid ourselves of the crime problem even if we succeeded overnight in lifting everyone above the poverty level. The role of poverty as a cause of the crime upsurge in America has been grossly exaggerated—and the incumbent Administration bears major responsibility for perpetuation of the myth."[80] Invoking the powder keg metaphor, Nixon used "social dynamite" as the trope that characterized race relations, though he obviously blamed black activists and citizens for lighting the fuse. Suggesting that cities were primitive spaces, Nixon offered a colonial perspective on riots, proclaiming, "We are trifling with social dynamite if we believe that the young people who emerge from these brutal societies in the central cities will come out as satisfied and productive citizens."[81]

The riots were important in the unfolding of the black freedom struggle because the riots from 1964 to 1968 prompted emergent disciplinary regimes to counter the political force of their anticolonial illegibility. In Wendy Brown's words, "Disciplinary power manages liberalism's production of politicized subjectivity by neutralizing (re-de-politicizing) identity through normalizing practices. As liberal discourse converts political identity into essentialized private interest, disciplinary power converts interest into normativized social identity manageable by regulatory regimes. Thus, disciplinary power politically neutralizes entitlement claims generated by liberal individuation, while liberalism politically neutralizes rights claims generated by disciplinary identities."[82] Martin Luther King speaks to this conversion of interest into regulated identity regimes in his 1968 essay "Showdown for Nonviolence." There he describes how riots short-circuit the evocations of shame and guilt that moral suasion sought out as psychic conversion: "We really feel that riots tend to intensify the fears of the white majority while relieving its guilt, and so open the door to greater repression. We've seen no changes in Watts, no structural changes that have taken place as a result of riots. We are trying to find an alternative that will force people to confront issues without destroying life or property."[83]

Law-and-order culture shaped itself against demands for white shame by black activists like King. But it also contoured itself against urban mobilization. The white backlash against Black Power and urban riots changed the racial landscape of America because "white America in the early 1970s no longer felt as guilty about racial matters. The collective white guilt toward blacks had arisen only in response to the media coverage of white southern racist brutality and the black nonviolent response. As a consequence of rioting and urban crime, blacks, once perceived by many whites as victims of American racism, became increasingly seen as victimizers. As a result, blacks were cut from liberal white America's short-lived financial conduit for the black militants' fear-induced, victim-status benefits. The riots became a symbol of black political autonomy when in fact, blacks, even those advocating rioting, were far from autonomous creatures."[84] But as Jerry Watts notes, the early militancy of Black Power rhetors produced a new emotional repertoire for black Americans through their own attempts at circulating political fear. "Over time, Cleaver, Carmichael, H. Rap Brown, Bobby Seale, Huey Newton, Karenga, Baraka, and other militants were temporarily successful in undermining and replacing the Martin Luther King, guilt-induced, victim status appeal," and they did so by marshaling the "fear of rebellious blacks."[85]

While this strategy gave rise to antiblack police violence and state repression, the response to Black Power's emotional shift holds a few political lessons. First, the entire guilt frame operated from a spectatorship to *white action*. It was *white* police violence in Birmingham that generated sympathy and guilt; watching bad behavior by white people produced guilt and shame among white people. Second, white support for nonviolent action decreased after Birmingham, even before Black Power emerged in 1966, suggesting that Black Power rhetoric was not *causal* in this affective shift. Third, the patronage of white liberals in the White House was singularly engaged when white violence marked black protest rather than when black feelings of urban despair unfolded as rebellion. Johnson's confusion and anger during and after Watts were born of his feelings of rejection as white patronage no longer served as a driving goal of black urban activism. However, even by 1968, Vice President Hubert Humphrey was still communicating from a place where white guilt was the dominant emotional frame for civil rights despite the increasing importance of Black Power rhetoric. In a 1968 speech, for example, Humphrey railed, "Ever since Watts, and particularly since Detroit and Newark, the discussion of equal rights has been distorted and sometimes even sidetracked by the very different issues of riots and civil disorders, of 'crime in the streets' and 'law and order'. . . . It is dangerous nonsense to believe that social progress and a respect for law are somehow in opposition to each other."[86] Fourth, as America's cities burned, white conservatives mobilized the fear frame better as a political emotion. In 1968, Richard Nixon campaigned against ideas about black victimhood, accelerating the collapse of "protest" into "crime." Segregationists like George Wallace who saw black equality as reverse racism and wanted to preserve unlimited white agency amplified this framework as their emotional repertoire emphasized *white rage* in response to *black despair*.[87]

Likewise, the urban rebellions of the mid-1960s produced affective discourses about property, poverty, and antiblack urban violence that helped black Americans articulate and harness political feelings that propelled precarious but enduring practices and institutions. Black and white rhetors used the language of *feelings* to interpret the meaning of rioting and of riots as temporal expressions of underdeveloped politics that eschewed hope as a master trope of the American experience. Rather than articulate American exceptionalism, discourses of urban rebellion complicated the tropes of progress that had traditionally characterized civil rights discourse since the end of the Second World War and centered the benevolence of white liberals on brokering changes in the distribution of black rights. Riot discourses demonstrated the ways in which Black Power, as an alternative political commitment, harnessed *fantasy* in the service of black liberation. Rebellions in places like Harlem, Watts, Detroit, and New York City exposed the tensions and obvious contradictions of black existence in America's largest cities, where black life was often painful, cruel, and short. Using speakers like Malcolm X and Stokely Carmichael and groups like the Black Panther Party as foils, white law-and-order rhetors mobilized *against* black anger and despair as a way of reconsolidating whiteness and white political power. But antiblack terror, despair, and hopelessness were also met with political impotence, particularly after 1965, giving rise to Black Power.

Chapter Five

MOURNING KING
Memory, Affect, and the Shaping of Black Power

It would be difficult to pinpoint a more poignant example of the social and political turmoil of 1968 than Martin Luther King Jr.'s assassination at the Lorraine Motel in Memphis on April 4. Although he had flown to Memphis to march with sanitation workers, King's assassination imperiled the Poor People's Campaign to end poverty. While press outlets scrambled to eulogize King, his Atlanta funeral on April 9 was a prominent rhetorical space where varying publics contested King's legacy and the future of the movement in the wake of his tragic murder. Nostalgia, love, disgust, and guilt mingled in the Ebenezer Baptist Church where King lay as his family and close friends sat alongside federal and state officials, Southern Christian Leadership Conference (SCLC) comrades, members of the Student Nonviolent Coordinating Committee (SNCC), and white liberal activists.

King's funeral highlighted divergent expectations about the future of the movement and competing assessments of civil rights ideology as attendants memorialized the fallen leader. Writing for the *New York Review of Books*, Elizabeth Hardwick described the scene at the funeral as one "bathed in memory." In a section that bears lengthy quotation for its emphasis on *feeling* and its relationship to memory, Hardwick writes:

> No one could doubt that there had been a longing for the reunion among the white ministers and students, the liberals from the large cities. The "love"-locked arms, songs, comradeship—all of that was remembered with nostalgia and feeling.... This love, if not actually refused, was seldom forthcoming in relations with new black militants, who were determined to break the dependency of the

black people even on the cooperation, energy, and checkbooks of the guilty, longing, loving whiteys. Everything separated the old Civil Rights people from the
new militants, even the use of language. The harsh, obscene style, the unforgiving
stares, the insulting accusations and refusal to make distinctions between bad
whites and good—this was humbling and perplexing. Many of the white people
had created their very self-identity out of issues and distinctions. They felt cast off,
ill at ease with the new street rhetoric of "self-defense" and "self-determination.[1]

The distance between ministers, white students, and Black Power activists
as they confronted King's absence was palpable to Hardwick as each cohort
expressed different *affective* connections to King and to the struggle that he
had helped to lead. Beyond the sentimentality of the white churchgoers is the
contrast between the positivity of their memories of solidarity with the stance
of the black militants, whose rejection of this affective positionality marked
a shift in both memory and political philosophy. Hardwick's description,
though, is part of the problematic rhetorical memory of this moment of the
movement, since the black militants who actually attended the funeral had
marched and organized *with* King. Rather than a completely oppositional
relationship, SNCC leaders had a much deeper relationship with King than
Hardwick suggests. For the black radicals who stayed in the South and suffered the beatings, jailings, and voter registration drives, these white home-
coming feelings were insulting, especially given the thousands of poor black
people waiting outside the church to pay their last respects. Additionally, such
a description (and descriptions of this sort were everywhere at the end of the
decade) relies on what Sara Ahmed has called "a nostalgia for whiteness," in
this case for a whiteness that wasn't under constant criticism for its nihilism.[2]
Still, the mere presence of SNCC members at the funeral served as a hedge
against the crippling nostalgia that can urge strategic forgetting.

Working against this narrative, former SNCC chairman Stokely Carmichael remembered King's funeral in his memoir, highlighting his proximity to
King and evoking a deep sense of belonging *near* the slain leader. Saying that
although it couldn't be helped, "Ain't never been so many high-up white folk
in that church, before or since. Celebrities, politicians. Powerful white folk
in that church."[3] Hubert Humphrey and Bobby Kennedy were there, despite
Kennedy having authorized the wiretaps on King, which bothered Carmichael, who recalled, "Thousands, I mean thousands, of poor black folk were
sweating outside in the sun, many of them crying. People who loved him
and whom he loved. Greater love hath no man than that he lay down his
life. . . . For a moment, I thought we should stand out here with Dr. King's
people. Then I saw the 'important' guests all going in. I said, hell no. Ain't

nothing going keep us out. We belong in there. So we crashed."[4] As someone who marched next to King and arguably radicalized him, Carmichael is clear about the importance of the physical location of black radicals in the *process* of the funeral. SNCC activist Cleveland Sellers remembers the funeral similarly in his own memoir, adding, "Jackie Kennedy, who had never shown any particular interest in Dr. King or black oppression, was conspicuously present. Unfortunately, there was no place in the church for the hundreds of thousands of poor blacks who loved Dr. King and believed in his beautiful 'Dream.'"[5] Both Carmichael and Sellers invoke *black feelings* at the funeral while also talking about the importance of *proximity* to King in the hierarchy of the struggle and its historical representation, noting the closeness of indifferent white liberals to King and the separation between King and the poor, loving black masses while exposing the paradox of King's liberal dream.

This chapter examines the ways in which Black Power activists used memories of King's assassination to legitimize Black Power discourse. I explore how King's assassination was used as an *instrumental* as well as an *affective* rhetorical resource to help shape the memory and direction of the Black Power movement after 1968. In their speeches and autobiographies, Black Power activists framed and remembered the assassination; thus I argue that King's murder provided context and clarity for the Black Power movement, justifying a more militant and assertive identity for black activists working in opposition to an increasingly hostile federal government even as these intellectuals expressed their closeness with King. King's death calcified an affective and rhetorical shift from black optimism to black pessimism because his assassination was a chronopolitical moment that not only ended integration politics but fundamentally *stopped time* and also spurred more riots. For Black Power activists, King's assassination confirmed both the impotence and duplicitousness of the federal government, particularly in the Johnson administration. Moreover, King's own class politics and militancy on Vietnam near the end of his life, shaped in part by the Black Power movement, allowed Black Power leaders to mobilize King's memory in the service of Black Power philosophy and tactics. Thus did King's assassination become an important site in the rhetorical and emotional remembrance of King, as well as a political watershed as Black Power filled the political vacuum his death left.

Rhetorical Memory and National Trauma

The discursive field surrounding King's assassination was complicated by President Lyndon Johnson's announcement, a week before, of his decision not to seek reelection. *Time* magazine described the complexity of the affective moment: "Rarely in American memory had *hope* and *horror* been so poignantly fused ... within a single week. Rarely had men's actions—voluntary and involuntary—seemed so ineluctably intertwined. President Johnson's announcement of a major peace offensive in Asia, coupled with his renunciation of another term, raised anticipation throughout the world that the long agony of Viet Nam might soon be ended."[6] Complicated by the violence surrounding the segregationist campaign of Alabama governor George Wallace, the assassination of Robert F. Kennedy, and the riots at the Democratic National Convention, and the popular new conservatism led now by Richard Nixon, pronouncements of "the end of an era" easily lent themselves to a periodization of civil rights that saw 1968 as the most tumultuous year in recent American memory. King's assassination became a repository of memories that exposed huge rifts in American cultural life, especially as riots again emerged across the country. This periodization, then, also reflects a *temporal finitude* as elites decried the end of an era. But temporally, the spring of 1968 saw massive cultural shifts that *amplified* social trauma through the dense language of *political feelings.*

King's death was a poignant cultural trauma, which, in the words of Jeffrey C. Alexander, "occurs when members of a collectivity feel they have been subjected to a horrendous event that leaves indelible marks on their group consciousness, marking their memories forever and changing their future identity in fundamental and irrevocable ways."[7] Grier and Cobbs explained how King's death shattered black America: "For a moment be any black person, anywhere, and you will feel the waves of hopelessness that engulfed black men and women when Martin Luther King was murdered. All black people understood the tide of anarchy that followed his death. It is the transformation of this quantum of grief into aggression of which we now speak. As a sapling bent low stored energy, which will be released in the form of rage—black rage, apocalyptic and final."[8] King's murder amplified hopelessness, grief, aggression, and rage, fundamentally shifting black assessments of civil rights, white liberalism, and social organizing. And the riots that followed were the outpouring of massive loss in the face of a cultural shift back toward white supremacy.

Consequently, King's assassination was a temporal touchstone for baby boomers, marking time with feelings and memories that amplified the moment. So as black Americans articulated the consequences of this cultural trauma, they asserted black solidarity to manage the "acute discomfort entering into the core of the collectivity's sense of its own identity."[9] When rhetorical actors represent and circulate traumas, they craft rhetorical frames that help publics make sense of the trauma by advancing competing arguments about how the change happened, who is responsible for the change, and the consequences of the change. The interlocutors lay "claim to some fundamental injury, an exclamation of the terrifying profanation of some sacred value, a narrative about a horribly destructive social process, and a demand for emotional, institutional, and symbolic reparation and reconstitution."[10] Thus does a public trauma become a precipitating event for social protest: as rhetors lay claim to public traumas, their goal is to convince publics to share trauma and respond in a certain way.[11] Convincing publics of a trauma's collectivity is "a complex, multivalent symbolic process that is contingent, highly contested, and sometimes highly polarizing," and for the narrative to have rhetorical power, the audience needs to be moved by the rhetor to understand the trauma as deeply meaningful.[12] Thus, in compelling a public to consider the identificatory dimensions of a public trauma, the rhetor faces a plethora of rhetorical work to enact.

While cohort studies of civil rights memory have showcased how generational differences influence perspectives on the movement, King's assassination has been overlooked despite the wealth of rhetorical memories and their rich affective dimensions. Alexander's cultural trauma theory articulates four ordinal points of contention for cohort rhetors framing a public trauma such as King's murder: (1) the nature of the pain, (2) the nature of the victim, (3) the relationship between the victim and the audience, and (4) the attribution of responsibility for the trauma.[13] These considerations become the rhetorical and emotional terrain of political life, especially because black intellectuals had admired King and worked with him and were deeply traumatized by his death. They sought to describe their pain at his loss as the death of the movement; to laud King and his work as heroic in the face of white supremacy; to compel people who admired King but had no proximity to him to engage in black struggle in particular ways; and to link King's assassination to structural racism and the failure of the Johnson administration.

After his assassination, King became, in Michael Schuyler's words, an "instant martyr," and his death marked a moment of keening grief and poignant reflection. The mythification of King prompted intense political struggle over meaning because it also secured King in public memory as a rhetorical resource for movement organizing and for state appropriation, indefinitely extending the kind of *time* that King occupied as an icon. As Kendall Phillips reminds us, memory is a "highly rhetorical process," where constitutive memories such as those of the King assassination "are open to contest, revision, and rejection."[14] This certainly happened through the recollections of black writers and artists, King comrades, and Black Power advocates. King himself had been "talking death" in Memphis only hours before his death.[15] There he uttered the now-famous line "I may not get there with you, but I want you to know tonight, that we as a people will get to the Promised Land," complicating accounts of memory about that fateful day.[16] King's prescience was prompted by immediate safety concerns in Tennessee, his opposition to the war in Vietnam along with Johnson's declining popularity, the continued violence against black activists in the Deep South, and the urban rebellions in northern cities. As Dyson rightly points out, in Memphis temporality is central: "It is clear that time is on [King's] mind. And so is death—the death of time, the death of the movement, the death of hope."[17]

Publishers and journalists understood King's murder as a repository of competing loyalties, feelings, and memories about King that needed to be framed. Although support among whites and blacks had been declining (due in no small part to his opposition to the Vietnam War), King's assassination fueled urban rage against the broken promises of the American Dream, high-lighting the divergent affective responses to King's death. This led John H. Johnson, chair of the Johnson Publishing Company and founder of *Ebony* magazine, to reflect on the black condition in America in 1968 in his eulogy for King: "And so we stand today, a nation more divided black against white than at any time in history. The promise of the March on Washington is dead. Dr. Martin Luther King is dead. Very much alive is a virulent white racism that threatens to destroy not only black people but American democracy."[18] Where King is divested of rhetorical power in John Johnson's declaration, white supremacy is invigorated as a monumental force of destruction in the days after King's assassination. Certainly, the notion that white supremacy had triumphed in snuffing out the life of the nation's most visible civil rights leader was inescapable, and it was an affective thread woven through many of the eulogies and remembrances of King's traumatic death. But Johnson's statement also characterizes the moment after King's death as *singular in time*, suggesting that black intellectuals saw his death as a singular cultural trauma but also as a chronopolitical *ending*, particularly of the notion of political hope.

The Death of Nonviolence: Romanticizing King's Dream

If anything, the rhetorical memory work assessing the meaning of King's death has been polysemic and hotly contested. Some people remembering King after the assassination talk about seeing him and falling in love with him, inscribing a kind of heterosexual desire for and devotion to him that fixes him as an infallible saint. Novelist and poet Alice Walker writes, "Like a good omen for the future, the face of Dr. Martin Luther King Jr. was the first black face I saw on our new television screen. And, as in a fairy tale, my soul was stirred by the meaning for me of my mission . . . and I fell in love with the sober and determined face of the Movement."[19] Walker describes King as a kind of wish fulfillment for black people, which amplifies the role of *longing* (a kind of elongated desire maintained because satisfaction is actively withheld) as a feeling in the black freedom struggle. She also emphasizes his singularity, saying: "He was The One, The Hero, The One Fearless Person for whom we had waited. I hadn't even realized before that we *had* been waiting for Martin Luther King Jr., but we had."[20] Walker's comments invoke temporality, invoking the *wait* (much as King himself did in Memphis) as an essential experience of the long arc toward black freedom.

In remembering a virile, heroic King, Walker's romanticizing suggests that *optimism*, too, was a central part of his legacy. Lauren Berlant explains, "Any object of optimism promises to guarantee the endurance of something, the survival of something, the flourishing of something, and above all the protection of the desire that made this object or scene powerful enough to have magnetized an attachment to it."[21] The optimism of King's quest for a nonviolent solution to segregation was heightened after his death by black rhetors who romanticized him, suggesting that heroic memories of the man would outlive his movement and denying that the movement died, since its ideas lived on. Optimism, central as it often is in social movement organizing, is an affective structure of longing, holding out hope for the future; optimism has a chronopolitics that elongates the object. But with King's assassination, optimism met rage. Aida Hussen explains that "the articulation of black rage is coextensive with a necessary affirmation of black humanity and a compelling reanimation of black political potential under tremendously hostile sociopolitical circumstances. Black rage, then, attempts to fill the generative and hopeful space that has been evacuated by the lost leader. It wards off the debilitating, defeatist alternative of black despair—a racialized variant of Freudian melancholia, in which the bereaved retreats from the social world and thus also from the space of political possibility."[22] Rage and hope, then, coconstitute political possibilities, though by 1968 rage was the primary ontological vector of blackness and is positioned *against* hope. In Calvin Warren's words, "The politics of hope posits that one *must* have a politics to have hope; politics is the natural habitat of hope itself. To reject hope in a nihilistic way, then, is really to reject the politics of hope, or certain circumscribed and compulsory forms of expressing, practicing, and conceiving of hope."[23] Because hope is compulsory in a world where whites control the entire political apparatus, Warren rightly concludes that "the Politics of Hope reconfigures despair and expectation so that black political action *pursues an impossible object*" through seductive appeals to "linear proximity—we can call this 'progress,' 'betterment,' or 'more perfect.'"[24] Certainly John Kennedy's discourses on hope reflect this perspective, but by the decade's close, hope was more obviously an "impossible object."

Nonetheless, King himself often commented on the necessity of optimism, though he recognized its cruelty, saying in one speech, for example, "I feel free to say that we who believe in non-violence often have an unwarranted optimism concerning man and lean unconsciously toward self-righteousness."[25] Far from offering naive optimism, King offered a pragmatic, moral optimism that helped activists embrace the nonviolent path in the face of increasing repression. Attributing his optimism to his childhood, King found Reinhold Niebuhr's view of human nature too pessimistic and instead borrowed from the Hegelian dialectic to explain how to operate in a world where conflicting views constrained social justice activism.[26] But King's optimism ebbed and flowed, especially after Watts, the disastrous organizing effort in Chicago, a never-ending war in Vietnam, and massive domestic repression ordered by a now-hostile democratic president. King's death signaled not just his own mortality but also a death of *optimism* as black intellectuals proclaimed the death of the civil rights movement.

For example, in his memoir, Stokely Carmichael recalls, "All over the country, black America was telling the nation: This time you went too far, killing this good, decent man, this man of peace. When you killed Dr. King, you killed nonviolence. Man, all the way to Atlanta, every station that came over the radio, more reports of riots, insurrection, disorder. Black folk signaling America, when you killed Dr. King, you killed nonviolence."[27] Arguing that the death of the man was the death of the movement made the trauma more significant and signaled that the time had come for new leadership, new ideas, and a new series of signs that acknowledged nonviolence and Christian moralizing as a dead end for the black freedom struggle. Floyd McKissick, director of the Congress of Racial Equality (CORE), echoed Carmichael: "Dr. Martin Luther King was the last prince of nonviolence. Nonviolence is a dead philosophy, and it was not the black people that killed it."[28] One major problem loomed as black intellectuals like Walker, Carmichael, and McKissick oriented King's assassination as a public trauma. In these rites of national grief,

the significance of the empty boots is predicated on a paradox: what is irretrievably lost must somehow be replaced. Moreover, in the economy of cultural memory, the more important the social role played by the departed, the more immutable the loss and the more critical that a substitute be found to fill the social cavity filled by the fallen. In memorializing the fallen leader, the ritual of mourning simultaneously and necessarily interpolates a replacement of recapitating a body politic that has literally lost its head.[29]

SNCC activist Cleveland Sellers laments the fragmentation of black liberation, echoing this assessment in his autobiography: "The assassination of Dr. King and the collapse of SNCC have left a tremendous void that no individual or organization has managed to fill."[30] Though impossible, replacing King's head in the aftermath of his assassination was imperative, particularly for SCLC supporters, since King's dream of nonviolent integration was the idea that had helped win him such broad support.

Given that King's dream has functioned as the pathway into the mythology of the slain leader and as an obvious extension of his head, ideas, rhetorical expressions, and tactical decisions, it seems important to understand King's dream as it was articulated in 1963 at the March on Washington for Jobs and Freedom. There King's dream emerged (as it had in speeches across the South) as an indictment of white invocations of the so-called American Dream. In the oft-replayed "I Have a Dream" speech, King explains that in the one hundred years since emancipation, "the life of the Negro is still sadly crippled by the manacles of segregation and the chains of discrimination. One hundred years later, the Negro lives on a lonely island of poverty in the midst of a vast ocean of material prosperity. One hundred years later, the Negro is still languished in the corners of American society and finds himself an exile in his own land. And so we've come here today to dramatize a shameful condition."[31] In using narrative devices like metaphor to dramatize the bankrupt dream of American life, King impugns the vision of America that ignores the material deprivation of black America. Acknowledging the southern violence that black citizens confronted daily, along with the jailings they endured for their part in the nonviolent crusade, King reimagined the American Dream not as an attainable ideal each day but rather as a futurist moment when segregation and racial fear would not characterize any communities in the United States. Repeating the motif of the dream to climax in the speech, King cites both hope and faith as the constitutive resources necessary to reach this imagined future, urging his audience to continue believing that such a future is possible.

But we would be remiss to consider King's "dream" without also attending to Malcolm X's assessment of the "nightmare" of white supremacy, especially in the context of civil rights activism in the South. In this classic dialectic, the notions of dream and nightmare competed as contextual frames for understanding the stakes and the strategies of the black freedom movement where the affective dimensions of hope and despair attenuate the contrast. Writing about this dialectic, James Cone argues: "White people's refusal to acknowledge the right of blacks to defend themselves against persons who violated their humanity was perhaps the main reason that Malcolm could never accept Martin King's idea of nonviolence and its capacity to prick the moral conscience of whites."[32] For example, in "The Ballot or the Bullet," Malcolm told black audiences, "America's conscience is bankrupt. She lost all conscience a long time ago."[33] Here, since he had no hope for changing white minds, Malcolm sought to change black people's consciousness, and he urged black people to understand themselves as perpetually alienated from the American Dream. Claiming that he was free from the aspirational delusion of the dream, Malcolm exclaimed: "I'm speaking as a victim of this American system," and "I see America through the eyes of a victim. I don't see any American dream; I see an American nightmare."[34] Malcolm's comments showcase how the "dream" can only exist in a place where the nightmare of black victimization is rampant, and they demonstrate a resistance to the dream predicated on shifts in white rather than black consciousness.

From the essays published on the anniversaries of King's assassination, we see that despite Malcolm X's early critique, the "dream" and "hope" continue as frames for understanding King's legacy, demonstrating that some black intellectuals held on to the dream trope as their enduring memory of King. For example, writing in the *Crisis* in 1998, editor Ida E. Lewis marks the thirtieth anniversary of King's death with the following words: "King left behind a monument of hope and opportunity for us all that the storm of time can never destroy."[35] For the fortieth anniversary of his death, activists including Rev. Al Sharpton and Rev. Jesse Jackson led a Recommitment March in Memphis, ending at the Lorraine Motel, where two of King's children placed a wreath on the spot where their father was slain. The march had one purpose, according to leaders, and it was to "remember King and what he stood for." Sharpton highlighted "love" as the important ingredient in the march, explaining, "This is a march of love, not a march of hate. . . . We are marching to say that a man gave his life for us 40 years ago and we are going to recommit ourselves and march in the glow of his spirit." In highlighting the importance of love to the march and to the process of remembering King, Sharpton added, "You can kill the dreamer, but you can never kill the dream."[36] Sharpton's remarks suggest that there was a vested interest, certainly by King's SCLC collaborators, in continuing the "dream" trope along with the sentimentality of earlier proclamations of love for King. This is not totally surprising, because the dream metaphor is bound up with the experiential and embodied dimension of the speakers' shared social movement activism. But it certainly works against more critical readings of King in popular memory that remember his own militancy on poverty and Vietnam after 1963.

Still, King's death left a vacuum in the black freedom movement, a fact that the singer and activist Harry Belafonte speaks quite eloquently about in his own memoir. Belafonte recalls how both Rev. Jesse Jackson and Rev. Ralph Abernathy were "angling for proximity to Coretta" as they fought for the mantle of King's successor in the movement."[37] He adds:

> Martin's death had seriously crippled the movement he'd begun; that was becoming all too clear. The old groups were sputtering, their leaders competing, the sense of purpose dispelled. The movement for equality among blacks and whites in America was like a peeling poster on a brick wall, papered over with images of Black Panthers raising their fists. All those who had denounced Martin, from either the left or the right, now had a vacuum they could fill with whomever they wanted.[38]

The fighting between Jackson and Abernathy was particularly nasty, lasting for decades after King's death, splashed across the pages of *Jet* magazine and waged through autobiographies and interviews as the close associates of King struggled for proximity to King and his dream long after the leader's assassination. It became clear that the death of King had created a vacuum that no one could fill; change was inevitable.

Even Alice Walker acknowledged that King's death was implicitly the death of the civil rights movement. Walker describes the generative affective force of civil rights as an enterprise that helped rebuild black culture through "hope" and reproductive futurity:

> If the Civil Rights Movement is "dead," and if it gave us nothing else, it gave us each other forever. It gave some of us bread, some of us shelter, some of us knowledge and pride, all of us comfort. It gave us our children, our husbands, our brothers, our fathers, as men reborn with a purpose for living.... It gave us heroes, selfless men of courage and strength, for our little boys and girls to follow. It gave us hope for tomorrow. It called us to life.[39]

This generative description of hope created by King's movement permeates Walker's writings and even characterizes Maya Angelou's memory of learning that King was assassinated on her birthday. She recalled, "Life stopped for me for a few days. It was terrible. I couldn't believe that this great man, this great dream, this great dreamer, this person who dared to love everybody, could be killed."[40] The memories of Walker and Angelou point to their faith that such a good man would never be harmed, that his nonviolence would protect him from violence as they equated or reduced King to his dream. However, intellectuals who were not SCLC associates had more critical assessments of King and their feelings about his assassination.

In her memoir, the musician and activist Nina Simone described King's assassination as "the traditional white American tactic for getting rid of black leaders it couldn't suppress in any other way." Simone wrote, "For a while people walked around in a kind of daze and I wept along with them, but I couldn't understand why they were surprised by Martin's assassination: we'd already lost Malcolm, Medgar Evers, Emmett Till, and hundreds, thousands of others down through our history." Simone saw King's assassination as "a desperate act by a country with nowhere to hide anymore. Stupid, too, because the thing that died along with Martin in Memphis that day was nonviolence, we all knew that. It was a time for bitterness—almost funny if it hadn't been so sad."[41] Simone's comments reflect a rhetorical memory that avoids nostalgia and optimism, articulating instead an affective rhetoric more reflective of Malcolm's disillusionment with the promise of white salvation, suggesting that the affective shift from optimism to pessimism was palpable. Her assertion that bitterness was a reasonable response to the sadness of King's murder suggests an alternative affective response, different from the romanticism of other artists who were intimate with King, demonstrating a formidable gulf between the two styles of remembrance as they harness affect to orient readers toward King and his assassination.

From Black Optimism to Black Pessimism

Time magazine's editorial eulogy of King provides a clear example of how hope oriented the nation differently in 1968 than it did in 1960, as a result of the constant violence of the decade. The editorial opined, "Rarely in American memory had hope and horror been so poignantly fused . . . within a single week. Rarely had men's actions—voluntary and involuntary—seemed so ineluctably intertwined. President Johnson's announcement of a major peace offensive in Asia, coupled with his renunciation of another term, raised anticipation throughout the world that the long agony of Viet Nam might soon be ended."[42] Again, we see the contrast between hope and horror here as an affective frame for King's assassination while this snippet also points to the war in Vietnam as an essential part of the political context that provided insight into memories of King (as well as Johnson).

While this framework was strong, we might expect Black Power rhetors to completely denounce King after his death. However, in doing the constitutive work to define the King assassination as cultural trauma, they did not seek to distance themselves from King; instead they sought to identify him as a proto–Black Power intellectual. For example, Stokely Carmichael used identification as a mode of rhetorical constitution by explaining that of all the people whom he "worked with, respected, and learned from—Julius Hobson, Cecil Moore, Malcolm X, Gloria Richardson, Assata Shakur, Robert Williams, Muhammad Ali, Jamil al-Amin (H. Rap Brown), and even Dr. King himself—*all* at some point, whenever they were seen to cross that media-imposed line of 'responsible' black protest, were subject to vicious character assassination by the press."[43] Writers like Carmichael invited the reader to see King as simultaneously above the movement (as a martyr) and of it (as an intellectual kindred), thus at least partially reclaiming him as one of them. Perhaps this was easier for Carmichael, since he and King were close.

But where Carmichael clearly used King's assassination as a way of marking his closeness with King, other Black Power leaders, particularly those in the Black Panther Party (BPP), had a more complicated deployment of affect in recalling King's death. For example, Black Panther minister of information Eldridge Cleaver used King's death to denounce President Johnson's repression of civil rights efforts. Cleaver's affective hostility reminds the reader that the political shift from black optimism to pessimism was spurred by continued internal repression, harassment, disruption, violence, and assassination. Cleaver explains how the BPP was formed in Oakland, California, in 1966, from this climate of unrelenting white violence: "The Black Panther Party was born under Johnson. Even Malcolm didn't call for the gun until after Kennedy was killed, which shows how reactionary violence begets reactionary violence, and why we have an internal war on our hands today.... We asked for our civil and human rights. Instead of getting our rights, we have been killed, jailed, and driven underground, en masse. Now we ask for nothing. Instead, we are moving to take what we want."[44] Tracing domestic repression of civil rights to Johnson as the catalyst of the BPP's resistance, Cleaver explains that the Panthers distanced themselves from Johnson, not just because of his lack of support for civil rights after the passage of the Civil Rights Act of 1964 and the Voting Rights Act of 1965, but also because, in Cleaver's words, "Both Malcolm and King were killed under Johnson, and Nixon has turned us into a nation of pallbearers and gravediggers. In the almost ten years since the killing of Kennedy, the official solution to the racial problem has shifted from integration to a policy that approaches apartheid."[45] Cleaver explains that while Kennedy and King had a symbiotic relationship that helped both men articulate a slow-moving vision of progress, Johnson's America bore nothing in common with the prior administration, especially on civil rights; consequently, Johnson's administration led a campaign that Cleaver characterized by its proximity to death. As Cleaver puts it, "King didn't fit at all into the cracker strategy plotted by Lyndon Johnson. Besides that, LBJ had made it crystal clear that he took a dim view of poor people marching, except off to war."[46] I examine the politics of black death at length in Chapter Six, but suffice it to say here that Cleaver's indictment of Johnson via King's assassination was powerful memory work, calcifying Johnson as a bad-faith actor on civil rights.

Cleaver's remarks resituate King's relationship with Johnson in the wake of King's assassination and create what Lauren Berlant calls "fantasmatic inter-subjectivity."[47] Berlant explains that in this mode of engagement, the speaker projects new possibilities in the absence of the displaced subject, which "creates a fake present moment of intersubjectivity in which, nonetheless, a performance of address can take place."[48] In the case of King's assassination, this move functions to help the reader understand the shared experience of King's death, to facilitate accurate judgment about King and his legacy, and to situate King within discourses that speak to institutional repression rather than, say, a lone gunman. Since King was a profound object of attachment for many, but also a figure who provoked affects ranging from extreme ambivalence to hatred, his assassination required rhetorical animation to decide what should come next, for America, for the civil rights movement, for black citizens.

The memories of Black Power members reveal deep attachments to King despite the often critical positions that Black Power leaders took against him publicly. Reading the memories of King's assassination by Black Power leaders demonstrates how they were grappling with the loss of their connection to King, evidencing his power to influence them despite their rhetorical aloofness. In Berlant's terminology, leaders like Cleaver are political depressives, who, "having adopted a mode that might be called detachment, may not really be detached at all, but navigating an ongoing and sustaining relation to the scene and circuit of optimism and disappointment."[49] It is in the navigation of optimism and pessimism after a public trauma like King's murder that citizens work through what Berlant calls the "infrastructures of belonging" that characterize political life.[50] The structures of belonging to King are keyed to blackness, black masculinity, martyrdom, southernness, the church and an emphasis on agape, physical attraction, love, respect, and resistance. But black intellectuals also needed to navigate their feelings about belonging to the nation-state in the wake of Johnson's decision not to seek reelection in the midst of a contentious and bloody democratic primary and the rise of new conservatism.

In negotiating this web of affect, Cleaver used King's assassination to denounce Johnson for failing to protect black intellectuals while simultaneously denouncing nonviolence as a strategy whose time had passed. In doing so, Cleaver makes the case that King knew that the movement had left him behind, explaining, "Certainly the center of the Afro-American struggle had shifted several notches to the left, and King knew that he no longer stood on that spot. When he kneeled down to pray now, he knew his was like a voice crying in the wilderness."[51] Cleaver's comments demonstrate a rhetorical posture that linked the assassinations of the decade to Johnson, signified a real sense of loss in the Black Power community because King's death confirmed their worst fears about white supremacy, and positioned King as having acknowledged the inevitability of Black Power as the orientation of future black struggle.

From Cruel Optimism to Black Pessimism

In the bitterness and hardness of Black Power commentary after King's death, we see a shift in both rhetoric and affect that moved black liberation from the "cruel optimism" of nonviolence to unbridled black pessimism about white liberals and the possibility of white consciousness-raising particularly in the federal government. Like Carmichael, many Black Power intellectuals used King's assassination to point to the widespread (and unwarranted, in their estimation) cultural attachment to nonviolence while also engaging with King's ideas in the wake of his death. As they did so, the death of King exposed the cruel optimism of nonviolence that catalyzed the complete shift to black pessimism. In the simplest terms, "cruel optimism" refers to "the condition of maintaining an attachment to a significantly problematic object."[52] Berlant says, "A relation of cruel optimism exists when something you desire is actually an obstacle to your flourishing."[53] It would be difficult to pinpoint a more "significantly problematic object" that was an "obstacle to flourishing" than nonviolence, especially by 1968. Berlant explains that cruel optimism "explains our sense of *our endurance in the object*."[54] I suggest that King's death shook the Black Power movement because activists saw themselves in him, even as they sought to define themselves as apart from him. Because cruel optimism is expressed through the fetishizing of an object or ideal, in this case King himself or his nonviolent dream, the destruction of that object or ideal is devastating. Berlant explains, "What's cruel about these attachments . . . is that the subjects who have *x* in their lives might not well endure the loss of their object/scene of desire, even though its presence threatens their wellbeing, because whatever the *content* of the attachment is, the continuity of its form provides something of the continuity of the subject's sense of what it means to keep on living and to look forward to being in the world."[55] For Berlant, though optimism is a mechanism of mediation that allows humans to process and understand life situations, it becomes cruel when it is linked to institutions that block the realization of the imagined, dreamed-of future. King's idea of a nonviolent America is an instance of cruel optimism because it is a dream that could not be realized even under Johnson, as Cleaver's brutal assessment suggests.

Time's major editorial about King's assassination expressed this sense of cruel optimism. The editors wrote, "Even as that hope blossomed, an older blight on the American conscience burst through with the capriciousness of a spring freeze. In Memphis, through the budding branches of trees surrounding a tawdry rooming house, a white sniper's bullet cut down Dr. Martin Luther King Jr., pre-eminent voice of the just aspirations and long-suffering patience of black America."[56] Referencing the hope of King's message while simultaneously pointing to the blight of white supremacy, the editorial uses weather and nature tropes to express the disillusionment that King's assassination brought to the nation. If the murders of southern civil rights workers and the assassination of a US president were not enough, King's murder certainly spoke to the death of an era defined by the loss of his life, the pronouncements of the end of the movement, and the end of Johnson's presidency.

Another aspect of the cruel optimism of nonviolence was found in King's religious loyalties. "One of the cruelties of the South and part of the pathos of King's funeral and the sadness that edges his rhetoric is that his same popular religion is shared by the poor, ignorant whites, and of course, by many white people not poor or without education. The religion does not seem to have sent any peaceful messages to them in so far as their brothers in Christ, the Negroes are concerned," writes Elizabeth Hardwick. This disconnect between the Christian values of white and black Americans made cruel optimism in nonviolence clear to Black Power rhetors like Malcolm and Cleaver, who spoke frequently about how even though they shared the same texts, precepts, and loyalties, white Christians still often condoned killing black Americans. Appealing to the moral conscience of whites regarding segregation, poverty, or war was made impossible by white privilege, white institutions, and cultural white supremacy.

But even as journalists and intellectuals were poised to identify the discontinuities that followed King's death, Black Power intellectuals made the opposite rhetorical choice, because continuity was a major rhetorical goal in asserting memories of King's murder. A shallow or cynical assessment of this rhetorical move would see Black Power leaders as agents co-opting King to radicalize him posthumously. But this move to see Black Power as an extension of the southern civil rights movement only appears disingenuous if readers insist on remembering the King of "I Have a Dream" and refuse to acknowledge King's class politics and internationalism. Certainly, King was a dreamer, constantly using the jeremiad as a rhetorical form to build optimism for social change and in him as a leader. King's use of the dream motif reflected the religious beliefs of his communities of practice and represented new possibilities for black organizing in the South. Harry Reed has suggested that King's use of "the dream" as a central symbol in his rhetorical discourse gave him "the opportunity to transcend the limited concerns" of the clerical communities that supported him.[57] And to a large extent, King was able to harness ecumenical rhetoric to help propel a more ambitious political agenda, certainly after the legislative civil rights victory of the 1964 Civil Rights Act.

However, the dream was no longer a central rhetorical motif for King by 1965. As his assessment of inequality turned to structural racism and classism, King's language, strategies, and goals changed. Historian Thomas Jackson explains that by 1965,

> King's radical voice rang more clearly when he confessed that his dream had turned into a "nightmare." The dream shattered when whites murdered voting rights workers in Alabama, when police battled blacks in Los Angeles, when he met jobless and "hopeless" blacks on desperate Chicago streets, and when he saw hunger and poverty in rural Mississippi and Appalachia. But King picked up the shards of his shattered dreams and reassembled them into more radical visions of emancipation for all poor people.[58]

Jackson contends that once King adopted Malcolm's language of the "nightmare," he acknowledged the "shattered dream," demonstrating how his own wishes for black America were a function of cruel optimism, as well as how more radical futurist impulses were necessary for civil rights activists. And yet King's death highlighted that nonviolence itself was a fantasy and an object of cruel attachment.

For political depressives—particularly radical political leaders—fantasies become "a life sustaining defense against the atrocities of ordinary violent history," especially when that violence is state sanctioned and targets similar leaders.[59] Exhausted from panic and the extreme emotional labor of disappointment, Black Power leaders looked for ways to make sense of King's murder. But the increasing number of political assassinations among the ranks of the civil rights and Black Power movements convinced many activists that their lives were fleeting and they had not much time on this earth, making optimism a less likely affective and rhetorical device for them. The constant harassment from the FBI and local police under the FBI's counterintelligence program (COINTELPRO), the sheer numbers of Panthers being shot and killed in unprompted police shoot-outs, the militantly anti-civil-rights posture and "southern strategy" of the Nixon administration (particularly in the Department of Justice), and the conservatism of Reagan's law-and-order rhetoric in California made optimism a foolish, passé, and untouchable feeling for black activists, especially after King's death.

As Garth Pauley has explained, understanding a speech act "means illuminating how the message both emerges from its historical moment and invites a recognition of the events about which it speaks."[60] Certainly Black Power intellectuals understood this maxim as they encouraged more critical reflection on the pitfalls of integration ideology after King's death. Eldridge Cleaver explains King's assassination thus: "Something may be dead a long time before its corpse begins to stink. If we focus on the assassination of Martin Luther King as marking the death of nonviolence, we may be dealing more with the stink than with the dirty deed. Pursuing this line of thought leads to the flip conclusion that King was Kennedy's puppet."[61] Cleaver's words suggest that King's death was not only the end of the man and his ideology but also the end of optimism about Camelot and, by extension, the end of white liberal interference in black organizing. As long as King was alive, activists and publics could indulge in the Kennedy administration's hope and optimism that segregation and racial violence would slowly ebb from American political life. However, the striking absence of other objects of optimistic attachment influenced the rhetorical choices of Black Power leaders, whose political depressiveness was also an attachment for emergent publics.

The dramatic loss of King (magnified by the assassinations of John Kennedy and Malcolm X, along with the countless strings of murders among civil rights leaders and workers) had the striking effect of narrowing the black rhetorical responses available in his absence. Counterfactuals, conspiracy theories, ad hominem attacks, paranoia and hyperbole, and guerrilla warfare all became much more prominent narratives and tropes in a world without King because his death exposed the cruelty of the dream as a trope of racial progress and racial liberalism. This is because, as Calvin Warren notes, "The Political and anti-blackness are inseparable and mutually constitutive. The utopian vision of a 'not-yet-social order' that purges anti-blackness from its core provides a promise without relief—its only answer to the immediacy of black suffering is to keep struggling. The logic of struggle, then, perpetuates black suffering by placing relief in an unattainable future, a future that offers nothing more than an exploitative reproduction of its own means of existence."[62]

Cleaver's texts reflect how the political is fundamentally antiblack, and are an important place to interrogate rhetorical memory, because his comments suggest that integration was a death wish, inverting the traditional media coverage of Black Power that blamed urban blacks for an inevitable race war. Suggesting that a change in the movement was inevitable because nonviolence was doomed, he explains that "one can be fed up with a certain way of doing something, and remaining in that same posture becomes a form of doom. When you know you're in a situation that is killing you, the thrust is toward another scene, another set of circumstances, to alter in some fundamental way the prevailing crisis, to shift, if possible, the odds in one's favor."[63] In casting integration or desegregation as folly, Cleaver is able to deflect some (but certainly not all) of the criticism of Black Power ideology.

I suspect that Black Power intellectuals were more steeped in fatalism than the SNCC folks because many of their leaders came straight from the penitentiary, a place where optimism barely penetrates. Cleaver would seem to agree and links the fatalism of early Black Power rhetors directly to the embodied knowledge of social corruption that prison provided, describing the conclusions that he had reached by the time he left prison:

> That secret, conspiratorial machinery existed in America involving some of the most powerful and best-known men in the land, and that this machinery had killed President Kennedy and Malcolm X; that the goal of this machinery was the fascization of the American social order; that black people faced the alternatives of genocide or war for liberation; that many more people, myself included, were going to be killed and that we had to do all that we could because time was short, and that it was possible, if we fought hard, to defeat this conspiracy and rebuild America along the lines of our dreams.[64]

Cleaver speaks to a deep knowledge of the scope and volume of violence against black people happening in the United States and directed at progressives in 1968. But even while recognizing this nightmare, Cleaver also recaptures the radicalism of King's dream.

King's assassination recalibrated black analyses of power, but material consequences also impacted black communities because of the riots that began in Washington and spread throughout the country.[65] Black Panther chairman Huey Newton explains that after King's assassination, Oakland police chief Charles Gain "had canceled all police leaves and doubled the number of occupying troops in our community, which only intensified the sense of anger and

despair."[66] Newton, like other black intellectuals critical of the romanticizing of hope, emphasizes how the affective shift to "anger and despair" was
an important component of Black Power organizing, but notes that it was a
response to increased police repression. Black Panther chief of staff David
Hilliard remembers being with Eldridge, coordinating a cookout fund-raiser
in De Fremery Park, when they heard the news that King had been shot,
writing, "This is our general consensus: no more hoses, whippings, and dogs.
People shouldn't be asked to bleed peacefully, Malcolm has said."[67] Invoking
Malcolm to push back against sentimentalizing King's assassination, the Panthers described the consensus about resisting white supremacy by refusing to
submit to white violence through nonviolence.

The riots after King's assassination, briefly discussed in the last chapter,
demonstrated how King's death exposed the limits of racial liberalism. Just two
days before his assassination, *Look* magazine published an interview with King
where he (correctly) anticipated, "If rioting continues, it will strengthen the
right wing of the country."[68] The riots after King's death burned down ten blocks
in Washington around the White House, and the extensive television coverage of the funeral was explicitly designed to keep black Americans at home
rather than in the streets.[69] Antiriot prevention plans in Washington helped
to de-escalate the riots, but they nonetheless confirmed that racial inequality
was a permanent part of the political. But with George Wallace running the
most successful third-party campaign for the presidency, the assassination of
Bobby Kennedy, and the protests at the 1968 Democratic National Convention
rounding out the political landscape of 1968 leading to Nixon's election, King's
prediction of a massive swing to the right deepened both the rage and despair
of black America, definitively ending King's dream of the beloved community.

Hopelessness in Black and White

King's assassination, at least to the Panthers, provided unequivocal evidence
that appeals to white conscience had failed, cooperation with liberal government officials was useless, and no black American was safe. These accounts
are dominated by a sense of precarity, along with an embrace of a more
oppositional posture toward state authority, which nurtured the pessimism
of young activists. Integration had failed as a concept because whites fundamentally did not want to know or feel blackness as a permanent part of public culture; whites didn't want to share the political world with black people.
King's assassination and the death of his dream presented irrefutable proof of
the antiblackness of the political.

Former SNCC leader James Forman helped to broker a short-lived merger of the SNCC and the BPP in 1967 and writes about the constant barrage of assassination threats plaguing black activist leaders and how they shaped the political climate of 1968. In his memoir, Forman recalls an ultimatum he made in Berkeley at a meeting of the Peace and Freedom Party in northern California, where he pledged full retaliation for the assassination of any black activist leader. He explained that any black assassination should be met by "ten war factories destroyed; fifteen blown up police stations; thirty power plants destroyed; one Southern Governor; two mayors; and five hundred racist cops dead."[70] He continued, "The price on Stokely and on Rap [Brown] is triple my price because all of them have been receiving assassination threats.... But we say to the CIA people who are in the audience, to the local police agents, to the FBI, and to everyone else that their deaths will not go unseen.... And I tell you this: the sky is the limit if you kill Huey Newton. The sky is the limit if Huey Newton dies."[71] Forman highlighted the visibility of assassination, a feature that makes its role in cultural trauma so prominent. Here the promise of retribution marked the visibility of resistance and demonstrates how Black Power advocates, in the face of brutal black assassination, became even more confrontational rhetorically. How else to combat the blatant public murder of so many black activists, when appealing to white conscience would not save even the most nonviolent among them? Because political assassinations were so widespread in the 1960s and were a source for the erasure of optimism as either a public or private rhetorical sentiment, it makes sense that Black Power activists would turn away from optimism and toward rhetorical devices that reflected this disillusionment as they moved from assessing assassination as a passive action to suicide as an active one, as we shall see in the next chapter. As Black Power ideology began to incorporate guerrilla warfare into its rhetorical programs, leaders showcased an irrational attachment to models that were not necessarily sustainable in the United States. George Jackson's *Blood in My Eye*, for example, is a lengthy treatise on the utility of guerrilla warfare in the Cuban style for black liberation in urban centers. How do we understand this attachment to such a model of resistance? One way is to remember how much low-level conflict like police brutality characterized black urban life in the 1960s and 1970s. Another is to understand the death of optimism. A third would highlight the importance of new modes of black Being that promoted pride, shunned state dependency, and acknowledged a more collective and global view of oppression, resistance, and (neo)colonialism.

So while the Black Power activists marked the death of King as the political death of nonviolence, I suggest that King's death exposed nonviolence and the racial liberalism of King's dream as *cruel optimism*. That exposure drove Black Power organizing. Bobby Seale explains that King's assassination had a direct effect on the size and scope of the Black Panther Party. In an interview for *Eyes on the Prize*, he explained how after King's assassination the BPP "grew from seven hundred to five thousand members plus. And with the assassination of Robert Kennedy later that year the young White radicals readily coalesced with us at our direction. . . . So it was whoever in the power structure who murdered Martin Luther King caused a lot of people who sided with Martin Luther King to say, 'The heck with it. Let's join the Panthers.' And they in effect tagged us as the vanguard of the revolution."[72] Seale's comments here can perhaps be read as a post facto rationale for his fugitivity, which began two days after King's assassination, after he persuaded Panthers to ambush the Oakland police in retaliation for the civil rights leader's murder. Still, the memories of Black Power advocates pushed back against bourgeois black memories of King and his legacy, but their resistance in the face of his assassination built their organization in his absence.

Contributing to this conundrum about King's memories is the elevation of the dream trope even today because, historical memory Harry A. Reed explicates, "the Dreamer is still a powerful motif guiding perceptions about King," in large part owing to the preference that white newspaper editors had for the "I Have a Dream" speech as opposed to King's hard-line stance against the Vietnam War.[73] Vincent Harding has lamented this "unremitting focus on the 1963 March on Washington, the never-ending repetition of the great speech and its dream metaphor, the sometimes innocent and sometimes manipulative boxing of King into the relatively safe categories of 'civil rights leader,' 'great orator,' harmless dreamer of black and white children on the hillside."[74] Probably the most egregious problem with using "the dream" as a synecdoche for King is that it eclipses his commitment to exposing class warfare, prison and police brutality, and the continuities of black repression since slavery. Harding, a King intimate, suggests that "the dream" enables "national amnesia" about King's radical transformation after 1963. Harding explains that King's move to Chicago highlighted his commitment to progressive class analysis. Harding writes that King "was driven by the fires of Watts and the early hot summers of 1964 and 1965. Challenged and nurtured by the powerful commitment of Malcolm X to the black street forces, he was also compelled by his own deep compassion for the urban black community—whose peculiar problems were not fundamentally addressed by the civil rights law so dearly won in the South."[75] Harding urges a more radical reading and writing of King in rhetorical memory: "We understand nothing about the King whose life ended in the midst of a struggle for garbage workers if we miss that earlier offering of himself to the struggle against poverty in America, to the continuing battle for the empowerment of the powerless—in this nation, in Vietnam, in South Africa, in Central America, and beyond."[76]

Harding's comments suggest that any assessment of King should acknowledge the way that he adapted and adopted new rhetorical and political strategies as the political landscape changed. Rather than fix King in time at the 1963 march, when the country had reached a height of jubilant optimism before the assassination of Kennedy, before the assassination of Malcolm X, before Watts and Detroit, and before the escalation of Vietnam, I would suggest that the memories of King highlight the pitfalls of such a one-dimensional account of the man, the movement, and his assassination. Rather, the memories of King's assassination point to his death as a reorientation of the movement where even cruel optimism was exposed as a fraud. The death of King was a moment of contention over representation and memory, not just between King's organization, the SCLC, and his family, but also for people across the globe who struggled to understand what role he played in a country where political assassinations were so common. "King was," in the words of cultural sociologist Ron Eyerman, "a powerful symbolic and representative figure well beyond the United States even before his death. His death, especially the way he died, was the catalyst to his transformation. King died a martyr to a cause that was, by this time, universally acknowledged as just."[77] What role could hope possibly play when his crusade, widely acknowledged as righteous, was destroyed by a sniper? As Elizabeth Hardwick wrote after his funeral in 1968, King's murder "was a national disgrace. This we said over and over and it would be cynical to hint at fraudulent feelings in the scramble for suitable acts of penance." Still, she adds, "Perhaps what was celebrated in Atlanta was an end, not a beginning—the waning of the slow, sweet dream of Salvation, through Christ, for the Negro masses."[78]

Although it often helps to read the past into the present, particularly from the standpoint of social movement activists, nostalgia can compel people "to do nothing more than remain where they stood, to keep old ways familiar, even to flee the present and the future into a nostalgically golden yesteryear secluded somewhere far off among remembrances of things past."[79] Activists must resist the urge to prefer "*things as they are perceived to have been*" and instead focus on what can be done now, in the present, with the resources available.[80] To simply indulge in nostalgia reifies the past in the present and acts as tacit consent for the status quo. In this case, King's death invigorated the new generation of Black Power radicals who saw his death as a confirmation of their proclamations about the nightmare of white supremacy, and it forced a more structural critique of imperialism, colonialism, and power, particularly in urban centers where King's dream seemed meaningless by 1968.

Chapter Six

REVOLUTIONARY SUICIDE
Necromimesis, Radical Agency, and Black Ontology

I never had a childhood. I was born dead.
—James Baldwin

In a 1969 prison interview, Chairman Huey Newton described the Black Panther Party's revolutionary impulse in this way: "The Black Panther Party, which is a revolutionary group of black people, realizes that we have to have an identity.... We believe that culture itself will not liberate us. We're going to need some stronger stuff."[1] Newton spoke at length about the class tensions of black America, suggesting that the Black Panther Party align itself with "the black have-nots, which represent about ninety-eight percent of blacks here in America. We're not controlled by the white mother country radicals nor are we controlled by the black bourgeoisie. We have a mind of our own and if the black bourgeoisie cannot align itself with our complete program, then the black bourgeoisie sets itself up as our enemy and they will be attacked and treated as such."[2] Critical of both white *and* black sellouts, Newton explained that white revolutionaries "have a choice between whether they will be a friend of Lyndon Baines Johnson or a friend of Fidel Castro. A friend of Robert Kennedy or a friend of Ho Chi Minh. And these are direct opposites. . . . After they make this choice, the white revolutionaries have a duty and a responsibility to act."[3] In pointing to this choice between fidelity to white liberal sellouts or Third World revolutionaries, Newton's dichotomies pointed to a new cognitive and affective map for what black resistance would orient itself to and away from.

Newton's comments demonstrate the importance of the revolutionary idiom and Third World politics to the Black Panther Party's philosophy, but they also highlight the pervasiveness of black vulnerability, not just to the police who were terrorizing black communities, but also to whites who expressed some solidarity with the black freedom struggle. In a collection of writings published posthumously, Newton wrote: "A true revolutionary realized that if he is sincere death is imminent. The things he is saying and doing are extremely dangerous."[4] Newton pointed to the constancy of antiblack violence in the United States and to political death as a certainty in the struggle for a more radical black consciousness. As Judith Butler explains, "In a way, we all live with this particular vulnerability, a vulnerability to the other that is part of bodily life, a vulnerability to a sudden address from elsewhere that we cannot preempt. This vulnerability . . . becomes highly exacerbated under certain social and political conditions, especially those in which violence is a way of life and the means to secure self-defense are limited."[5] For political pessimists and social revolutionaries like the Panthers—operating as they did in a climate of political and social precarity, where self-defense was intrinsic to their platform—their confrontational rhetorical posture was grounded in the assumption that death by the state was a foregone conclusion given their political vulnerability. The Panthers saw the necessity for new modes of political engagement, particularly those that moved away from "spontaneous riots," because, as Black Panther Party chairman Huey Newton argued, "the outcome was always the same: the people might liberate their territories for a few short days or hours but eventually . . . the oppressor would wipe out their gains. . . . In the final analysis, riots caused only more oppression."[6] This was especially true after the assassination of Martin Luther King, as we saw in Chapter Five.

The Panthers, more than any other radical black organization, centered the negative feelings that preoccupied black America at the end of the 1960s by describing how black bodies are ontologically immobilized as non-Beings who provide complete contrast with those, in Frank Wilderson's words, "who do not magnetize bullets."[7] The escalation of the war in Vietnam, along with the assassinations of Malcolm X, Martin Luther King Jr., and so many others, barred the possibility of hope as a guiding emotion of the black freedom struggle and militarized the Panthers as urban police forces purchased decommissioned military-grade weapons to repress race riots. As riots "swept cities like Watts and Detroit, the Panthers provided a concrete alternative to more traditional civil rights protest and government-sponsored community action programs, on the one hand, and the outpouring of frustration and anger of the 'long hot summers,' on the other," writes Donna Murch, whose work demonstrates the ways in which black feelings shaped responses to urban antiblack public policy.[8] James Baldwin argued that precisely because the Panthers demonstrated how to perform black autonomy, they were "a great force for peace and stability in the ghettoes," though he acknowledged that white America was unwilling to admit this fact because it refused black grievances and could not permit the "unprecedented measure of authority for ghetto citizens" that the Panthers demanded, noting that "no one in authority is prepared to face this overwhelmingly obvious fact."[9]

In this chapter, I argue that Black Panther Party chairman Huey Newton's rhetorical invention of the meme "revolutionary suicide," in his 1973 memoir of the same name, functions as an exploration of necromimesis, where the speaker believes themself to be socially, juridically, and politically dead as a subject.[10] Necromimesis is the essence of political sacrifice, whereby one's death can only be comprehended by those who share their liminal positionality as the walking dead. Theoretically, necromimetic discourses—exemplified most clearly in *eulogies*—complement what Achille Mbembe calls "necropolitics" and "necropower," or the means by which deathworlds are created alongside lifeworlds.[11] Revolutionary suicide is, in Mbembe's words, "a gesture of self-determination, a way of being present to oneself and looking inward" "as a utopian critique."[12] The intimate exchanges among the living dead and between the dead and those still living that operate in Newton's writings function as rhetorical and political interventions in a space where political futures have been violently foreclosed on. Newton borrows from classic revolutionary hermeneutics, with clear heroes and enemies, to make his case for necromimesis. The structures are describable and the political asks are straightforward. But where Kennedy's language of hope at the beginning of the sixties charts a political futurity of optimism, by the publication of *Revolutionary Suicide*, the semantics and feelings of progress receded and were replaced with more complicated assessments of the limits of white progressivism. In animating and replicating the living dead, necromimetic discourses create political and aesthetic interventions that highlight the forms of death that create encounters between hegemonic and subaltern peoples. In Wendy Brown's parlance, these discourses "consider freedom in existing figurations of power—economic, social, psychological, political."[13] And as Alex Houen has argued, "Necromimesis thus helps to draw together reified transcendence, death, and social exchange into a sacrificial compound for a particular community."[14] Given the tremendous surveillance, harassment, and disruption of the Black Panther Party by COINTELPRO in the late 1960s, we might even go so far as to say that California (the Bay Area, in particular) was a necropolis after the election of Ronald Reagan as governor in 1966 ushered in the era of mass incarceration.[15]

Black Pessimism, Black Assassination, Black Suicide

Huey Newton begins his memoir *Revolutionary Suicide* by documenting the incredible rates of black suicide in the United States, noting that the foremost psychologists of the era saw suicide as an individual failure of will rather than a symptom of social forces. Using the pioneering psychological work of Dr. Herbert Hendin, however, Newton described what he called "reactionary suicide," which was the result of black men who "had been deprived of human dignity, crushed by oppressive forces, and denied their right to live as proud and free human beings."[16] If people do not have dignity, Newton asserts, suicide emerges as a reaction to persistent *feelings* of fear, despair, and hopelessness in the face of economic and social poverty. "Connected to reactionary suicide, although even more painful and degrading, is a spiritual death that has been the experience of millions of Black people in the United States.... Many Blacks have been driven to a death of the spirit rather than of the flesh, lapsing into lives of quiet desperation. Yet all the while, in the heart of every Black, there is the hope that life will somehow change in the future," Newton writes.[17] This notion of reactionary suicide contextualized black suicide within a matrix of social forces operating to undermine black health and welfare and echoes what Martin Luther King called "suicidal longing."

Hendin's research pointed to variables like access to solid public education, employment opportunities, safe housing, health care, healthy food, and communities free from white-on-black violence as factors that have continuously undermined the mental health of black people. Grier and Cobbs demonstrated that the dearth of black clinicians in the United States willing and able to treat black patients experiencing psychiatric distress and negative emotions contributed to high rates of depression and suicide. But simply providing more black clinicians would not be a solution; the authors pointed instead to a certain range of *feelings* that new black clinicians must access to be successful. They reasoned that the black therapist's "real usefulness will come into play only when he begins to grabble with his own feelings about being black, ineffective, and victimized in a powerful white nation."[18] Huey Newton's articulation of the relationship between black health and black pride underscored Malcolm X's contributions to discourses of black feelings but circulated them more widely as Newton theorized the relationship between black mental health and structural oppression, even as it influenced black therapists.

The research and language of mental and social health also underscored how black discourse has been shaped by "slavery, colonization, and apartheid," and it pointed to the generational effects of exclusion and violence marking American housing, employment, and educational policy.[19] These processes of estrangement distance black people from their authentic selves, creating an alterity that must be overcome through new modes of identification (what Malcolm described as being detached from their "African minds") in what Tommy J. Curry has called a "political economy of niggerdom."[20] But they also speak to modernity's demand for the perpetual dispossession of black people around the globe. The result of these historical structures is "maximal exteriority and ontological impoverishment" that feed into the degradation of black people and their inner selves by whites.[21] As bodies rather than people, black men especially were viewed as material goods despite liberalism's articulation of freedom, producing the alienation that Fanon, himself a psychiatrist, described so clearly.

Newton's assessment established black mental health as a legitimate vector of BPP inquiry and demonstrated the necessity of political pessimism as an emotional discourse. This is particularly true as police brutality figured so clearly in psychological assessments of black communities after the Harlem riot of 1964, but it amplified after Martin Luther King's assassination in 1968, as demonstrated in the last chapter. Newton, like other black intellectuals critical of the romanticizing of hope especially after King's death, emphasized how the affective shift to "anger and despair" formed an important component of Black Power organizing, but noted that it came in response to increased police repression.

While Peniel Joseph warns of viewing Black Power as the death of the civil rights movement,[24] we should have no doubt that Black Power activists framed the political moment in this way because of shifting *feelings* about racial liberalism, blackness, and violence. King's assassination, at least to the Panthers, provided unequivocal evidence that appeals to white conscience had failed, cooperation with liberal government officials was useless, and no black activist was safe. A sense of precarity dominates these accounts, along with a total resignation to a more oppositional posture toward state authority, which nurtured the pessimism of young activists. In the words of Kennerly and Pfister, "Mimetic pedagogies draw attention to the argumentative architecture, figurative dimensions, and contexts of emergence for a given text, or genre, or, today, a meme."[25] In offering "revolutionary suicide" as a meme that encapsulated the racial politics of death, Newton articulated a new ontology of blackness that was, in James Baldwin's estimation, inevitable.[26] Eulogies of movement activists (including but beyond King) helped to frame the meme and transmit it as a powerful meditation on the death politics of the 1960s.

The Eulogy as a Form of Political Address

Because political assassinations were so widespread in the 1960s and were
a source for the erasure of optimism as either a public or private rhetorical
sentiment, it makes sense that Black Power activists would turn away from
optimism and toward rhetorical modes and devices that reflected disillusionment as they moved from assessing assassination as a passive action to suicide as an active one. Exhausted from panic and the extreme emotional labor
of disappointment, Black Power leaders looked for ways to make sense of a
future without King as a foil. But the increasing number of political assassinations within the ranks of the civil rights and Black Power movements
convinced many activists that their lives were fleeting, making optimism a
less likely affective and rhetorical device for them. Fredrika Newton speaks of
this feeling in the preface to *Revolutionary Suicide*: "There was an unspoken,
ever-prevailing sense between us that our life together was fleeting. Some of
Huey's closest comrades in the party had been gunned down, and the constant presence of an armed bodyguard in our lives was a constant reminder
that Huey might meet the same fate."[27]

As a meme, revolutionary suicide emerged from political precarity that
only intensified after King's assassination, and it found its voice in the eulogies of the period because Black Power was producing itself necromimeti-
cally, through black death and black sacrifice. Because eulogies are the clearest
form of mimetic rhetorical oration, they occupy a unique position in the discourse of tragedy. One of the major reasons that eulogy is unique is that it is
overdetermined by temporality. Thomas Farrell reminds us that eulogy is the
rhetorical form that comes the closest to "bring[ing] together all the mystery
and paradox surrounding the aesthetic language of rhetoric."[28]

These paradoxes often find their articulation through political feelings. In
the eulogy, *feeling* "links the final interruption of the individual life to *the
continuity* of public life."[29] In eulogy, as Hans Robert Jauss has suggested in
his readings of Gorgias and Aristotle, "*katharsis* names the pleasure produced by one's own affects when they are stimulated by oratory or poetry and
which can change the listener's and liberate the spectator's mind." This process, found especially in elegiac rhetoric, has the power to justify "norms of
action."[30] The catharsis of movement activism is often propelled by the kinds
of pleasure gained in narrating a new relationality, particularly to the state
or to oneself, that is often found in black freedom eulogies. That catharsis
comes from the production of discourses of freedom. In an interview with
Paul Rabinow, Foucault explains: "Liberty is a *practice*. . . . The liberty of men
is never assured by the institutions and laws that are intended to guarantee

them. . . . Not because they are ambiguous, but simply because 'liberty' is what must be exercised. . . . The guarantee of freedom is freedom."[31] In this way, revolutionary suicide, as it circulated as a meme of liberty in Newton's eulogies, was an assertion of radical black agency.

Given that such a large portion of civil rights and Black Power memory is fixed to eulogies and other elegiac rhetorical moments, it seems clear that this form of address constitutes an essential form in shaping the Black Power vernacular. And this is certainly true of Huey Newton's public eulogies, which meditated on black sacrifice, sovereignty, and freedom. "The relation of individuality to foreknowledge of death creates an ambiguous context for the exercise of freedom," writes William Connolly.[32] This complicates the eulogy as a discourse of Black Power, since death was a foregone conclusion. Nonetheless eulogy figures as a primary mode of rhetorical engagement that, in Campbell and Jamieson's words, "transforms the relationship between the living and the dead" and "reknits the fabric of the community," in this case around new values.[33] Given that Newton was not a famous preacher as King was, his eulogies are also animated by different political orientations and feelings. Take, for example, Newton's eulogy for Samuel Napier, the distribution and circulation manager of the *Black Panther* newspaper, who was executed in April 1971. Napier was found bound, gagged, and facedown on a mattress, his body riddled with bullet holes delivered execution style. In his eulogy, Newton explained: "Death comes to all of us, but it varies in its significance. To die for the reactionaries, the racists, the capitalists is lighter than a feather. But to die in the service to the people is heavier than any mountain and deeper than any sea."[34] Newton's words perform the "mimetic genius" of producing a "field of signs that, once decrypted, opened the way for an array of practices that moved constantly away from orthodoxy."[35] He does so by introducing necromimetic sacrifice as a lens through which to interpret the repetition of black death.

Nowhere is that more clear than in *Revolutionary Suicide* as Newton praises the sacrifice of San Quentin prisoner and Black Panther George Jackson as the model of revolutionary sacrifice. Jackson was first incarcerated at eighteen and charged with being an accessory to the theft of $71.00 from a service station. His friend Robert Early Young allegedly stole the money on his way back to Jackson's car from the restroom. Jackson was sentenced to serve one year to life in prison after his court-appointed lawyer suggested that he plead guilty for a reduced sentence. Thereafter Jackson spent seven and a half years of his prison time in solitary isolation in "adjustment centers" within maximum security, where he wrote the best-selling book *Soledad Brother*. There he argued that "capture, imprisonment, is the closest to being dead that one is likely to experience in this life."[36] In describing the psychic alienation of blackness in America, compounded as it is under mass incarceration, Jackson demonstrates the importance of new frameworks of agency as black Americans struggle against the domination and violence structuring their lives. Grier and Cobbs explain that, for the black man living under such strain, the "net effect is an alienation from his roots with no substitute available. He cannot go forward and he cannot go back. He may try to bind himself to blackness and voice the spirit of dark people; he may attack the white man, taking up the sword for his people; he may try in a thousand ways to become engaged in the battle, but always he enters from the outside and his contribution is that of an outsider. As the giants move toward battle, his is the voice of the bystander begging for engagement."[37] When black life itself is a prison, black people run out of options.

Jackson's theoretical writings on black prison resistance elucidate what Fred Moten calls "blackness-in-fugitivity" by describing how capture, escape, and death have been the fundamental experiences of black life in America.[38] In 1971 a prison guard shot Jackson in the back in retribution for allegedly killing a prison guard and attempting a prison escape, and Jackson's death became a catalyst for the Attica prison rebellion in New York, demonstrating the importance of his performance of fugitivity as an intellectual activity and as a practical matter of life or death, particularly for other prisoners in solitary confinement. Newton's eulogy of Jackson transforms his killing into a political suicide. *Revolutionary Suicide* is important precisely because it converts narratives of trauma (in this case, death, assassination, and suicide) into narratives of political triumph. Political suicide, then, becomes the only truly autonomous act in a white supremacist culture where hope is long dead. Writing about the institutionalization of slavery, Paul Gilroy comments that "in many respects, the plantation inhabitants live non-synchronously," and in fact, the same is true of prisoners, giving them a different perspective on the chronopolitics of black life and death.[39]

Newton gave the eulogy at Jackson's public funeral, saying that even in death, "George Jackson is a legendary figure and hero. . . . a superman. And we will teach our children to be like George Jackson, to live like George Jackson, to fight like George Jackson fought for freedom. . . . He showed us how to act. He demonstrated how the unjust would be criticized by the weapon."[40] Jackson was the embodiment of someone who was juridically dead but very much engaged with black life. His resistance in San Quentin, knowing that he would die there, provided an example of revolutionary suicide that formed the foundation of Newton's meditation and demonstrated Moten's idea that blackness itself functions "as a criminality that is before the law."[41] Likewise,

Jackson centralized the prison as a space where meditations on fugitivity and death were necessary and useful calibrations of black agency. Jackson's writings augmented the momentum against the "civil death" doctrine, which inspired prisoners to agitate to restore citizenship rights to felons.[42] As Saidiya Hartman notes, "It is a tricky matter to detail the civil existence of a subject who is socially dead and legally recognized as human only to the degree that he is criminally culpable."[43] This conundrum is precisely the point on which the revolutionary suicide meme meditates, because it describes the psychologically treacherous arena of the penitentiary as a way of understanding sovereignty, empire, and capital as mechanisms of antiblack death. More importantly, these prison writings interrogated the deathworlds created by capitalism and mass incarceration. As Katherine Stanutz so eloquently argues, "Jackson's textual strategies give shape to his grief and reframe mourning" by "converting intimate grief into public idiom" to redistribute "the emotional impact of loss."[44] In converting private feelings into political strategy—in this case, revolution—Jackson's writings and his life stood as the ultimate example of how black feelings could be mobilized "enough to alter the structural relation between living and dead," in the words of Frank Wilderson.[45]

Jackson provided a central case study for Newton to discuss the liminality of black masculinity. Jackson's discourses on revolutionary sacrifice and civil death helped create the foundation for what would be revolutionary suicide. By praising Jackson and men like him as heroes (especially in death), Newton affirms that revolutionary suicide is the state wherein the "Black Man affirms of himself that he is that which cannot be captured or controlled; the one who is not where they say he is, and even less where they are looking for him. Rather, he exists where he is not thought."[46] Jackson provides an example of the "refusal to adjust to existing conditions of capture, enslavement, and incarceration"; he is mobile, shifting, fugitive.[47] Praising these characteristics, Newton's eulogy transforms Jackson into the Dragon, which Newton describes thus: "He was a strong man, he was determined, full of love, strength, dedication to the people's cause, without fear. He lived the life that we must praise. It was a life, no matter how he was oppressed, no matter how wrongly he was done, he still kept the love for the people. And this is why he felt no pain in giving up his life for the people's cause."[48] Newton's description of Jackson animates him as a resource for the movement, connecting this rhetorical intervention to the chronopolitics of (black) death and life and seeing Jackson's death as a point of regeneration for Black Power activism. Newton proclaims: "George's body has fallen, but his spirit goes on, because his ideas live. And we will see that these ideas stay alive, because they'll be manifested in our bodies and in those young Panther bodies, who are our children. So it's a true saying that there will be revolution from one generation to the next."[49] In this invocation of reproductive futurity, Newton sees Jackson's spirit as something that can be taught and modeled for black children as part of a pedagogy of resistance and radical black agency. Thus was George Jackson a central figure of revolutionary suicide as a meme. But Newton's tenure as chairman of the BPP was characterized almost exclusively by his own incarceration, cementing their connection beyond organizational affiliation. As Gilbert Moore has suggested, "Probably no prisoner in Oakland's penal history was held in tighter security."[50] With stretches of several months to several years in solitary confinement, "it is inconceivable that incarceration had no impact on Newton."[51] This kind of existence is what Spillers calls "*being for* the captor*," where imprisonment is what structures black Being.[52] Newton's own experience in the California penal system gave his eulogy of a heroic Jackson more gravity.[53]

Revolutionary Suicide as Necromimesis

At the heart of the notion of revolutionary suicide is Newton's disavowal of political optimism, driving him to oppose the forces that cripple the souls of black folk, even as he acknowledges the importance of hope as a driving force of social change. Because death is the price for fighting for a humane (black) existence, Newton sees revolutionary suicide not as fatalism but as a radical form of black agency. He writes:

> Although I risk the likelihood of death, there is at least the possibility, if not probability, of changing intolerable conditions. This possibility is important, because much in human existence is based upon hope without any real understanding of the odds. Indeed, we are all—Black and White alike—ill in the same way, mortally ill. But before we die, how shall we live? I say with hope and dignity; and if premature death is the result, that death has meaning that reactionary suicide can never have. It is the price of self-respect.[54]

Newton explains, "Revolutionary suicide does not mean that I and my comrades have a death wish; it means just the opposite. We have such a strong desire to live with hope and human dignity that existence without them is impossible. When reactionary forces crush us, we must move against these forces, even at the risk of death."[55] He continues, "Che Guevara said that to a revolutionary death is the reality and victory the dream. Because the revolutionary lives so dangerously, his survival is a miracle."[56] Thus does Newton understand revolutionary suicide as an acceptance of the inevitability of (black) death and the importance of dying on one's own terms in opposition to brutality and despair. Glossing Guevara and Mikhail Bakunin, Newton explains that in his estimation, "to a revolutionary death is a reality and victory is the death," and "the first lesson a revolutionary must learn is that he is a doomed man."[57] Indeed, as the COINTELPRO papers show, the state was hell-bent on eradicating Black Power leadership at all costs, certainly while J. Edgar Hoover still had breath in his body.

Newton also knew that revolutionary suicide is what ultimately separated black revolutionaries from white radicals. He explains, "Considering how we must live, it is not hard to accept the concept of revolutionary suicide. In this we are different from the white radicals. They are not facing genocide." This distinction marked black suffering and death as having revolutionary power and demonstrated the power of revolutionary suicide as a meme invoking black reason. Mbembe argues, "It is on the basis of a distinction between reason and unreason (passion, fantasy) that late-modern criticism has been able to articulate a certain idea of the political, the community, the subject—or, more fundamentally, of what the good life is all about, how to achieve it, and, in the process, to become a fully moral agent. Within this paradigm, reason is the truth of the subject and politics is the exercise of reason in the public sphere. The exercise of reason is tantamount to the exercise of freedom, a key element for individual autonomy. The romance of sovereignty, in this case, rests on the belief that the subject is the master and the controlling author of his or her own meaning."[58] Newton's attempt to wrest control of the meaning of his life and the narration of himself as a national subject and moral agent demonstrates how black activists were living with constant trauma and how they resisted seeing the violence as exceptional, choosing instead to underscore the violence as quotidian. Revolutionary suicide functioned as a meme that helped scaffold black agency on systems of black death.

In characterizing Black Power as an assertion of history, sovereignty, and self-defense of a colonized people, Newton's use of the meme differed greatly from assimilationist politics that held out for the optimistic possibility of constructive interracial alliances in the 1960s and 1970s. Using postcolonial thinkers to map American necropolitics, Newton explains, "Mao and Fanon and Guevara all saw clearly that the people had been stripped of their birthright and their dignity, not by any philosophy or mere words, but by gunpoint. They had suffered a holdup by gangsters, and rape; for them, the only way to win freedom was to meet force with force."[59] Thus revolutionary suicide, as an organizing principle of Black Power, is exactly the kind of necromimetic philosophical intervention that reproduced itself in and through the discourses of assassination that evidenced precisely the kind of civic death that activists were facing (above and beyond the juridical death they faced through imprisonment). The invocation of Jackson in his collected writings and Newton's memoir belongs to a genre I see as productively hauntological and is part of what Derrida has called "a phantomatic mode of production": a mimetic death-in-life rhetorical possibility, a modern aesthetic space for producing paradoxes where the dead are conjured.[60] Because Newton advocates suicide as a rhetorical and political posture for the living, his writings engage the paradoxical nature of black life and death. Revolutionary suicide, then, became a way of replicating Black Power ideology through necrotic, rather than biophiliac, means.

In the earliest rhetorical studies of the Black Power movement, Scott and Smith elaborated on what was then described as a nihilistic impulse: "Part of the attraction of confrontation is the strong sense of success, so strong that it may be a can't-lose strategy," because after suffering for so long, the Black Power activist has nothing left to lose.[61] Black Power activists, particularly in the Panthers, articulated this "nothing left to lose" posture in several ways. They argued that black people are already socially dead and therefore can't be killed again. They argued that they could be reborn, perhaps as martyrs. They argued that they had the tenacity for a revolutionary fight where white conservatives did not. And they argued that black people have a global understanding of oppression and how to work together to destroy it.[62] But it is possible to rebel against political fatalism "in two ways: we deny the idea that the future is an already existing reality and we reject the fate of an inevitable destiny against which we cannot intervene. . . . The future is a conjecture about what is possible, not the knowledge of something that is necessarily going to happen."[63] But insofar as Black Power embraces forms of black nihilism, they "reject[ed] this 'trick-of-time' and the lure of emancipatory solutions. To refuse to 'do politics' and to reject the fantastical object of politics is the only 'hope' for blackness in an antiblack world."[64] Black nihilism is a rhetorical elaboration of what Warren calls "the bio-political grotesque," this discursive and material violence enacted on black bodies in the streets and in the prisons.

In *Revolutionary Suicide*, Newton is critical of this early posture, acknowledging that while they were attempting to perform the Fanonian move to highlight the vulnerability of the state, the ideograph of the Panther with the gun actually alienated the Panthers from the community. In discussing the importance of self-defense, Newton suggests that the aesthetic practices of the Black Panther Party compromised its political efficacy. His writing embraces some ambivalence about the party's guerrilla aesthetics: "We soon discovered that weapons and uniforms set us apart from the community. We were looked upon as an ad hoc military group, acting outside of the community fabric and too radical to be a part of it. Perhaps some of our tactics at the time were extreme; perhaps we placed too much emphasis on military action."[65] Newton suggests that the gun as a symbol of the struggle against white supremacy compounded the alienation of black people and contributed to the downfall of the Panthers. While he doesn't denounce the decision to militarize, couching his assessment in the context of the time, he does seem to acknowledge that taking up the gun against the oppressor also contributed to the repression of black people and complicated their feelings about resistance and liberation. While it might be tempting, especially for white interlocutors, to read Newton's comments on the gun as exculpatory for law-and-order politics, I want to suggest that a closer reading would lead us to understand how entangled black death is with black life. Rather than shunning the gun as a tool of liberation, Newton's writings seem to highlight the tensions between building coalitions to transform communities (as the Panthers did with their survival programs) and guerrilla warfare. And the use of guerrilla warfare (in a police state) as the language of the party provided rhetorical resources to rethink black life and death in American while also undercutting the political efficacy of the Panthers because the presence of the gun as the ideograph of struggle guaranteed massive resistance by the state, compounding everyday struggles for urban black Americans.

In proposing revolutionary suicide as a philosophical meme to unpack black life and death, Newton's memoir provides a template for intimate engagement with the living and the dead as a way of negotiating the boundaries of power and possibilities of identification within the nation. For example, Newton concludes the book with an old African proverb: "I am we." In this proverb, Newton sees the origins of revolutionary suicide as an understanding that the individual only exists in intimate relation to the communal:

> So many of my comrades are gone now. Some tight partners, crime partners, and brothers off the block are begging on the street. Others are in asylum, penitentiary or grave. They are all suicides of one kind or another who had the sensitivity and tragic imagination to see the oppression. Some overcame: they are the revolutionary suicides. Others were reactionary suicides who either overestimated or underestimated the enemy, but in any case were powerless to change their conception of the oppressor.

Speaking to those lost, Newton describes the conditions of their despondency as structural. He explains their deaths as inevitable given the scale and scope of antiblack violence, especially as it has been targeted at black men. But he also describes the affective dimensions of this kind of misery as it shapes reactive versus revolutionary suicide: "The difference lies in hope and desire. By hoping and desiring, the revolutionary suicide chooses life; he is, in the words of Nietzsche, 'an arrow of longing for another shore.'" In longing for the other shore, the revolutionary passes through death on the way to something greater, articulating a consciousness about oppression that transcends life and permits an expanded view on political resistance to white supremacy.

For Newton, necromimesis allows the writer and the reader to long for shores that seem impossible to comprehend through the landscape of violence that characterized urban America in the late sixties and early seventies. In embracing a different affective or emotional register, Newton sees necromimetic practices as transcendent ones, where fear, resignation, and hostility no longer exert control over mortal decision making. He sees the choice to embrace revolutionary suicide as an act of radical agency that creates new possibilities for identification, political agitation, and social resistance. And he underscores the importance of radical intimacy as the transformative act that can bridge oppositional social locations and create a strong foundation for community action.

Necropolitical Agency

Activists like Newton were meditating on civic death and its utility to building stronger black life, and they were extremely aware of "the intimate exchanges that take place between death and representation."[66] In representing black death via a meditation on the rates of black male suicide, as well as the relationship between state-sanctioned murder-assassination and suicide, Newton's memoir transcends the political moment in which it is written to create a space for black fellowship among both the living and the dead. His expressions of hope and freedom were exoteric, concrete, understandable, if difficult to confront. For the writer as well as the reader, necromimetic representation ties the text to ancestors, kin, and community in ways that sustain black life and demonstrate its continuity alongside the constancy of antiblack trauma and civil death. And in sacrificing and representing sacrifice, books like *Revolutionary Suicide* reframed black suicide not as an individual mental state but as a response to collective racial trauma. The memoir became a reconstitutive rhetorical intervention that reframed back life and death in ways that demonstrated how death and life exist simultaneously for black America. Mbembe argues that necropolitics describes the process by which sovereignty "becomes the refusal to accept the limits that the fear of death would have the subject respect." To me, this is probably the most profound contribution of Newton and the BPP; they fundamentally embraced a notion of black sovereignty that was more oppositional and fundamentally more confrontational, which prompted the collision between lifeworlds and deathworlds as the FBI systematically targeted black leaders for assassination.

But revolutionary suicide was also a tenacious assertion of black political and social agency. Winters explains, "Within [black] culture, agency typically means something like self-determination, the ability to act and make decisions without being determined by something outside of the self. Following the Kantian tradition, agency is usually associated with autonomy and either assumes or imagines a coherent self, that can act rationally and individually. The coherence of the self, however, relies on avoiding or disavowing threats to that coherence—such as vulnerability, death, radical alterity, and trauma, all qualities and conditions that are inescapable for humans."[67] In this vein, Newton's writings signal the possibility for political redemption and personal transformation through death. As a movement text, *Revolutionary Suicide* is important precisely because it converts narratives of trauma—imprisonment, murder, and also suicide—into political triumph. Political suicide becomes the only truly autonomous act in a white supremacist culture where hope is long dead. Thus revolutionary suicide is a subjectivity that aggressively interrogates antiblack death to make room for black life.

Newton's life ended in a drug deal gone bad, marking him as a tragic figure of the late sixties and early seventies. It should come as no surprise that prison affected Newton tremendously. Joe Street observes that although Newton

> protested that he had prevailed over his captors, his post-release behavior exhibited many of the symptoms that characterize those who have become damaged by prison. These symptoms indicate that his descent into crime and drug addiction was firmly enmeshed in his prison experience. Newton's prison experience, then, must be acknowledged as a defining period in his life and as a key moment in the transformation of California's prisons into locations for the punishment rather than rehabilitation of its prisoners.[68]

Given Newton's experiences in the California penal system and his relationship to political repression and black death, *Revolutionary Suicide*, both as a memoir and as a meme, offers us a powerful meditation on the hyperfuturism of liberalism's hope and a return to political presentism for black folks. It is a powerful reminder of the material conditions that preclude productive future imaginaries by black communities. And it is an indictment of white political structures that prohibit hopeful futurism for black Americans after a decade of longing for the colorblind hope circulating early in the decade. It exposes the cruelty of colorblind hope in the age of political assassination and confirms that the conceptual horizon of civil rights had, indeed, changed by the early 1970s. The complexity of conversation and decision making about racial issues had made race a much more difficult political terrain to traverse because there were so many *competing* feelings. Where whites overwhelmingly disapproved of direct action by the end of the 1960s, many black Americans felt hopeless and trapped between white conservatism and the failures of white liberalism. As discussed in the last chapter, King's assassination exposed the cruelty of white liberal hope and the optimism of colorblind federal policy, and as the tremendous antiblack violence of America's cities escalated, necromimetic representational strategies and philosophies shaped black ontology for a new generation.

But beyond Newton's own affective and rhetorical strategies in describing the necropolitics of black life in the long sixties, it was clear that Black Power's descriptive influence had become pervasive as the Black Power era wound down. Writing in 1969, the sociologist James Turner cautioned:

> It is apparent that as the black power movement gains more strength and becomes more aggressive and defines its objective in terms of specific Afro-American interest, and not on (white) liberal terms and its increasingly politicized Afro-American element, it will appear more threatening and separatist to the dominate group. It would be a mistake, however, to dismiss such development as a futile and sectarian obsession with self—a kind of black narcissism. In the larger context of Afro-American experience, it represents, for many, the ultimate and perhaps most stable of self-awareness.[69]

Turner's assessment foretold the white backlash cycle that would follow Black Power and all but predicted the rise of Reagan. In cautioning any critical reading of Black Power that described it as narcissism, Turner's prescient perspective highlighted a mode of self-awareness that continues to be (deliberately) misunderstood.

Conclusion: Black Feelings in the Age of Obama

In this book, I have attempted to demonstrate how public feelings shaped the nation's racial politics in the long sixties through an examination of the discursive field surrounding the nation's ambivalent commitment to racial equality. Through a dense examination of presidential addresses, administration documents, federal commission reports, activist speeches and writings, and press accounts, I have showcased the vibrant and dynamic landscape of racial liberalism in this period. With hope as the frame for the New Frontier, the nation was asked to participate in futurist imaginings that fused technological progress and liberal values for the largest youth generation in the nation's history. But for all the euphoria about a new era in American politics—one that rejected fears of nuclearism for the promise of technological progress—the whiteness and masculinity of hope were exposed by black leaders and activists, who were unmoved by the Kennedy administration's productions of hope in light of its lack of commitment to racial justice. Black feelings, then, were provoked and disciplined by the successes and failures of liberalism's rebirth.

Beyond black political ambivalence about Kennedy himself, the resistance to white liberal conceptions of postwar political feelings deepened as the civil rights struggle expanded and transformed through the Johnson administration. The rhetorical productions of Martin Luther King Jr., Malcolm X, Eldridge Cleaver, Huey Newton, and others navigated a political milieu steeped in discourses about racial feelings. Hope, despair, rage, resentment, grief, and suicide commingled to create a political landscape of intense cognitive feelings that informed public policy and political resistance. This dense, flexible field of affective discourses (rather ironically) organized and deployed liberalism's classic tropes of hope, change, progress, and equality while also invigorating black discourses critical of liberalism's shortcomings, failures, and compromises. *Black Feelings* sees Black Power as an inevitable consequence of midcentury racial liberalism, as well as an enduring assemblage and as a racial formation that exposed the pathways of white power while reconstituting blackness in sometimes contradictory or short-sighted ways, but always with the goal of manufacturing new political attachments.

While the tensions between white hope and black despair were a dynamic that characterized politics in the long sixties, their structure is recursive. That is, the (positive and negative racial) feelings that undergird racial liberalism did not stop emerging and receding after law-and-order campaigns destroyed civil rights and Black Power organizing in the mid-1970s. Nowhere is this clearer than in the entrance and disappearance of the so-called Obama coalition in 2008 to elect Barack Obama as the first biracial/black president in US history. In considering how hope continues to be inextricably linked to rage, contempt, and despair, this brief conclusion considers hope as an ironic discourse of liberalism, particularly as it is racialized. The birth of Afro-pessimism as a coterminous discourse with what we now call the "postracial"

Obama coalition is important because we can see how black feelings in the long sixties continue to shape national political discourse, demonstrating how affective politics are iterative as well as how they change over time. In doing so, we can perhaps draw some conclusions about the increasing reliance of black activists on negative feelings to characterize their political subjectivity. We can also see calls for reparations as an ossification of black feelings that have emerged in response to new versions of law-and-order culture appearing under the cloak of postracialism, and we can see how property relations are being restratified in ways that mirror the kinds of politics for which Malcolm X and the Black Panthers were criticized in the 1960s and early 1970s.

THE OBAMA COALITION

Reinvigorating Liberal Hope

When Barack Obama won the presidential election in 2008, pundits proclaimed the success of the "Obama coalition," which was shorthand for people of color, young people (18–29 years old), the highly educated, and white working-class people outside the South, who propelled the freshman senator to victory. His autobiography, *The Audacity of Hope: Thoughts on Reclaiming the American Dream* (2006), presented Obama to the country as a representative anecdote of a changing American landscape where multiracial people of color would offer leadership paradigms that moved the country forward. Emphasizing opportunity, fairness, equality, and accountability, *The Audacity of Hope* charted a values-driven perspective and offered a transformational candidate.[1] In discussing America's modest hopes for a better future, Obama's memoir calibrated expectations about futurist longings that made his proposals seem achievable.[2] Obama explained, "We will need to understand how we got to this place, this land of warring factions and tribal hatreds. And we will need to remind ourselves, despite all our differences, just how much we share: commons hopes, common dreams, a bond that will not break."[3] Invoking a notion of commonality that connects the populations he energized to vote for him through the familiar polyglot narratives popularized by earlier democratic presidential candidates (notably Jimmy Carter), Obama praised everyday Americans for their "determination," "self-reliance," and "relentless optimism in the face of hardship."[4] Obama's narrative offered a new affective identity for Americans weary of the austerity of the Bush years.

The "audacity of hope" anchored the Obama narrative, a heroic turn of phrase designed to advance a bold vision and to elicit bravery to do the unthinkable. Just as John F. Kennedy's Pulitzer Prize–winning book *Profiles in Courage* (1957) offered a blueprint for a new and daring liberalism leading up to the 1960 election, so too did Obama's *Audacity of Hope* propose a similar political intervention in 2006. Explaining that the book's title came from a sermon that his Chicago pastor, Rev. Jeremiah A. Wright Jr., had used, Obama articulated the ethos of the hope that he was invoking: "This was the best of the American spirit, I thought—having the audacity to believe despite all the evidence to the contrary that we could restore a sense of community to a nation torn by conflict; the gall to believe that despite personal setbacks, the loss of a job or illness in the family of a childhood mired in poverty, we have some control—and therefore responsibility—over our own fate."[5] Obama invokes hope here as the spirit of his orientation toward public service while also attempting to resuscitate liberalism's loftiest goals, rooted as they are in individualism.

But beneath his pursuit of a fearless new path for American politics lies the fact that Obama is also characterizing hope as a political feeling held *despite evidence to the contrary*. Here audacity is a foolish optimism, grounded in the endurance of liberal tropes like the American Dream that mystify structural negligence and antiblack violence. Obama describes this hope as a galling one, as a kind of praiseworthy political impudence. Likewise, embedded in Obama's notion of this kind of audacious political hope is an acknowledgment of its explicit limitation. Rather than offering government as the solution to the ills that undermine political hope, Obama offers an extremely conservative notion of personal control and responsibility as the answer to this political anguish. Where systematic neglect and intentional community destruction propel despair, Obama offers individual hope as the palliative. Obama sees the personal sphere as the one to shift, since he relies on liberal political *feelings* to buttress his candidacy.

The return to hope reanimated *the language* of the 1960s without *the politics* of the 1960s, and it was ironic because it created the very exclusion that it denounced.[6] As Joan Didion explained, with the election of Obama, "Irony was now out. Naiveté, translated into 'hope,' was now in." She adds:

> I couldn't count the number of times I heard the words "transformational" or "inspirational," or heard the 1960s evoked by people with no apparent memory that what drove the social revolution of the 1960s was not babies in cute T-shirts but the kind of resistance to that decade's war that in the case of our current wars, unmotivated by a draft, we have yet to see. It became increasingly clear that we were gearing up for another close encounter with militant idealism—by which I

mean the convenient but dangerous redefinition of political or pragmatic questions as moral questions—"convenient" because such redefinition makes those questions seem easier to answer, "dangerous" because this was a time when the nation was least prepared to afford easy answers.[7]

Didion's critique of militant idealism is useful here because it demonstrates how dedicated Obama was to mobilizing idealism (and, dare I say, misguided nostalgia) at the expense of policy. Here sincerity and civility were a form of erasure of both race and history.

His connection to hope was permanently fixed in guerrilla artist Shepard Fairey's famous and now-iconic poster of Obama with the hope slogan underneath a mod portrait of the candidate in red, white, and blue. The posters (and their parodies) served to further associate Obama with this resurgent liberal hope.[8] Likewise, on the presidential campaign trail, Obama's stump message amplified tropes of hope as well as change, though hope perhaps overshadowed change. The journalist Richard Wolffe critiqued Obama's stump speech, saying that it "amounted to little more than a defense of Hope—not a plan to change the nation."[9] Wolffe's critique and others like it highlighted the personality politics of the Obama campaign while also demonstrating the candidate's reliance on affect as a controlling rhetorical intervention in the political sphere. In 2008 this affective intervention was important, since (George W.) Bush fatigue was profoundly evident given his poll numbers, which, by the end of December 2008, were at a shocking 29 percent approval and 61 percent disapproval.[10] Highlighting this fatigue in the opening of his announcement speech, Obama reiterated the goals of liberalism and accentuated the affective contrast between his vision of the future and the eight years under George W. Bush: "In the face of war, you believe there can be peace. In the face of despair, you believe there can be hope. In the face of a politics that's shut you out, that's told you to settle, that's divided us for too long, you believe we can be one people, reaching for what's possible, building that more perfect union."[11] Emphasizing hope rather than despair, Obama articulated a vision of harmony and civility (certainly not the message of the social movements of the 1960s) in contrast to the economic turmoil and war of the Bush years.

These campaign themes reached their apex in Obama's inaugural address, where (a young) Obama echoed (a young) John F. Kennedy in urging hope over fear, proclaiming:

> On this day, we gather because we have chosen hope over fear, unity of purpose over conflict and discord. On this day, we come to proclaim an end to the petty grievances and false promises, the recriminations and worn-out dogmas that for

far too long have strangled our politics. We remain a young nation. But in the words of Scripture, the time has come to set aside childish things. The time has come to reaffirm our enduring spirit; to choose our better history; to carry forward that precious gift, that noble idea passed on from generation to generation: the God-given promise that all are equal, all are free, and all deserve a chance to pursue their full measure of happiness.[12]

Obama depicted his vision and the possibility of his presidency as a fresh start and a new path, one that promised to reverse the hostility and ambient negativity of the Bush years through a commitment to the "American spirit," a notion of vague pluralism that undergirds much of Obama's campaign discourse. With language that was explicitly chronopolitical as it expressed *change* as the transmission of values between generations, Obama's inaugural address pointed to his election as a defining moment in shifting American values for more mature (as opposed to childish) *public feelings*.

Nevertheless, Obama didn't just anchor his persona to hope in his orations. In *Change We Can Believe In: Barack Obama's Plan to Renew America's Promise*, his blueprint for the administration, Obama characterizes hope both as a political feeling nurtured against evidence of neglect and as an unseen spirit, moving America toward a different, though undefined, political future. Obama opines, "I'm not talking about an idle hope that's little more than blind optimism or willful ignorance of the problems we face. I'm talking about hope as that spirit inside us that insists, despite all evidence to the contrary, that something better is waiting for us if we're willing to work for it and fight for it. If we are willing to believe."[13] Writing about the election as a critical moment in American history with the potential to define the American character, the book's authors add, "But in critical moments of transition like this one, success has also depended on national leadership that moved the country forward with confidence and a common purpose."

Here John Kennedy is the example of what national leadership looks like in the transition from fear to hope. As a way to both return to and augment Kennedy's hope in the early 1960s, *Change We Can Believe In* explicitly compares the two men in age, generational sensibility, and emotional orientation. For example, the text points to Kennedy's program as the ultimate example of invigorating progressive hope for progress, contending, "That's what Kennedy did in the dark days of the Cold War, when he called us to a new frontier, created the Apollo program, and put us on a pathway to the moon."[14] Citing the space race as an anchor of Kennedy's hope in the American spirit, the book hails Kennedy's New Frontier as the prototype for Obama's vision of a hope that could overcome pessimism and corruption.

In addressing the profound national cynicism after almost eight years of foreign wars, the authors write, "We've been warned against offering the people of this nation false hope." But in citing America's exceptionalism, they add, "There has never been anything false about hope. For when we have faced down impossible odds; when we've been told that we're not ready, that we shouldn't try; or that we can't, generations of Americans have responded with a simple creed that sums of the spirit of the people. Yes we can." As a slogan of the campaign, "Yes we can" was an interesting addition to the language of hope and change because of its rich history as a refrain for the United Farm Workers (UFW) in the 1970s. Then, UFW leaders Dolores Huerta and Cesar Chavez adopted "Sí se puede" (Yes, it can be done) as their motto during a twenty-five-day fast in Phoenix, Arizona.[15] The Obama campaign's use of this slogan broadened the candidate's appeal to Latinx voters and racialized his program of hope and change by connecting it to a rich labor history of Hispanic organizers. This intentional rhetorical maneuver harnessed support for movement organizing and co-opted it in a presidential campaign, where movement activism had been thoroughly demonized since Reagan.

"Yes we can" was part of the Obama campaign's explicit (and, yes, ironic) rejection of cynicism, one that appealed to the groups in his coalition. But given that cynicism is a sticky feeling, Obama's win in 2008 is even more impressive. William Chaloupka writes, "Once started, charges of cynicism spiral and multiply. Cynicism recruits, captures, and encloses. It is remarkably agile and hard to escape."[16] Where hope provided an antidote to nuclear fears during the Kennedy campaign, here it functioned as a turn away from the disappointment of the Bush administration, "eight years," in the words of the scholar Tony Monchinski, "marked by war and economic collapse at staggering costs in dollars, in loves, and in worldwide prestige, eight years of disillusionment and fear. Barack Obama appeared as a beacon of hope to many, a symbol that cut across ideologies and political opinions. Obama the man and Obama the administration have brought optimism to many, an optimism that government can care, that government can be and will be made to work for the people in these dark times."[17] Obama's appeal to hope, then, was deeply rooted in an affective reversal as he campaigned against the most unpopular president in modern American history on a rhetorical platform that mobilized historicized sentiment without the attendant historical politics attached.

To amplify this affective shift, campaign discourses repeated over and again, "Yes we can," which both constituted a new American identity, "we," and also reassured voters that the hope Obama promised was not vain but rooted in action, much like Kennedy's New Frontier service programs. Pointing to the nation's founding documents, as well as the perseverance of slaves, abolitionists, and immigrants in the face of collective disenfranchisement, the blueprint repeats the phrase "Yes we can." Locating the power of assent in the collective "we" of the polis, the section continues: "It was the call of workers who organized; women who reached for the ballot; a President who chose the moon as our new frontier; and a King who took us to the mountaintop and pointed the way to the Promised Land."[18] Obama's blueprint offers a collective vision for the future that points to the achievability of hope by using unions, women's suffrage, Kennedy's New Frontier, and Martin Luther King's civil rights campaigns as examples of the endurance of hope in the American spirit. "Yes we can" functions as a chronopolitical refrain to reorient the nation toward a new, optimistic future (and perhaps a revisionist past) inclusive of Obama as its first biracial president, but it also elides presidential power and movement activism in a mélange of achievements crowed mostly by violence.

Thus we would be remiss to consider Obama's hope only in the context of Kennedy and the long sixties. Civil rights activist, Baptist minister, and politician Jesse Jackson's 1988 "Keep Hope Alive" presidential campaign "sought to configure the relationship between injury, identity, and desire" in a rainbow coalition whose idiom would reposition "wants, hope, desires, dreams" against more antagonistic postures within the regime of racial liberalism.[19] So named for the climax of his address at the 1988 Democratic National Convention in Atlanta, Jackson's exclamation of "keep hope alive" functions within explicitly black discourses that nonetheless seek to find "common ground" within the American electorate and to "never surrender" to the despairs of inequality. Invoking the trope of King's dream dozens of times in the context of liberalism, Jackson's speech provides implicit notions of hope in the face of policy failures and political tragedy. But "keep hope alive," though invoked in Jackson's speech as declarative, is undercut by the litany of political offenses Jackson lists and is underdeveloped and not operationalized for the audience. In short, "keep hope alive" is an incomplete articulation of a new form of racial liberalism, too steeped in civil rights and Black Power, too close to the activism of midcentury. With Rosa Parks in the room; with memories of Martin Luther King's connection to Jackson still fresh; with references to Fannie Lou Hamer's exclusion from the 1964 Democratic National Convention; and with the memorialization of civil rights martyrs like Jimmie Lee Jackson, Viola Liuzzo, the four little girls in Birmingham, and Michael Schwerner, Andrew Goodman, and James Chaney, Jackson's speech was too close to the terror and brutality of the civil rights era to build the patchwork quilt of futurism that he desperately tried to weave. Following Jackson by twenty years, Obama's discourse benefited from the distance between 2008 and midcentury black activism and was, in some ways, constrained more by colorblind liberalism than conservative backlash. Obama's discursive landscape was not the thinly theorized hope of 1988 but a dense field of language about hope and change that would propel the electorate to embrace him in ways that they would never have embraced King's colleague Jesse Jackson. Said another way, Jackson's hope was too black.

Obama's brand of postracial hope formed the bedrock of his campaign and presidency and created a veritable cottage industry in publishing. Administration faith outreach director Michael Wear's memoir, for example, was titled *Reclaiming Hope: Lessons Learned in the Obama White House about the Future of Faith in America* (2018). David Litt's tongue-in-cheek memoir about his time in the Obama White House is titled *Thanks, Obama! My Hopey, Changey White House Years* (2017). The title of Jean Marie Laskas's chronicle of the president's mail includes more than just hope as an affective dimension of the administration: *To Obama: With Love, Joy, Anger, and Hope* (2018) reprinted letters to the president and some of his responses while describing the White House mail operations from 2009 to 2017. Even Evan Schaffer's completely ridiculous "Obama/Biden" mystery series peddles hope as the hook in *Hope Never Dies* (2018) and *Hope Dies Again* (2019). Children's books about Obama also magnified his campaign themes. Nikki Grimes and Bryan Collier's *Barack Obama: Son of Promise, Child of Hope* (2008), for example, echoed a close relationality between liberal futurism and hope. Even Joe Biden cashes in on the hope train in his memoir *Promise Me, Dad: A Year of Hope, Hardship, and Purpose* (2018). Biographies of Michelle Obama adopted the same tactic. For example, Elizabeth Lightfoot's *Michelle Obama: First Lady of Hope* (2008) connected the First Lady to her husband through hope discourse. And Molly Dillon's *Yes She Can: Ten Stories of Hope and Change from Young Female Staffers of the Obama White House* (2019) feminizes hope. The self-help guru John Pavlovitz capitalizes on all of the Obama hope hype in his book *Hope and Other Superpowers: A Life-Affirming, Love-Defending, Butt-Kicking, World-Saving Manifesto* (2018).

Change was regularly paired with hope in campaign discourses and their ilk. The edited collection of Obama's speeches curated by E. J. Dionne and Joy-Ann Reid is titled *We Are the Change We Seek* (2017). Likewise, monographs and collections focused on the importance of hope and change as rhetorical frames for Obama and, when mentioned in this order, indicated that the transformation from fear to hope would be the change that the nation needed. For example, Ted Rall's *The Book of Obama: From Hope and Change to the Age of Revolt* (2012), Jacob Snively's *Hope, Change, and Pragmatism: Analyzing Obama's Grand Strategy* (2016), and *The Obama Presidency and the Politics of Change* (ed. Edward Ashbee and John Dumbrell, 2017) all high-lighted change as the goal of the Obama campaign and presidency. Katrina vanden Heuvel (editor at the *Nation*) published a memoir titled *The Change I Believe In: Fighting for Progress in the Age of Obama* (2011). Likewise, female staffers in the Obama White House helped to produce a children's book titled *Yes She Can: Ten Stories of Hope and Change from Young Female Staffers of the Obama White House* (2019).

Finally, even in critiques of Obama, hope continues to define him as a president, as in Roger D. Hodge's *The Mendacity of Hope: Barack Obama and the Betrayal of American Liberalism* (2010); Kevin McCullough's *No He Can't: How Barack Obama Is Dismantling Hope and Change* (2011); and Kate Oben-shain's *Divider-in-Chief: The Fraud of Hope and Change* (2012). In all these cases (which are but a small sample of the hundreds of books that connect Obama to hope), the authors amplify hope as the organizing affective dis-course of the Obama years and as a reinvigorated liberalism. And especially because so many of the books about hope and change (regardless of ideo-logical orientation or audience) were published after the election of Donald Trump, there seems to be an investment in continuing hope as a defining political feeling for liberals, despite its pitfalls.

Because Obama's hope echoed Kennedy's New Frontier rhetoric, and because he used change as a point of contrast with Bush, Obama's articula-tion of new political feelings provided a launching point for imagining a new/old political future/past. But the lineage of Obama's hope was compli-cated by the history of the 1960s, as he employed Kennedy's language while simultaneously invoking King's vision. This dual lineage, juggling memories of both Kennedy and King, is what amplified hope and change for Obama's campaign as well as for his presidency. Obama employed Kennedy and King as a way of mediating his own blackness, leading pundits like Joe Klein to explain (in 2006, no less) that Obama "transcends the racial divide so effort-lessly."[20] Transcendence functioned as a way of de- and reracializing Obama and catapulting him into a category of his own. Gerald Early concedes that Obama "brought together the privileged majority and the aggrieved minor-ity in a new way: instead of each complaining about how the other is depen-dent on it, each cooperated to achieve a common goal, electing Obama as a way to restart or redefine American history." And while this was true, it was also true that "many hoped that Obama could permanently unify the two worlds of race: this was the prospect they found so exciting about his candidacy. Obama the bridge, the mixed race messiah, Obama the blended beneficence."[21] Obama's own (racialized) body became the repository of anxieties and optimism about a new racial context and future for American political life, and consequently this notion of transcendence dehistoricized and depoliticized the language and activism of the 1960s, which his appeals explicitly evoked.

This notion of a transcendental racial messiah was crafted partly by Obama and partly by the wishful thinking of (mostly) white pundits (who wanted rapid change without the difficult political work). Contributing to this heroic and futurist frame was the fact that Obama was pushing both hope and change, with their synchronic and diachronic connections. For example, in a speech he delivered on November 3, 2007, in South Carolina, Obama described his decision to run for the presidency. Like Dr. Martin Luther King Jr., he said, he believed "in the fierce urgency of now," saying, "There is such a thing as being too late."[22] Rejecting "the politics of fear and cynicism," Obama provided an extended critique of the venal and violent policies of Bush era corruption. But in couching his candidacy in the chronopolitics of King in 1963, Obama anchored his hope in the groundswell of goodwill for King after Birmingham and after the rhetorical power of the March on Washington. This is to say that Obama's hope is attached to the period before the terrorist bombing of the Sixteenth Street Baptist Church, before the assassinations of John Kennedy, King, and Robert Kennedy. Obama's hope is secured to images of King's liberalism in 1963 even as it critiques Bush's use of the military-industrial complex, suggesting that Obama's use of black hope here is recursive, inviting the reader to elide 1963 and 2007 to imagine a time where King's dream (still alive and not killed by a sniper's bullet) was imagined in and through Obama himself.

Civility Politics, Deracializing Hope

In articulating hope as a foolish but necessary feeling required for change, Obama set the path for a campaign that propelled him into the limelight and into the White House. Rather than the confrontations with antiblack state violence that Jesse Jackson offered in his presidential campaigns, Obama's path to victory was paved with appeals to civility, which pacified liberals about his blackness. In *Reading Obama: Dreams, Hopes, and the American Political Tradition* (2010), James T. Kloppenberg writes, "Obama remains committed to treating his adversaries with a degree of respect that his supporters find worrisome and his foes find spineless."[23] Obama's civility politics were deeply connected to hope as the affective vehicle of his presidency.

Obama's civility was partly framed by his perceptions about the limitations of appeals (made by a black/biracial man) that focused on white guilt.

In *The Audacity of Hope*, Obama explained, "Rightly or wrongly, white guilt has exhausted itself in America; even the most fair-minded of whites, those who would genuinely like to see racial inequality ended and poverty relieved, tend to push back against suggestions of racial victimization—or race-specific claims based on the history of race discrimination in this country."[24] In arguing that appeals to white guilt have no power, Obama makes the case that these strategies backfire (despite his invocations of King) and calcify white fragility. Obama elaborates that being a black man performing emotional tone (anger, especially) in a political climate fed a steady diet of what he calls "the politics of resentment" makes it difficult to know how to navigate the affective terrain. Here Obama acknowledges the affective limitations on him *as a result of his blackness*, suggesting that civility was the way that he operationalized his blackness with the keen awareness of the limitations of inventional possibilities about emotional tone. That is, civility was a way that Obama avoided white guilt and performed white hope, deracializing his tone and avoiding the affective constraints on black men feeling in public.

Given that Obama's campaign was historic because of his race, there was considerable debate over Obama's rhetorical style even before he was elected.[25] The debates about Obama's civility politics were shaped, in part, by a March 2008 media storm about his Chicago pastor, Rev. Jeremiah Wright. Wright's criticisms of the US government and his sermonic style gave rise to criticisms that he was fundamentally hostile to liberalism. The following quotation from one of Wright's sermons focused attention on the relationship between Obama and Wright: "The government gives them [African Americans] the drugs, builds bigger prisons, passes a three-strike law and then wants us to sing 'God Bless America.' No, no, no, God damn America, that's in the Bible for killing innocent people. God damn America for treating our citizens as less than human. God damn America for as long as she acts like she is God and she is supreme."[26] Using black prophetic style (not easily transcribed by the white press, with its complete ignorance about black discursive forms, particularly those from the pulpit), Wright's comments pointed to the war on drugs, the prison-industrial complex, and the three strikes law as intentional structural impediments to black equality as well as to black health and welfare. In essence, Wright's comments here point to the ways in which the vehicles of liberalism (law-and-order culture, particularly in the 1980s) foreclosed black political and personal agency. But Wright's arguments also reinvigorate Black Power critiques of liberalism and ineffective resource management by white liberals. Wright's comments were controversial precisely because their amplification in the news cycle re(circulated) a Black Power perspective on race relations that was more like Malcolm than Martin.

Obama's 2008 "More Perfect Union" speech, perhaps his most famous, attempted to address the firestorm of comments that assailed his candidacy after the publication of Wright's critiques of racial liberalism through a reassertion of deracialized hope. Michael Fletcher at the *Washington Post* called it "the speech on race that saved Obama's candidacy" and described the exigency that produced it thus: "Wright's unsparing critique was at odds with both Obama's message of hope and his multiracial family history. The discrepancy raised pointed questions—gleefully fanned by Obama's political opponents—about the true sentiments of the first African American candidate with a real shot at being elected president."[27] Rev. Wright's comments had the potential to create a different context for Obama's civility, and pundits questioned if candidate Obama shared his pastor's positions, particularly on the failures of liberalism.

Delivered at the National Constitution Center in Philadelphia, Obama's speech began by describing the 1787 convention that produced the Declaration of Independence. Obama's futurist imaginings invoke the tropes of the 1960s early on in the speech, focusing on the civil rights march as the chronopolitical intervention of activism at midcentury:

> This was one of the tasks we set forth at the beginning of this presidential campaign—to continue the long march of those who came before us, a march for a more just, more equal, more free, more caring and more prosperous America. I chose to run for president at this moment in history because I believe deeply that we cannot solve the challenges of our time unless we solve them together, unless we perfect our union by understanding that we may have different stories, but we hold common hopes; that we may not look the same and we may not have come from the same place, but we all want to move in the same direction—toward a better future for our children and our grandchildren.[28]

Emphasizing unity as a goal worthy of the country's children and grandchildren, Obama's reproductive futurity directs the nation toward justice, equality, freedom, care, and prosperity.

While defending these goals as constitutive of a new vision, Obama also needed to reconcile his racial politics with Rev. Wright's. Describing Rev. Wright as controversial, but as a member of his family, Obama explains:

> I can no more disown him than I can disown the black community. I can no more disown him than I can disown my white grandmother—a woman who helped raise me, a woman who sacrificed again and again for me, a woman who loves me as much as she loves anything in this world, but a woman who once confessed

her fear of black men who passed her by on the street, and who on more than one occasion has uttered racial or ethnic stereotypes that made me cringe.[29]

This move to refuse a disavowal of Wright is interesting as a strategy of rapprochement and as a precursor to Obama's call for unity and dialogue precisely because he invokes his racist white grandmother as a reason to defend Wright and his perspective, clearly a move that would appeal to white listeners.

As he refused to denounce Wright as a person or preacher, Obama was clear to talk about how antiblack animus has driven much of contemporary American politics. In a passage that bears quoting at length, Obama describes anger and resentment as the *feelings* that mobilize conservatism, particularly as they manifested in the Reagan era:

> Like the anger within the black community, these resentments aren't always expressed in polite company. But they have helped shape the political landscape for at least a generation. Anger over welfare and affirmative action helped forge the Reagan Coalition. Politicians routinely exploited fears of crime for their own electoral ends. Talk show hosts and conservative commentators built entire careers unmasking bogus claims of racism while dismissing legitimate discussions of racial injustice and inequality as mere political correctness or reverse racism.
>
> Just as black anger often proved counterproductive, so have these white resentments distracted attention from the real culprits of the middle class squeeze—a corporate culture rife with inside dealing, questionable accounting practices and short-term greed; a Washington dominated by lobbyists and special interests; economic policies that favor the few over the many. And yet, to wish away the resentments of white Americans, to label them as misguided or even racist, without recognizing they are grounded in legitimate concerns—this too widens the racial divide and blocks the path to understanding.[30]

With a false equivalency that compared historical black anger (think, perhaps, of Watts) to white resentment, Obama chooses to denounce both, to walk in the middle on the terrain of civility. Notably, unlike Rev. Wright, Obama does not harness righteous black anger. Instead, in describing the white anger over federal policies designed to ameliorate black inequality, Obama impugns the Reagan coalition, describing the architecture of neoconservatism as a deliberate, white affect. Obama also demonstrates how that white anger was augmented by a shrinking middle class, corporate greed, and special interests, obliquely suggesting that the stratification of power and wealth pushed white people together in rage despite class differences. This is precisely the rhetorical move that undermines the historicizing of black feelings as a product of temporal material policies. Said another way, this is why Malcolm is read as a "prophet of rage" and why Watts is illegible to white people as a product of decades of antiblack urban policy.

According to Obama, Wright's mistake was that "he spoke as if our society was static; as if no progress had been made."[31] Resisting this conclusion, Obama reiterates his affective position, although it is undercut by the white class politics of the history lesson in neoconservatism that he has just offered: "But what we know—what we have seen—is that America can change. That is the true genius of this nation. What we have already achieved gives us hope—the audacity to hope—for what we can and must achieve tomorrow."[32] Ending with an anecdote about a speech he gave at Martin Luther King's Ebenezer Baptist Church, perhaps as a way of suggesting that Obama was part of the realization of King's dream, Obama tells the story of a twenty-three-year-old white campaign worker in South Carolina and her struggles with food insecurity. At a roundtable, she told her story, and a black man cited her as the reason he was working for the Obama presidential campaign. This synecdoche provides the moment of reconciliation that transcends blame and cements interracial alliances as part of the Obama coalition while also deradicalizing the 1960s and (deliberately mis)reading the goal of black activism, in particular, as conciliatory. Here civility becomes the goal, although it did not yield the successes that Obama wants to champion here.

Postracialism and Afro-pessimism

The success of his "More Perfect Union" speech, as Ebony Utley and Amy L. Heyse have noted, was that "Obama successfully maintained a post-racial rhetorical stance that appealed to extremely diverse audiences."[33] This postracial positionality is interesting given that 2008 was the most obviously racialized election in history, particularly with the racist imagery that circulated of Obama, reminiscent of animalist representations of black Americans during and after slavery. Likewise, the postracialism is puzzling (dare I say, ironic) given the tremendous amount of violence against people of color after the election of Obama, particularly after the 2012 killing of Trayvon Martin, a black teenager in Miami Gardens, Florida, and the unfolding #BlackLivesMatter activism in response to the killing of unarmed black citizens (many of them children), like Martin. In particular, the 2014 killing of Michael Brown, a black teenager in Ferguson, Missouri, sparked a huge national conversation about police accountability, racial profiling, and state violence targeting black boys and men.[34]

The success of the "postracial" frame, despite the pervasive and extremely publicized antiblack state violence that characterized much of Obama's second term, appealed to white Americans who wanted to see themselves as more progressive on race than they actually were or are. Adia Harvey Wingfield and Joe R. Feagin have located three major features of postracialism, including "an emotion-laden accent on the decades-old idea of a major decline in racism; the emotion-laden idea that Obama is white-assimilated, acceptable, mixed-race, and/or less black (or not really black); and, somewhat contradictorily, the rather new view that President Obama himself has an obligation to be a racial healer who should not articulate a renewed civil rights agenda and whose election proves the fallacy of the view that white racism is still a serious barrier in the United States."[35] These rationalizations and delusions, rooted in the constellation of feelings that constitute white fragility, are what allowed a biracial/black presidential candidate like Obama to create a coalition of voters who were able to briefly overcome the ambivalence and instability of racial politics in the United States to support him in two presidential campaigns.

But Obama's rhetoric and his embodiment of racial reconciliation, particularly in light of #BLM activism prompted by excessive antiblack police force, is problematic. Eduardo Bonilla-Silva has argued that Obama's language of postracial reconciliation is a form of "new racism" built from subtle, though institutionalized, practices that have supplanted Jim Crow. For Bonilla-Silva, colorblind postracialism is built on the back of civility and offers an invigorated and calcified form of racial domination, since it normalizes the erasure of race talk as what he has called "cultural racism."[36] Similarly, Ian F. Haney López suggests that "Obama's post-racialism, rather than serving as a claim about our racial present, operates as a political or perhaps even an ideological approach toward the continuing astringent of race."[37] Postracialism "constitutes a liberal embrace of colorblindness," writes Haney López, "in a way likely to limit progress toward increased racial equality."[38] This view is compelling because it suggests that colorblindness (rather ironically) fundamentally undermines racial equality because it never ends white supremacy and, in fact, calcifies white power in the avoidance of racial reflection or critiques of racial liberalism.

The idea of Obama as a postracial messiah was deeply connected to the use of hope as a trope of new racial liberalism. Obama strategically invoked "a reconciliation narrative in order to portray himself as the vehicle through which America can, once again, leave the past behind in a dream-cloud of hope."[39] Suggesting that Obama refused the politics of Jesse Jackson (and, say, James Baldwin or Black Power intellectuals), which were more honest about "the price at which hope for future change is earned," Brendese argues that Obama "blurred the key distinctions in memories needed to make legible and confront the systemic nature of racial inequality" and also "sidestepped engagement with the stigma of blackness wherein memory conditions habituated practices of self-segregation."[40] So, for example, in the places where Obama invoked King's civil rights campaigns, he did so without acknowledging that King's assassination (in the midst of a liberal revival) was the cruel optimism that Chapter Five explores.

In fact, it was precisely Obama's rhetorical style of employing deliberate racial amnesia that caused Jesse Jackson to remark in July 2008 that he wanted to castrate Obama. Or to be more precise, Jackson suggested, "I want to cut his nuts out," because, as Jackson suggested, Obama was "talking down to black people."[41] Jackson's objection to Obama's style, especially his articulation of hope in the context of the political realities of black life in 2008, prompted the following tirade on a hot mic at Fox News. The underlying disagreement between the men revolved around "the apportionment of responsibility for the breakdown of some African-American families." Obama's 2008 Father's Day speech suggested that African American fathers needed to take more responsibility for their children—a point made by entertainer Bill Cosby and others. That line of argument has rankled those on the left, including Jackson, who wanted to hold government policies accountable for "the impoverishment of African-American families."[42] Jackson's interest in structural accountability was at odds with Obama's persistent emphasis on personal responsibility, and Jackson saw Obama's rhetorical posture as a fundamental problem for black America, even if his choice of words about Obama unfortunately invoked lynching imagery.[43] And this incident with Jackson exposes the problems with Obama's mobilization of colorblindness and 1960s rhetoric *as a black man*. Jackson's critique, while unfortunate, does point to the irony of Obama's articulation of hope.

Nonetheless the election of Barack Obama *did* seem to confirm that his candidacy improved optimism about American race relations. That is, Obama's campaign briefly transformed white *feelings* about the possibility of a biracial/black president. Opinion polls just after the election showed increases in optimism of both black and white citizens, but that bump quickly settled to pre-2008 election levels, and in fact, white support for Obama declined dramatically by the time of his reelection in 2012.[44] As Michael Tesler has convincingly demonstrated, "Mass politics was indeed more polarized *by and over race* during Barack Obama's presidency than it was before his 2008 presidential campaign."[45] We should not be surprised, then, that racial animus increased as the Obama administration continued, particularly as

conservatives used race as a way of undermining Obama's executive authority (particularly in Congress) and as a means of propelling the white backlash
cycle that elected Donald Trump. Journalists like Matt Bai asked, "Is Obama
the End of Black Politics?," suggesting that Obama's election completed some
sort of political assimilation.[46]

At the same time that white pundits proclaimed the election of Barack
Obama as evidence that America had become "postracial," black intellectuals
began writing about black feelings through the lens of what they called Afro-
or black pessimism as a political and ontological orientation toward state
power. While the bump in optimism quickly abated after the 2008 election,
pessimism quickly emerged as a dominant affective dimension of the Obama
years. And this pessimism was a distinctly racialized pessimism, political in
its concerns. Joshua Dienstag writes that political pessimism functions as
a ballast to the failure to achieve progress. "Precisely because it asks us to
rethink our sense of time, pessimism is an idea that challenges our notions
of order and meaning in dramatic ways." He adds, "In suggesting that we
look at time and history differently, it asks us to alter radically our opinion
both of ourselves and of what we can expect from politics. It does not simply tell us to expect less. It tells us, in fact, to expect nothing."[47] While black
intellectuals like Malcolm X certainly practiced pessimism as a political and
affective exercise in thinking about liberalism differently as a racialized process of safeguarding white power, the notion that pessimism was a primary
affective strain of modern black rhetorical invention really began to shape
the public imaginary during the Obama administration as the irony of his
campaign of hope and change was exposed as a cruel optimism. And where
Huey Newton meditated on reactionary versus revolutionary suicide, here
were black intellectuals thinking about the necropolitics of American life as
they watched unarmed black citizens being killed, sometimes on camera, by
police officers. No wonder, then, that the Obama years prompted a consideration of pessimism as a particularly black feeling as old as slavery and as a
pervasive racial *mood* during and after Obama's presidency. Obama's invocation of King, then, as a touchstone of liberalism, should be read as a kind of
double irony, since King's hope for nonviolence was ultimately exposed as
cruel through his assassination, and since Obama, as a black man, embraced
the very liberalism that destroyed the black hero he so consistently invokes.

In addition to pessimism, however, there was an increasing strand of public thought about black rage. Particularly after the 2014 shooting of Michael
Brown in Ferguson, Missouri, journalists and public intellectuals began talking about how rage was fueling what ultimately became #BlackLivesMatter
demonstrations. There was an "overwhelming focus on black rage" after the

shooting of Michael Brown.[48] Pundits and reporters debated whether Brown (or the victims who came afterward) were assaulting police officers; whether the victims were threats or "thugs"; and whether the police were justified in their use of excessive force. "The operative question seemed to be whether African Americans were justified in their rage," writes Carol Anderson.[49] This focus on rage was amplified in articles like Lili Loofbourow's widely circulated essay in *Slate* titled "The Price of Rage: The Incivility of Anger in America" (2018), as well as in books defending black rage, most notably Ta-Nehisi Coates's *Between the World and Me* (2015) and Brittney Cooper's *Eloquent Rage: A Black Feminist Discovers Her Superpower* (2018). With the tremendous success of Marvel's *Black Panther* film (2018), pop culture also explored the history of black rage as a postcolonial adaptation strategy. So there were no shortages of spaces within which to examine black rage as a historically contingent phenomenon, even as white rhetors sought to fix black rage within the pathological frames of the past and into a notion of what Tommy J. Curry has called the "hegemonic black male," a category of Being that mobilizes regressive public policy and social attitudes.[50]

But then an interesting turn emerged, where academics like Carol Anderson began to talk about *white rage* as the Obama administration waned and the world witnessed the rise of Trumpism after the inauguration of Donald Trump. Where the affective politics of the long sixties had mostly focused on victim blaming, the new political critique focused on demystifying racial liberalism much as Mbembe, Turner, and Mills outline in the introduction. That is, critics pointed to white rage as a response to the election of America's first black/biracial president. Rather than theorizing about black pathology, or what was interpreted as inappropriate black rage in the 1960s, liberal critics pointed to white rage as the fuel for the destruction of American institutions after the Obama era. Anderson explains that white rage "is not about visible violence, but rather it works its way through the courts, the legislatures, and a range of government bureaucracies. It wreaks havoc subtly, almost imperceptibly."[51] As Anderson demonstrates, the "trigger for white rage is black achievement. It is not the mere presence of black people that is the problem; rather, it is blackness with ambition, with drive, with purpose, with aspirations, and with demands for full and equal citizenship."[52] It was Obama's articulation of black excellence that unleashed the feelings of white rage so prevalent as a response to King, Malcolm X, and Black Power from 1965 to 1975. In fact, a tremendous amount of ink was spilled talking about triggers and trigger warnings as the Obama administration came to an end, echoing the language of powder kegs and fuses from the mid-1960s, suggesting that gun metaphors had replaced metaphors about TNT. In the wake of gun violence against unarmed black citizens perpetrated almost exclusively by white police, the trigger metaphor invites a discussion about how violence and trauma are precipitated, what the duration of that violence will be, the magnitude of the consequences of the trigger, and all the language of sparks, fuses, provocation, and flames that are corollary to the powder keg at mid-century. Given the history of antiblack political assassinations, though, this shift in metaphor is noteworthy as yet another example of liberalism's ironies and as a foreshadowing of another tragic moment in antiblack social policy in the United States.

While the bulk of this book has examined black feelings as a way of understanding the modes of expression that delineated political feelings within the black liberation struggle, these feelings were not produced in a vacuum. White writers and politicians regularly articulated their opposition to civil rights, desegregation, and black liberation through the language of feelings (often while denigrating the language of black protest as "too emotional"). As Antoine J. Banks notes, "Very little empirical attention has been devoted to the beliefs of white racial liberals—let alone the emotional undertones of this belief system."[53] Banks discusses the connection between white liberal supporters of civil rights reform and their black counterparts, arguing that "the feelings of disappointment, bitterness, frustration, anger and anxiety" were shared among both groups.[54] But that is changing. With the publication of Anderson's *White Rage* and historical treatments like Dan T. Carter's *The Politics of Rage: George Wallace, the Origins of the New Conservatism, and the Transformation of American Politics* (1995), scholars are increasingly interested in thinking about how the negative feelings of white people in America undermine their fidelity to liberalism, as well as how those feelings foreclose the possibility of racial liberalism's best promises about racial equality. As David L. Eng and Shinhee Han write, "We inhabit a putatively colorblind and postracial society suffused with proliferating discourses of multiculturalism and diversity; on the other hand, we witness on a daily basis ongoing and escalating racial discord and violence, prominently underscored by the recent 2016 presidential election as well as the 'Black Lives Matter' campaign that emerged in response to police racism and violence."[55] Thus does the (ironic) promise of inclusion also reveal the necessity of exclusion as part and parcel of liberalism.

Additionally, as scholarship and public debate about white rage have been circulating, so too has much of the Afro-pessimist literature that frames this book. This literature sought to address racial colorblindness, new racial liberalism, and the period that was colloquially called "postracial." Saidiya Hartman, Fred Moten, and Frank Wilderson introduced and explicated

Afro-pessimism as a critical analytic employed to trace the consequences of historical structures of antiblack oppression and violence that shape empire. As a chronopolitical intervention, Afro-pessimism is deeply invested in the recursive structure of antiblack violence as it shapes generations of black people. In books like *The Future Is Black: Afropessimism, Fugitivity, and Radical Hope in Education* (2018), black writers engage the possibilities of fugitivity and radical hope post-Obama and explore the potential to escape the capture that Mbembe has so clearly delineated. Afro-pessimism has begun to trace the tropes and themes of black hopelessness, but for the most part, it has been a literary analytic, not a political one. This despite the fact that, in Eric King Watts's words, the "affective economies of postracial fantasies" create a landscape where blackness and black people are a biothreat to the body politic.[56] As a political analytic and as a rhetorical invention, Afro-pessimism was a central theoretical midcentury discourse resisting the hegemonic white masculine hope of the Kennedy years. This is to say that Afro-pessimism has a political history grounded in black skepticism and operationalized through black feelings that reorient black people in the face of negligent or destructive social policy. Perhaps no political rhetoric yields this strain of thought more clearly than Newton, Cleaver, and the Black Panthers, who persistently theorized about black precarity, black death, fugitivity, and revolution. In rejecting liberalism as a failed political experiment, the Panthers, more than any other organization of the long sixties, took seriously the work of exposing liberalism's failures and ironies in the service of black liberation.

Today, at the intersection of colorblindness and putative antiblack public policy, a renewed and reinvigorated call for black reparations is emerging to make sense of how overpolicing, the prison-industrial complex, white generational wealth, and disaster capitalism have destroyed black futures. Articulated perhaps most clearly in a 2014 *Atlantic* essay by Ta-Nehisi Coates titled "The Case for Reparations," this conversation about reparations, now a major part of the 2020 presidential campaign, is fundamentally about the chronopolitics of slavery, generational wealth, capitalism, and restorative justice. Coates writes, "To celebrate freedom and democracy while forgetting America's origins in a slavery economy is patriotism à la carte." But the historical amnesia is nothing without the consequences of white generational wealth. Coates adds, "Perhaps no statistic better illustrates the enduring legacy of our country's shameful history of treating black people as sub-citizens, sub-Americans, and sub-humans than the wealth gap. Reparations would seek to close this chasm."[57] This call for reparations recognizes that whiteness itself functions as property and reminds us that liberalism can only fulfill its highest calling with the redistribution of wealth.[58]

But even with calls for reparations challenging business-as-usual in Washington, the black pessimism that circulated at midcentury is still a vibrant part of public life. As Michael Dawson writes:

> What should not seem surprising is that at the turn of the century African Americans continue to believe that American democracy is broken—and the 2000 elections did nothing to convince blacks that the nation was on the road to recovery. African Americans are still waiting for black visions of a just and egalitarian society to become American visions. It [is] increasingly clear, though, that many African Americans fear that Malcolm X was right when he worried that blacks held a vision of freedom larger than America is prepared to accept.[59]

Dawson perfectly captures the sense of pessimism pervading black America, especially after the election of Obama and the return to a politics of white resentment. Where Obama had pitched himself as the embodiment and fulfillment of King's dream, the material situation for black America (after the financial crisis of 2008) and the ontological situation for black America (in the face of unprecedented public killings of black Americans) spoke to the contrary. Obama was not the racial messiah, and black Americans were doing worse after his election than before it.

Black (and Brown) Pessimism after Obama

Instead of the racial reconciliation that the election of Obama portended (at least in the minds of white America), black America recognized a culture of predation, dating back to enslavement, that was augmenting rather than receding after the election of Barack Obama. With a hyperfocus on urban centers as spaces for overpolicing and police brutality, pessimism again was the only affective space possible, particularly when Obama was unable or unwilling to stop the violence against black citizens. Mbembe has been clear that the convergence of economic and biological racism produces resegregation: "Capture, predation, extraction, and asymmetrical warfare converge with the rebalkanization of the world and intensifying practices of zoning, all of which point to a new collusion between the economic and the biological. Such a collusion translates in concrete terms into the militarization of borders, the fragmentation and partitioning of territories, and the creation of more or less autonomous spaces within the borders of existing states."[60] The border wall debate, the Muslim ban and the ban on transgender military service, and the forced separation of immigrant families are but a few examples of how postracialism's failures have spawned regressive antiblack and antibrown public policy during the presidency of Donald Trump, creating a continuity that is legible only to critics of colorblind liberalism, regardless of its champion.

So while Eng and Han suggest that colorblindness has finally produced "a collective psychic state of racial dissociation," the black intellectuals of this study described and agitated against this dissociation decades ago (Malcolm and Newton being the most vociferous critics), though it is different for model minorities than it is for former slaves. In fact, it seems more productive to trace how racial dissociation has been an intrinsic *demand of liberalism* since the nation's inception, as well as to investigate moments where grievances about racial (particularly black) dissociation have been raised as part of new political formations that cluster around affective rhetorics. While the Asian American dissociation that Eng and Han examine is rooted in what they call "suspended assimilation," that process for black Americans is compounded by all the technologies of erasure, surveillance, imprisonment, segregation, and police violence that are specific to black life after "emancipation." Historically, Black Power, as an acknowledgment of these processes of antiblack public life, seems to be a fundamental assertion of dissociation as a permanent consequence of segregation and unequal resource distribution, whose apotheosis is reached with Newton's *Revolutionary Suicide*. This is why discussions of psychological and psychic consequences of white supremacy feature so prominently in black liberation discourses: they help to explain the psychic and cognitive *feelings* produced by political and social dissociation. Especially in moments where racial anxieties are reanimated and white supremacist agitation proliferates, racial dissociation becomes a strategy of survival and an obvious social location from which to theorize racial oppression. In this way, then, black *feelings* are an extension of antiblack public policy in circulatory and augmented ways across time. As Gianni Vattimo reminds us, modernity's modality of "linear time, a continuous and unitary process that moves toward betterment," is not a suitable metaphysics for colonial contexts.[61]

Such is the case with black feelings and black time, which respond to material and psychic trauma in circular ways that always return to liberalism as a panacea, even for the racial problems it creates. Where contagion is the general metaphor used to describe the harms of antiblack policy, it presumes an external cause to what is fundamentally an internal psychic process that is intentionally produced as a result of the combination of segregation and colorblindness in contemporary public life. The black pessimism perhaps most famously embodied by Malcolm X, but articulated so clearly by Huey Newton, recommends an assessment of liberalism that is clear about how it has buttressed slavery, segregation, and economic and political disenfranchisement of black people while touting a belief in liberal ideals of equality. Black pessimism, in particular, is about a reassessment of black time, especially in the face of crises in progress; and as a locus of inquiry, black pessimism remains a fruitful space from which to engage the limitations of racial liberalism after Obama.

NOTES

Introduction

1. Ameer Baraka, "We Are Our Feeling: The Black Aesthetic," *Negro Digest*, September 1969, 5.

2. Baraka, "We Are Our Feeling," 5.

3. Barbara Ritchie, *The Riot Report* (New York: Viking Press, 1969), 125.

4. Agnes Heller, *A Theory of Feelings*, 2nd ed. (Lanham, MD: Rowman and Littlefield, 2009), 97.

5. Michael Omi and Howard Winant, *Racial Formations in the United States*, 3rd ed. (New York: Routledge, 2014).

6. Jeffrey Santa Ana, *Racial Feelings: Asian America in a Capitalist Culture of Emotion* (Philadelphia: Temple University Press, 2015), 2.

7. Frank B. Wilderson III, *Red, White, and Black: Cinema and the Structure of U.S. Antagonisms* (Durham, NC: Duke University Press, 2010), 279.

8. Achille Mbembe, *Critique of Black Reason* (Durham, NC: Duke University Press, 2017), 121.

9. Quoted in Aram Goudsouzian, *Down to the Crossroads: Civil Rights, Black Power, and the Meredith March against Fear* (New York: Farrar, Straus and Giroux, 2014), 16.

10. Heller, *A Theory of Feelings*, 93.

11. Michael Orrom and Raymond Williams, *Preface to Film* (London: Film Drama, 1954); Raymond Williams, *Marxism and Literature* (New York: Oxford University Press, 1977). In response to Antonio Gramsci's notion of hegemony, which can be understood as "common sense," or the dominant mode of understanding, Williams used "structure of feeling" to describe the process by which new thoughts and political formations occurred in various historical moments. His use of the term signaled that responses to official policy discourses were sometimes partial and incomplete, always in process, and often found in cultural texts where critics create interpretive schemas to name the ideas and processes in conflict with hegemonic ideals or norms. Though Williams was not talking about political feelings in precisely the way that I am, he was certainly indicating that these oppositional discourses had a temporality, a chronopolitics of emergence, precipitated by ways of thinking and feeling that undermined hegemonic practices.

12. Heller, *A Theory of Feelings*, 51.

13. See Devin Fergus, *Liberalism, Black Power, and the Making of American Politics, 1965–1980* (Athens: University of Georgia Press, 2009), 48. This book is in conversation

with Fergus's wonderful book, along with Karen Ferguson, *Top Down: The Ford Foundation, Black Power, and the Reinvention of Racial Liberalism* (Philadelphia: University of Pennsylvania Press, 2013); and Tom Adam Davies, *Mainstreaming Black Power* (Oakland: University of California Press, 2017). Together, these three books have started to chart the relationship between Black Power and liberalism as the racial terrain in the United States shifted at midcentury.

14. Robert E. Johnson, "Black Power: What It Really Means," *Jet*, July 28, 1966, 18.

15. Stokely Carmichael, "Berkeley Speech," in *Stokely Speaks: From Black Power to Pan-Africanism* (Chicago: Chicago Review Press, 2007), 51–52.

16. Carmichael, "Berkeley Speech," 55.

17. Hasan Kwame Jeffries, *Bloody Lowndes: Civil Rights and Black Power in Alabama's Black Belt* (New York: New York University Press, 2009), 188; italics mine.

18. Johnson, "Black Power," 16.

19. Lisa M. Corrigan, *Prison Power: How Prison Influenced the Movement for Black Liberation* (Jackson: University Press of Mississippi, 2016).

20. Martin Luther King Jr., "Civil Rights," *Ebony*, January 1967, 36.

21. In Johnson, "Black Power," 18.

22. Sianne Ngai, *Ugly Feelings* (Cambridge, MA: Harvard University Press, 2005).

23. The "long sixties" refers to the period beginning with the Supreme Court's decision in *Brown v. Board of Education* in 1954 and extending into the early 1970s as the Nixon presidency declined. It acknowledges the problems associated with periodization, particularly when those periods attempt to define American political epochs by decade. Recent scholarship has acknowledged that the idea of the long sixties is also useful in reminding us that the sixties have never left us. See, e.g., Tom Hayden, *The Long Sixties: From 1960 to Barack Obama* (New York: Routledge, 2009).

24. Foucault explains that the paradox of liberalism is that "it must produce freedom, but this very act entails the establishment of limitations, controls, forms of coercion, and obligations relying on threats, etc." In Michel Foucault, *The Birth of Biopolitics: Lectures at the Collège de France, 1978–1979*, trans. Graham Burchell (New York: Palgrave Macmillan, 2008), 64.

25. See, most recently, Charles W. Mills, *Black Rights/White Wrongs: The Critique of Racial Liberalism* (Oxford: Oxford University Press, 2017). Mills explains that liberalism "has historically been predominantly a *racial* liberalism, in which conceptions of personhood and resulting schedules of rights, duties, and government responsibilities have all been racialized" (29).

26. Harold Cruse, *Rebellion or Revolution?* (1968; Minneapolis: University of Minnesota Press, 2009), 191.

27. Mbembe, *Critique of Black Reason*, 42.

28. Mbembe, *Critique of Black Reason*, 10.

29. Mbembe, *Critique of Black Reason*, 13.

30. Mbembe, *Critique of Black Reason*, 27.

31. Claude Lévi-Strauss, *La Pensée sauvage* (Paris: Librairie Plon, 1962). Lévi-Strauss coined the term *bricolage* to describe the kind of tinkering and experimentation with language that accompanied indigenous thinking in response to colonial domination. This unexpected architecture of thought relied on the inversion and production of myth. Derrida's critique of this conception is explicated in *Structure, Sign, and Play* (1970).

32. Wendy Brown, *States of Injury: Power and Freedom in Late Modernity* (Princeton, NJ: Princeton University Press, 1995), 55.

33. Any discussion of Afro-pessimism and optimism must include the following partial but representative list: Jared Sexton, "Afro-Pessimism: The Unclear Word," *Rhizomes* 29 (2016), http://www.rhizomes.net/issue29/sexton.html; Jared Sexton, "All-Black Everything," *e-flux* 79 (2017), http://www.e-flux.com/journal/79/94158/all-black-everything; Frank B. Wilderson III, *Red, White, and Black: Cinema and the Structure of U.S. Antagonisms* (Durham, NC: Duke University Press, 2010); Frank B. Wilderson III, *Incognegro: A Memoir of Exile and Apartheid* (Durham, NC: Duke University Press, 2008); Frank B. Wilderson III, "The Prison Slave as Hegemony's (Silent) Scandal," in *Warfare in the Homeland: Policing and Prison in a Penal Democracy*, ed. Joy James (Durham, NC: Duke University Press, 2007); Jared Sexton, "Racial Profiling and the Societies of Control," in James, *Warfare in the Homeland*; Fred Moten, "Knowledge of Freedom," *CR: The New Centennial Review* 4, no. 2 (2004): 269–310; Fred Moten, *In the Break: The Aesthetics of the Black Radical Tradition* (Minneapolis: University of Minnesota Press, 2003); Achille Mbembe, *On the Postcolony* (Berkeley: University of California Press, 2001); Saidiya Hartman, *Scenes of Subjection: Terror, Slavery, and Self-Making in Nineteenth Century America* (Oxford: Oxford University Press, 1997); Hortense Spillers, *Black, White, and in Color: Essays on American Literature and Culture* (Chicago: University of Chicago Press, 2003); Derrick Bell, *Faces at the Bottom of the Well: The Permanence of Racism* (New York: Basic Books, 1992); Hortense Spillers, "Mama's Baby, Papa's Maybe: An American Grammar Book," *Diacritics* 17, no. 2 (1987): 64–81; Orlando Patterson, *Slavery and Social Death: A Comparative Study* (Cambridge, MA: Harvard University Press, 1982); and Doug McAdam, *Political Process and the Development of Black Insurgency, 1930–1970* (Chicago: University of Chicago Press, 1982).

34. Sara Ahmed, *The Cultural Politics of Emotion* (New York: Routledge, 2004), 33.

35. Santa Ana, *Racial Feelings*, 2.

36. Martin Luther King Jr., "Our Struggle," in *A Testament of Hope: The Essential Writings and Speeches of Martin Luther King, Jr.*, ed. James M. Washington (New York: HarperOne, 2003), 240.

37. Martin Luther King Jr., "Nonviolence: The Only Road to Freedom," in *A Testament of Hope: The Essential Writings and Speeches of Martin Luther King, Jr.*, ed. James M. Washington (New York: HarperOne, 2003), 59.

38. Erin Rand, "Bad Feelings in Public: Rhetoric, Affect, and Emotion," *Rhetoric and Public Affairs* 18, no. 1 (Spring 2015): 174.

39. Mbembe, *Critique of Black Reason*, 6.

40. James Turner, "The Sociology of Black Nationalism," *Black Scholar* 1, no. 2 (1969): 26.

41. Wendy Brown, *States of Injury*, 11.

42. Deborah Gould, *Moving Politics: Emotion and ACT UP's Fight against AIDS* (Chicago: University of Chicago Press, 2009), 30; italics mine.

43. Wendy Brown, *States of Injury*, 25.

44. Calvin L. Warren, "Black Nihilism and the Politics of Hope," *CR: The New Centennial Review* 15, no. 1 (2015): 218.

45. Ann Cvetkovich, *An Archive of Feelings: Trauma, Sexuality, and Lesbian Public Culture* (Durham, NC: Duke University Press, 2003), 7.

46. Heller, *A Theory of Feelings*.

47. Heller, *A Theory of Feelings*, 11.

48. Jeff Goodwin, James M. Jasper, and Francesca Polletta, "The Return of the Repressed: The Fall and Rise of Emotions in Social Movement Theory," *Mobilization: An International Journal* 5, no. 1 (2000): 69.

49. Neil Smelser, *Essays in Sociological Explanation* (New York: Prentice Hall, 1968), 92.

50. Smelser, *Essays in Sociological Explanation*, 121. He adds, "On the one hand there is the unqualified love, worship, and submission to the leader of the movement, who articulates and symbolizes 'the cause.' On the other hand there is the unqualified suspicion, denigration, and desire to destroy the agent felt responsible for the moral decay of social life and standing in the way of reform, whether he be a vested interest or a political authority" (119–20).

Eric Hoffer's influential work on demagoguery informed Smelser's thesis and suggested that leadership cults were an important facet of social movement mobilization. Hoffer's work focused on the idolatry of communism and Nazism as evidence of Oedipal impulses. See Eric Hoffer, *The True Believer: Thoughts on the Nature of Mass Movements* (New York: Harper and Row, 1951).

51. Goodwin et al., "The Return of the Repressed," 68.

52. Goodwin et al., "The Return of the Repressed," 69.

53. Ruth Searles and J. Allen Williams, "Negro College Students' Participation in Sit-Ins," *Social Forces* 40, no. 3 (1962): 215–20.

54. William H. Grier and Price M. Cobbs, *Black Rage: Two Black Psychiatrists Reveal the Full Dimensions of the Inner Conflicts and the Desperation of Black Life in the United States* (New York: Basic Books, 1992), 73.

55. Grier and Cobbs, *Black Rage*, 107.

56. In recounting the tremendous success of *Black Rage*, Price Cobbs writes that the book's success was due, at least in part, to the fact that they had "written it with an authentic black voice that had authority and credibility." Cobbs, *My American Life: From Rage to Entitlement* (New York: Simon and Schuster), 219. The notion of authenticity in the articulation of black voice is an important one in the airing of public feelings.

57. Robert Hariman and John Louis Lucaites, "Dissent and Emotional Management in a Liberal-Democratic Society: The Kent State Iconic Photograph," *Rhetoric Society Quarterly* 31, no. 3 (2001): 6.

58. Ahmed, *The Cultural Politics of Emotion*, 54.

59. Martha Nussbaum, *Political Emotions: Why Love Matters for Justice* (Cambridge, MA: Harvard University Press, 2013), 2.

60. Anne Anlin Cheng, *The Melancholy of Race: Psychoanalysis, Assimilation, and Hidden Grief* (New York: Oxford University Press, 2001), 4.

61. Cheng, *The Melancholy of Race*, 10.

62. For more on pedagogies of disidentification in politics, see Lisa M. Corrigan, "White 'Honky' Liberals, Rhetorical Disidentification, and Black Power during the Johnson Administration," in *Reading the Presidency: Advances in Presidential Rhetoric*, ed. Mary E. Stuckey and Stephen J. Heidt (New York: Peter Lang, 2019), 300–326.

63. Judith Butler, *Precarious Life: The Powers of Mourning and Violence* (New York: Verso, 2004), xiv.

64. Mbembe, *Critique of Black Reason*, 39.

65. Achille Mbembe, "Necropolitics," trans. Libby Meintjes, *Public Culture* 15, no. 1 (2003): 13.

66. See, e.g., Alison Jagger, "Love and Knowledge: Emotion in Feminist Epistemologies," in *Women, Knowledge, and Reality*, ed. Ann Garry and Marilyn Pearsall (Boston: Unwin Hyman, 1989), 129.

67. Laura Micciche, *Doing Emotion: Rhetoric, Writing, Teaching* (Boston: Boynton/Cook, 2007), 24.

68. Thomas R. West, *Signs of Struggle: The Rhetorical Politics of Cultural Difference* (Albany: State University of New York Press, 2002), 73.

69. Moira Gatens and Genevieve Lloyd, *Collective Imaginings: Spinoza, Past and Present* (New York: Routledge, 1999), 28.

70. Warren, "Black Nihilism," 218.

71. Thomas West, *Signs of Struggle*, 76.

72. Daniel Innerarity, *The Future and Its Enemies: In Defense of Political Hope*, trans. Sandra Kingery (Stanford, CA: Stanford University Press, 2012), 5.

Chapter One: Postwar Feelings: Beyond Hope

1. John F. Kennedy, "Acceptance Speech at the Democratic National Convention," July 15, 1960, in *Official Report of the Proceedings of the Democratic National Convention and Committee* (Los Angeles: National Document Publishers, 1964), 243. See also https://www.jfklibrary.org/learn/about-jfk/historic-speeches/acceptance-of-democratic-nomination-for-president.

2. Kennedy's New Frontier introduced and passed more new legislation than at any point since FDR's New Deal and represented a tremendous legislative success for the young president. By the congressional recess at the end of 1961, 33 out of 53 bills that Kennedy had submitted to Congress were enacted. A year later, 40 out of the 54 bills proposed by the administration had passed, and in 1963, 35 out of 58 major bills proposed were enacted by Congress. Thus did the New Frontier mark a major moment of collaboration between the executive and legislative branches that transformed public life in the United States.

3. Robert Dalleck, *An Unfinished Life: John F. Kennedy, 1917–1963* (Boston: Back Bay Books, 2004), 393.

4. See, e.g., Klaus P. Fischer, *America in White, Black, and Gray: A History of the Stormy 1960s* (New York: Bloomsbury, 2006).

5. Michael J. Hogan, *The Afterlife of John Fitzgerald Kennedy* (New York: Cambridge University Press, 2017), 63.

6. Arthur M. Schlesinger Jr., *A Thousand Days: John F. Kennedy in the White House* (1965; New York: Houghton Mifflin, 2002), 116.

7. Daniel Innerarity writes, "Modern society has in principle been optimistic regarding its ability to determine its own reality, when this optimism has been frequently contradicted in various ways." See Innerarity, *The Future and Its Enemies: In Defense of Political Hope* (Stanford, CA: Stanford University Press, 2012), 52.

8. Schlesinger, *A Thousand Days*, 740.

9. Schlesinger, *A Thousand Days*, 663.

10. Arthur M. Schlesinger Jr., *The Politics of Hope and the Bitter Heritage: American Liberalism in the 1960s* (Princeton, NJ: Princeton University Press, 2008), 8–9.

11. Schlesinger, *A Thousand Days*, 663.

12. John F. Kennedy, "First Inaugural Address," in *Let the Word Go Forth: The Speeches, Statements, and Writings of John F. Kennedy, 1947–1963*, ed. Theodore Sorensen (New York: Dell, 1991), 14.

13. Stanley Meisler, *When the World Calls: The Inside Story of the Peace Corps and Its First Fifty Years* (Boston: Beacon Press, 2012), 6.

14. Eldridge Cleaver, *Target Zero: A Life in Writing* (New York: St. Martin's Press, 2007), 70.

15. Heller, *A Theory of Feelings*, 81.

16. See, e.g., Paul Ricoeur, "Hope and the Structure of Philosophical Systems," *Proceedings of the American Catholic Philosophical Association* 44 (1970): 55.

17. Heller, *A Theory of Feelings*, 115.

18. Casey Nelson Blake, "Pragmatist Hope," *Dissent* 54, no. 2 (Spring 2007): 95.

19. Stan van Hooft, *Hope* (Durham, UK: Acumen, 2011), 81.

20. Paulo Freire, *Pedagogy of Hope: Reliving Pedagogy of the Oppressed*, trans. Robert R. Barr (London: Bloomsbury, 1992), 2.

21. Gilles Deleuze, *Difference and Repetition*, trans. Paul Patton (New York: Columbia University Press, 1994), 94.

22. Theodore O. Windt, *Presidents and Protesters: Political Rhetoric in the 1960s* (Tuscaloosa: University of Alabama Press, 1991), 17.

23. Windt, *Presidents and Protesters*, 22; italics mine.

24. Van Hooft, *Hope*, 83.

25. Schlesinger, *The Politics of Hope*, 9.

26. Tom Kemp, *The Climax of Capitalism: The U.S. Economy in the Twentieth Century* (New York: Routledge, 1990), 115. Kemp's assessment of the goodwill produced by the postwar boom includes the following observations: "The Second World War opened a new phase in the history of American capitalism, launching it on a long-term expansion which encountered no major setback until the late 1960s. The factors which now propelled it were different from those responsible for the 1920s boom and it did not end in a crash or a slump of the 1930s type. History did not simply repeat itself. . . . There was no post-war slump and the feared return of the depression did not happen. On the contrary, as early as the mid-1950s, and certainly during the early 1960s, there was a confident feeling that the expansionist trend would continue indefinitely with only the mild and short-lived recessions experienced up to that time since 1945" (115).

27. Paul Ricoeur, "Foreword," in *The Politics of Hope*, by Bernard P. Dauenhauer (New York: Routledge, 1986), xiv.

28. Ricoeur, "Foreword," xiv.

29. Ricoeur, "Foreword," xiv.

30. Ricoeur, "Foreword," xiv–xv.

31. John F. Kennedy, "Remarks by Senator John F. Kennedy at the Democratic National Convention, Conrad Hilton, Chicago, Illinois, on August 16, 1956," accessed August 12, 2018, https://www.jfklibrary.org/Research/Research-Aids/JFK-Speeches/Chicago-IL-Democratic-National-Convention_19560816.aspx.

32. Gary Donaldson, *The First Modern Campaign: Kennedy, Nixon, and the Election of 1960* (New York: Rowman and Littlefield, 2007), 82.

33. For a robust discussion of the gendered politics of Kennedy's "new man," see Steven Watts, *JFK and the Masculine Mystique: Sex and Power on the New Frontier* (New York: St. Martin's Press, 2016), 41. See also Marquis Childs, "Shifting the Burden to New Man," *Washington Post*, January 17, 1961, A12.

34. Quoted in Thurston Clarke, *Ask Not: The Inauguration of John F. Kennedy and the Speech That Changed America* (New York: Penguin, 2010), 32.

35. Quoted in Vincent Bzdek, *The Kennedy Legacy: Jack, Bobby, and Ted and a Family Dream Fulfilled* (New York: St. Martin's Press, 2009), 97.

36. Bernard P. Dauenhauer, *The Politics of Hope* (New York: Routledge, 1986), 3.

37. Warren, "Black Nihilism," 222.

38. Ricoeur, "Foreword," xv.

39. Ricoeur, "Foreword," xv.

40. Ricoeur, "Foreword," xvi.

41. Ondine Park, Tonya K. Davidson, and Rob Shields, "Introduction," in *Ecologies of Affect: Placing Nostalgia, Desire, and Hope*, ed. Ondine Park et al. (Waterloo, Ontario: Wilfrid Laurier University Press, 2011), 12.

42. Schlesinger, *A Thousand Days*, 116.

43. Arthur M. Schlesinger Jr., "The Decline of Greatness," in *The Politics of Hope and the Bitter Heritage: American Liberalism in the 1960s* (Princeton, NJ: Princeton University Press, 2008), 39.

44. Michel Foucault, *Death and the Labyrinth* (London: Continuum, 1963), 165.

45. Watts, *JFK and the Masculine Mystique*, 194.

46. Watts, *JFK and the Masculine Mystique*, 16.

47. Joel Dinnerstein, *The Origins of Cool in Postwar America* (Chicago: University of Chicago Press, 2017), 440–41.

48. Norman Mailer, "Superman Comes to the Supermarket," in *Mind of an Outlaw: Selected Essays*, ed. Phillip Sipiora (New York: Random House, 2014), 126.

49. Mailer, "Superman Comes to the Supermarket," 126.

50. Nelson George, *The Death of Rhythm and Blues* (New York: Pantheon, 1988), 61.

51. Theodore H. White, *The Making of the President, 1960* (1961; New York: Harper Perennial, 2009), 323.

52. Steven Levingston, *Kennedy and King: The President, the Pastor, and the Battle over Civil Rights* (New York: Hachette, 2017), 17.

53. Kenneth Mayer, *With the Stroke of a Pen: Executive Orders and Presidential Power* (Princeton, NJ: Princeton University Press, 2001), 8.

54. Gerald N. Rosenberg, *The Hollow Hope: Can Courts Bring About Social Change?* 2nd ed. (Chicago: University of Chicago Press, 2008), 77.

55. Dean J. Kotlowski, "With All Deliberate Delay: Kennedy, Johnson, and School Desegregation," *Journal of Policy History* 17, no. 2 (2005): 156–57.

56. Kotlowski, "With All Deliberate Delay," 157.

57. Wendy Brown, *States of Injury*, 11.

58. Ghassan Hage, *Against Paranoid Nationalism: Searching for Hope in a Shrinking Society* (Sydney: Pluto Press, 2003).

59. David Farrier, *Postcolonial Asylum: Seeking Sanctuary before the Law* (London: Oxford University Press, 2013), 53.

60. Larry J. Sabato, *The Kennedy Half-Century: The Presidency, Assassination, and Lasting Legacy* (New York: Bloomsbury, 2013), 254.

61. James W. Douglass, *JFK and the Unspeakable: Why He Died and Why It Matters* (New York: Simon and Schuster, 2010), 381.

62. Douglass, *JFK and the Unspeakable*, 381.

63. Todd Gitlin, *The Sixties: Years of Hope, Days of Rage* (New York: Bantam, 1987), 312.

64. Gitlin, *The Sixties*, 312.

65. Gitlin, *The Sixties*, xvi.

66. Stan van Hooft, *Hope* (Durham, UK: Acumen, 2011), 86.

67. Hogan, *Afterlife*, 64.

68. Quoted in Hogan, *Afterlife*, 65.

69. Quoted in Hogan, *Afterlife*, 65.

70. Mary Dudziak, *Cold War Civil Rights: Race and the Image of American Democracy* (Princeton, NJ: Princeton University Press, 2000), 205.

71. Gitlin, *The Sixties*, 150.

72. Hogan, *Afterlife*, 57.

73. Hogan, *Afterlife*, 64.

74. Sean Wilentz, "Introduction," in *The Politics of Hope and The Bitter Heritage: American Liberalism in the 1960s*, by Arthur M. Schlesinger (Princeton, NJ: Princeton University Press, 2007).

75. Matthew Holden, "President, Congress, and Race Relations," Ernest Patterson Memorial Lecture, University of Colorado at Boulder, 1986, 103.

76. Kenneth O'Reilly, "The FBI and the Civil Rights Movement during the Kennedy Years—from the Freedom Rides to Albany," *Journal of Southern History* 54, no. 2 (1988): 201–32.

77. Gitlin, *The Sixties*, 311.

Chapter Two: Contouring Black Hope and Despair

1. Martin Luther King Jr., "Fumbling on the New Frontier," *Nation*, March 3, 1962, 190–91.

2. Joseph Winters, *Hope Draped in Black: Race, Melancholy, and the Agony of Progress* (Durham, NC: Duke University Press, 2016), 20.

3. Winters, *Hope Draped in Black*, 19. See also Anne Anlin Cheng, *The Melancholy of Race: Psychoanalysis, Assimilation, and Hidden Grief* (New York: Oxford University Press, 2001).

4. Martin Luther King Jr., *The Autobiography of Martin Luther King, Jr.*, ed. Clayborne Carson (New York: Warner Books, 1998), 143–44.

5. The Declaration of Constitutional Principles (commonly known as the Southern Manifesto), written mostly by Strom Thurmond (R-SC) and signed in 1956 by 99 southern Democrats and 2 Republicans in the US Congress, opposed desegregation and refuted *Brown v. Board of Education* as a "clear abuse of judicial power." The document urged southerners to use all "lawful means" to resist the "chaos and confusion" that would stem from school desegregation. Only three Senate Democrats refused to sign: Lyndon B. Johnson (TX), Albert Gore Sr. (TN), and Estes Kefauver (TN). For a historical account, see John Kyle Day, *The Southern Manifesto: Massive Resistance and the Fight to Preserve Segregation* (Jackson: University Press of Mississippi, 2015).

6. Baldwin, "The Dangerous Road before Martin Luther King," in *The Price of the Ticket: Collected Nonfiction, 1948–1985* (New York: St. Martin's Press, 1985), 246; originally published in *Harper's Magazine*, February 1961.

7. King, "Fumbling on the New Frontier," 191.

8. Daniel Innerarity, *The Future and Its Enemies: In Defense of Political Hope*, trans. Sandra Kingery (Stanford, CA: Stanford University Press, 2012), 79.

9. Martin Luther King Jr., "Love, Law and Civil Disobedience," November 16, 1961, in *A Testament of Hope: The Essential Writings and Speeches of Martin Luther King, Jr.*, ed. James M. Washington (New York: HarperOne, 2003), 51.

10. King, "Love, Law and Civil Disobedience," 51.

11. King, "Love, Law and Civil Disobedience," 52.

12. King, "Love, Law and Civil Disobedience," 52.

13. Martin Luther King Jr., "Pilgrimage to Nonviolence," in *A Testament of Hope: The Essential Writings and Speeches of Martin Luther King, Jr.*, ed. James M. Washington (New York: HarperOne, 2003), 40. Reprinted from *Christian Century* 77 (April 13, 1960): 439–41. This was a restatement of Chapter Six of Martin Luther King Jr., *Stride toward Freedom: The Montgomery Story* (New York: Harper and Row, 1958).

14. Baldwin, "The Dangerous Road," 245–46.

15. He writes that King was not "particularly outgoing or warm. His restraint is not, on the other hand, of that icily uneasy, nerve-wracking kind to be encountered in so many famous Negroes who have allowed their aspirations and notoriety to destroy their identities and who always seem to be giving an uncertain imitation of some extremely improbably white man" (in Baldwin, "The Dangerous Road," 246).

16. Baldwin, "The Dangerous Road," 250.

17. Ken Plummer, *Intimate Citizenship: Private Decisions and Public Dialogues* (Seattle: University of Washington Press, 2013), 15.

18. Martin Luther King Jr., "Nonviolence and Racial Justice," in *A Testament of Hope: The Essential Writings and Speeches* (New York: Harper, 2003), 8; originally published in *Christian Century* 74 (February 6, 1957): 165–67.

19. Martin Luther King Jr., "Facing the Challenges of a New Age," address delivered at the First Annual Institute on Nonviolence and Social Change, December 3, 1956, in *The Papers of Martin Luther King, Jr.*, vol. 2, *Rediscovering Precious Values: The Birth of a New Age, December 1955–December 1956* (Berkeley: University of California Press, 1997), 451.

20. Silvan Tomkins, "Shame-Humiliation and Contempt-Disgust," in *Shame and Its Sisters: A Silvan Tomkins Reader*, ed. Eve Kosofsky Sedgwick and Adam Frank (Durham, NC: Duke University Press, 2015), 133.

21. King's ideas about the beloved community were heavily influenced by his professors at Boston College, especially Josiah Royce, who introduced King to this concept. See Judith M. Green, *Deep Democracy: Community, Diversity, and Transformation* (Lanham, MD: Rowman and Littlefield, 1999). Royce develops his observations about community in *The Hope of the Great Community* (1916) and *The Problem of Christianity* (1918).

22. Peter Coviello, *Intimacy in America: Dreams of Affiliation in Antebellum Literature* (Minneapolis: University of Minnesota Press, 2005), 61.

23. Green, *Deep Democracy*, 216.

24. Green, *Deep Democracy*, 216.

25. Green, *Deep Democracy*, 122.

26. Martin Luther King Jr., "The Power of Nonviolence," in *A Testament of Hope: The Essential Writings and Speeches* (New York: Harper, 2003), 12–13.

27. King, "The Power of Nonviolence," 13.

28. Martin Luther King Jr., "Speech at Glenville High School," April 26, 1967, *Cleveland Plain Dealer*, http://blog.cleveland.com/pdextra/2012/01/martin_luther_king_jr_april_26.html.

29. King, "Speech at Glenville High School."

30. Martin Luther King Jr., "Our Struggle," in *A Testament of Hope: The Essential Writings and Speeches* (New York: Harper, 2003), 80.

31. Andrew W. Manis, *A Fire You Can't Put Out: The Civil Rights Life of Birmingham's Reverend Fred Shuttlesworth* (Birmingham: University of Alabama Press, 1999), 4.

32. Manis, *Fire You Can't Put Out*, 98.

33. Martin Luther King Jr., *The Autobiography of Martin Luther King, Jr.*, ed. Clayborne Carson (New York: Warner Books, 1998), 173.

34. Martin Luther King Jr., *Why We Can't Wait* (1964; Boston: Beacon Press, 2011), 36.

35. Eric King Watts, "'Voice' and 'Voicelessness' in Rhetorical Studies," *Quarterly Journal of Speech* 87, no. 2 (2001): 180.

36. Christopher J. Lebron, *The Color of Our Shame: Race and Justice in Our Time* (New York: Oxford University Press, 2015), 25.

37. The emotional dynamic of Birmingham was achieved through visual mediation, as many monographs have argued. See, e.g., Leigh Raiford, *Imprisoned in a Luminous Glare: Photography and the African American Freedom Struggle* (Chapel Hill: University of North Carolina Press, 2011); Maurice Berger, *Seeing Through Race: A Reinterpretation of Civil Rights Photography* (Berkeley: University of California Press, 2011); Maurice Berger, *For All the World to See: Visual Culture and the Struggle for Civil Rights* (New Haven, CT: Yale University Press, 2010).

38. Kenneth B. Clark, *The Negro Protest* (Boston: Beacon, 1963), 42.

39. Sara Ahmed, *The Cultural Politics of Emotion* (New York: Routledge, 2004), 111.

40. Ahmed, *The Cultural Politics of Emotion*, 111.

41. Ahmed, *The Cultural Politics of Emotion*, 111.

42. Thandeka, *Learning to Be White: Money, Race, God and America* (New York: Bloomsbury, 1999).

43. Robin DiAngelo, "White Fragility," *International Journal of Critical Pedagogy* 3, no. 3 (2011): 54–70.

44. Eve Kosofsky Sedgwick and Adam Frank, eds., *Shame and Its Sisters: A Silvan Tomkins Reader* (Durham, NC: Duke University Press, 1995).

45. Ahmed, *The Cultural Politics of Emotion*, 109.

46. King, *Why We Can't Wait*, 157.

47. Martin Luther King Jr., *The Autobiography of Martin Luther King, Jr.*, ed. Clayborne Carson (New York: Warner Books, 1998), 198.

48. Jonathan Rieder, *Gospel of Freedom: Martin Luther King Jr.'s Letter from Birmingham Jail and the Struggle That Changed a Nation* (New York: Bloomsbury Press, 2014), 76.

49. Ian Klinke, "Chronopolitics: A Conceptual Matrix," *Progress in Human Geography* 37, no. 5 (2013): 674.

50. Martin Luther King Jr., "Letter from Birmingham City Jail," in *A Testament of Hope: The Essential Writings and Teachings of Martin Luther King, Jr.*, ed. James M. Washington (1986; New York: HarperCollins, 1991), 292.

51. King, "Letter from Birmingham City Jail," 292.

52. King, "Letter from Birmingham City Jail," 293.

53. King, "Letter from Birmingham City Jail," 293.

54. King, "Letter from Birmingham City Jail," 292.

55. King, "Letter from Birmingham City Jail," 295.

56. King, "Letter from Birmingham City Jail," 296.

57. Martin Luther King Jr., "Loving Your Enemies," March 7, 1961, in *The Papers of Martin Luther King, Jr.*, vol. 1, *Advocate of the Social Gospel, September 1948–March 1963* (Berkeley: University of California Press, 2007), 425.

58. King, *Why We Can't Wait*, 102.

59. King, *Autobiography*, 25.

60. King, *Autobiography*, 25.

61. John F. Kennedy, "Civil Rights Address," June 11, 1963.

62. King, *Why We Can't Wait*, 107.

63. Jeffrey C. Alexander, *The Civil Sphere* (New York: Oxford University Press, 2006).

64. Martin Luther King Jr., "I Have a Dream," in *A Testament of Hope: The Essential Writings and Teachings of Martin Luther King, Jr.*, ed. James M. Washington (1986; New York: HarperCollins, 1991), 217.

65. King, "I Have a Dream," 217.

66. Deborah Gould, "On Affect and Protest," in *Political Emotions*, ed. Janet Staiger, Ann Cvetkovich, and Ann Reynolds (New York: Routledge, 2009), 18–44.

67. Malcolm X, "Message to the Grassroots," in *Malcolm X Speaks: Selected Speeches and Statements*, ed. George Breitman (New York: Grove Press, 1965), 12.

68. Rieder, *Gospel of Freedom*, 41.

69. King, "Letter from Birmingham City Jail," 298.

70. Charles Marsh, *The Beloved Community: How Faith Shapes Social Justice, from the Civil Rights Movement to Today* (New York: Basic Books, 2005), 4.

71. Julius Lester, "The Angry Children of Malcolm X," in *Black Protest Thought in the Twentieth Century*, ed. August Meier et al. (New York: Bobbs-Merrill, 1971), 447.

72. Lester, "Angry Children of Malcolm X," 447.

73. King, *Why We Can't Wait*, 171.

74. King, *Why We Can't Wait*, 171.

75. King, *Why We Can't Wait*, 171.

76. King, *Autobiography*, 243.

77. Michael W. Flamm, *Law and Order: Street Crime, Civil Unrest, and the Crisis of Liberalism in the 1960s* (New York: Columbia University Press, 2007), 30.

78. Nick Kotz, *Judgment Days: Lyndon Baines Johnson, Martin Luther King Jr., and the Laws That Changed America* (New York: Houghton Mifflin, 2005), 20.

79. Guido van Rijn, *Kennedy's Blues: African-American Blues and Gospel Songs on JFK* (Jackson: University Press of Mississippi, 2007), xiv–xv.

80. Warren, "Black Nihilism," 221.

81. Warren, "Black Nihilism," 222.

82. Baldwin, "The Dangerous Road," 248.

83. Martin Luther King Jr., "Showdown to Nonviolence," in *A Testament to Hope: The Essential Writings and Speeches of Martin Luther King, Jr.*, ed. James M. Washington (New York: HarperCollins, 1991). 71–72.

84. King, "Showdown to Nonviolence," 71.

85. Quoted in David J. Garrow, *Bearing the Cross: Martin Luther King, Jr., and the Southern Christian Leadership Conference* (New York: Perennial, 2004), 523.

Chapter Three: American Negritude: Black Rage and the Restoration of Pride

1. Mike Wallace and Louis Lomax, *The Hate That Hate Produced*, produced by *News Beat*, distributed by WNTA-TV, New York, July 13–17, 1959.

2. Mike Wallace, "Malcolm X, 1925–1965," in *Voices of Freedom: An Oral History of the Civil Rights Movement from the 1950s through the 1980s*, ed. Henry Hampton and Steve Fayer (New York: Bantam, 1990), 247.

3. Finbarr Curtis, *The Production of American Religious Freedom* (New York: New York University Press, 2016), 113.

4. Kambiz GhaneaBassiri, *A History of Islam in America: From the New World to the New World Order* (New York: Cambridge University Press, 2010), 243.

5. Ron Simmons and Marlon Riggs, "Sexuality, Television, and Death: A Black Gay Dialogue on Malcolm X," in *Malcolm X: In Our Own Image*, ed. Joe Wood (New York: St. Martin's Press, 1992), 141.

6. Donna Murch, *Living for the City: Migration, Education, and the Rise of the Black Panther Party in Oakland, California* (Chapel Hill: University of North Carolina Press, 2010), 81.

7. In *Voices of Freedom: An Oral History of the Civil Rights Movement from the 1950s through the 1980s*, ed. Henry Hampton and Steve Fayer (New York: Bantam, 1990), 248.

8. Louis A. DeCaro, *On the Side of My People: A Religious Life of Malcolm X* (New York: New York University Press, 1996), 134.

9. Louis A. DeCaro, *Malcolm and the Cross: The Nation of Islam, Malcolm X, and Christianity* (New York: New York University Press, 1998), 191.

10. Audre Lorde, "The Master's Tools Will Never Dismantle the Master's House," in *Sister Outsider: Essays and Speeches* (1984; Berkeley: Crossing Press, 2007), 110–14.

11. Malcolm's psychological interventions were welcomed because they provided a different lens to understand racism in the United States, one that the civil rights movement had not engaged. See Jeffrey O. G. Ogbar, *Black Power: Radical Politics and African American Identity* (Baltimore, MD: Johns Hopkins University Press, 2004), 191.

12. Thomas J. Scheff, "Alienation, Love, and Hate as Causes of Collective Violence," in *Emotions, Crime and Justice*, ed. Susanne Karstedt, Ian Loader, and Heather Strang (Oxford: Hart, 2011), 275–94.

13. Agnes Heller, *A Theory of Feelings*, 2nd ed. (Lanham, MD: Lexington Books, 2009), 105.

14. Heller, *A Theory of Feelings*, 52.

15. Darieck Scott, *Extravagant Abjection: Blackness, Power, and Sexuality in the African American Literary Imagination* (New York: New York University Press, 2010, 25). He continues, "Thus, one can see through the invented prism of blackness both the deprivation on which the person in Western civilization is created and the possibilities for the transformation of that person—and the first step in the process of coming to this consciousness involves working through an experience of trauma (a forced recognition of his blackness)."

16. Robert Terrill, *Malcolm X: Inventing Radical Judgment* (Lansing: Michigan State University Press, 2004), 13.

17. Keith Miller, "Plymouth Rock Landed on Us: Malcolm X's Whiteness Theory as a Basis for Alternative Literacy," *College Composition and Communication* 56, no. 2 (2014): 199–222; Bruce Horner, "Students' Rights, English Only, and Re-imagining the Politics of Language," *College English* 63, no. 6 (2001): 741–58. See also Theresa Perry, *Teaching Malcolm X: Popular Culture and Literacy* (New York: Routledge, 2014).

18. Cornel West, "Malcolm X and Black Rage," in *Malcolm X: In Our Own Image*, ed. Joe Wood (New York: St. Martin's Press, 1992), 50.

19. Cornel West, "Malcolm X and Black Rage," 53.

20. See Jay Garcia, *Psychology Comes to Harlem: Rethinking the Race Question in Twentieth-Century America* (Baltimore, MD: Johns Hopkins University Press, 2012).

21. Wallace and Lomax, *The Hate That Hate Produced.*

22. Rodolfo Torres and Christopher Kyriakides, *Race Defaced: Paradigms of Pessimism, Politics of Possibility* (Stanford, CA: Stanford University Press, 2012).

23. Clark was the first black president of the American Psychological Association (APA), the first black American to earn a doctorate in psychology at Columbia University, and the

first to become a tenured instructor in New York's City College system. See Daniel Matlin, *On the Corner: African American Intellectuals and the Urban Crisis* (Cambridge, MA: Harvard University Press, 2013).

24. Kenneth B. Clark, "Effect of Prejudice and Discrimination on Personality Development," Midcentury White House Conference on Children and Youth, 1950. Clark's research plus the experiments that he conducted (known colloquially as the "Clark Doll Tests") with his wife Mamie Phipps Clark informed much of the background for the *Brown* decision. For an assessment of Clark's impact on *Brown* and on the American Psychological Association's credibility in American life, see Ludy T. Benjamin Jr. and Ellen M. Crouse, "The American Psychological Association's Response to *Brown v. Board of Education*: The Case of Kenneth B. Clark," *American Psychologist*, January 2002, 38–50.

25. Abram Kardiner and Lionel Ovesey, *The Mark of Oppression: A Psychosocial Study of the American Negro* (New York: Norton, 1951), 43.

26. Kardiner and Ovesey, *Mark of Oppression*, 43.

27. Kardiner and Ovesey, *Mark of Oppression*, 49.

28. Norman Duncan et al., eds., *Self, Community and Psychology* (Lansdowne, Australia: UCT Press, 2004), 28.

29. E. Franklin Frazier, *Black Bourgeoisie* (New York: Free Press, 1957), 213.

30. Frazier's groundbreaking work expanded on Erving Goffman's popular book *The Presentation of Self in Everyday Life* (1956), which argued that in any communication situation, an individual is "expected to suppress his [or her] immediate heartfelt feelings, conveying a view of the situation which he feels the others will be able to find at least temporarily acceptable." Erving Goffman, *The Presentation of Self in Everyday Life* (New York: Anchor, 1959), 9.

31. Frazier, *Black Bourgeoisie*, 131.

32. Frantz Fanon, *Black Skin, White Masks*, trans. Richard Philcox (1952; New York: Grove Press, 2008), xvi.

33. Fanon, *Black Skin, White Masks*, 15.

34. Fanon, *Black Skin, White Masks*, xvi.

35. Fanon, *Black Skin, White Masks*, xvii.

36. Fanon, *Black Skin, White Masks*, xiv.

37. Fanon, *Black Skin, White Masks*, xv.

38. Black Power leaders like H. Rap Brown, Stokely Carmichael, Eldridge Cleaver, Huey Newton, Fred Hampton, and Angela Davis (among others) acknowledged the centrality of Fanon in their thinking. See Alice Kaplan, "Dreaming in French: On Angela Davis," *Nation*, March 14, 2012, https://www.thenation.com/article/dreaming-french-angela-davis; David Macey, *Frantz Fanon: A Biography* (London: Verso, 2000); Bobby Seale, *Seize the Time: The Story of the Black Panther Party and Huey P. Newton* (New York: Random House, 1970).

39. Kwame Ture and Charles Hamilton, *Black Power: The Politics of Liberation* (New York: Vintage Books, 1992), 31.

40. Ture and Hamilton, *Black Power*, 81.

41. Damas, cited in René Piquion, *Manuel de négritude* (1965; Paris: Présence Africaine, 1979), 66.

42. See Max Silverman, ed., *Frantz Fanon's "Black Skin, White Masks": New Interdisciplinary Essays* (Manchester, UK: Manchester University Press, 2005); Nigel Gibson, *Fanon: The Postcolonial Imagination* (Cambridge, UK: Polity, 2003); David Macey, *Frantz Fanon: A Life* (London: Verso, 2000); Nigel Gibson, *Rethinking Fanon: The Continuing Dialogue* (New York: Humanity Books, 1999); Lewis R. Gordon, *Fanon and the Crisis of European Man* (New York: Routledge, 1995).

43. Babacar M'Baye, *Black Cosmopolitanism and Anticolonialism: Pivotal Moments* (New York: Routledge, 2017), 89.

44. See Reiland Rabaka, *The Negritude Movement: W. E. B. Du Bois, Leon Damas, Aime Cesaire, Leopold Senghor, Frantz Fanon, and the Evolution of an Insurgent Idea* (Lanham, MD: Lexington, 2015); Lilyan Kesteloot, *Black Writers in French: A Literary History of Négritude* (Washington: Howard University Press, 1991).

45. Michael Fabre, *From Harlem to Paris: Black American Writers in France, 1840–1980* (Urbana: University of Illinois Press, 1991); Jock McCulloch, *Black Soul, White Artifact: Fanon's Clinical Psychology and Social Theory* (Cambridge: Cambridge University Press, 1983).

46. Black American writers and speakers used Négritude, New Negro, and Harlem Renaissance writers to argue that the enslaved could not use enslavement as a vehicle of self-realization or liberation, thus rejecting Hegel's assertion that the master-bondsman dialectic was one that could humanize both parties. See, e.g., Donna V. Jones, *The Racial Discourses of Life Philosophy: Négritude, Vitalism, and Modernity* (New York: Columbia University Press, 2010).

47. Dozens of books have been devoted to Malcolm's relationship with Africa. See, e.g., Tunde Adeleke, *Africa in Black Liberation Activism: Malcolm X, Stokely Carmichael and Walter Rodney* (New York: Routledge, 2016); Regina Jennings, *Malcolm X and the Poetics of Haki Madhubuti* (Jefferson, NC: McFarland, 2006); William W. Sales Jr., *From Civil Rights to Black Liberation: Malcolm X and the Organization of Afro-American Unity* (Boston: South End Press, 1984).

48. Robert Terrill, arguably the foremost Malcolm X scholar in communication, never cites the influence of Négritude or Harlem Renaissance writers on Malcolm, despite their clear relationality, though he does acknowledge the connection between Malcolm and Garvey. See Robert E. Terrill, ed., *The Cambridge Companion to Malcolm X* (Cambridge: Cambridge University Press, 2010).

49. Peter Louis Goldman, *The Death and Life of Malcolm X* (Urbana: University of Illinois Press, 1973), 185.

50. Malcolm X, "An Appeal to African Heads of State: OAU Memorandum," in *Malcolm X Speaks: Selected Speeches and Statements*, ed. George Breitman (New York: Grove Press, 1965), 73.

51. Mbembe, *Critique of Black Reason*, 43.

52. Sara Ahmed, *The Cultural Politics of Emotion* (New York: Routledge, 2004), 120.

53. Ahmed, *The Cultural Politics of Emotion*, 111.

54. John Henrik Clarke, "Introduction," in *Malcolm X: The Man and His Times*, ed. John Henrik Clarke (1969; Trenton, NJ: Africa World Press, 1991), xi.

55. In this way, he disavowed the mimicry of whites that Homi Bhabha so famously described in "Of Mimicry and Man: The Ambivalence of Colonial Discourse," *October* 28 (Spring 1984): 125–33.

56. Whereas the Francophone writers focused mostly on the colonial situation, Damas deals with slavery at length in *Black Label*, one of several of his books still not translated into English. See Léon-Gontran Damas, *Black label et autres poe* (1956; Paris: Gallimard, 2011). See also Kathryn Batchelor and Claire Bisdorff, eds., *Intimate Enemies: Translation in Francophone Contexts* (Liverpool: Liverpool University Press, 2013).

57. Malcolm X, "Message to the Grassroots," November 10, 1963, in *Malcolm X Speaks: Selected Speeches and Statements*, ed. George Breitman (New York: Grove Press, 1965), 4.

58. Lauren Berlant, "'68, or Something," *Critical Inquiry* 21, no. 1 (1994): 128. See also Rajagopalan Radhakrishnan, "Nationalism, Gender, and the Narrative of Identity," in *Nationalisms and Sexualities*, ed. Andrew Parker et al. (Routledge: New York, 1992), 81.

59. Malcolm X, "Message to the Grassroots," 11.

60. Malcolm X, "Message to the Grassroots," 12.

61. Malcolm X, "The Ballot or the Bullet," April 3, 1964, in *Malcolm X Speaks: Selected Speeches and Statements*, ed. George Breitman (New York: Grove Press, 1965).

62. Malcolm X, "The Black Revolution," April 8, 1964, in *Malcolm X Speaks: Selected Speeches and Statements*, ed. George Breitman (New York: Grove Press, 1965), 50.

63. Mbembe, *Critique of Black Reason*, 104.

64. Mbembe, *Critique of Black Reason*, 105.

65. Achille Mbembe, *On the Postcolony* (Berkeley: University of California Press, 2001), 15.

66. Mbembe, *On the Postcolony*, 16.

67. Grier and Cobbs, *Black Rage*, 26.

68. Grier and Cobbs, *Black Rage*, 23.

69. Grier and Cobbs, *Black Rage*, 28.

70. Malcolm's use of the house Negro / field Negro expressed a tremendous ambivalence toward the black middle class: "He hated and emulated them; he ridiculed and admired them; he was part of a movement that tried to turn the most lumpen Negroes into respectable (by bourgeois standards, at least), well-mannered, 'civilized' black men and women. And through it all, Malcolm's critique of the black bourgeoisie floated somewhere between an intuitive hatred born of his past to an insightful analysis of the race/class matrix." Robin D. G. Kelley, "House Negroes on the Loose: Malcolm X and the Black Bourgeoisie," *Callaloo* 21, no. 2 (1998): 419.

71. Dennis A. Doyle, *Psychiatry and Racial Liberalism in Harlem, 1936–1968* (Rochester: University of Rochester Press, 2016), 6–7.

72. Mbembe, *Critique of Black Reason*, 93.

73. Goldman, *Death and Life of Malcolm X*, 401.

74. Goldman, *Death and Life of Malcolm X*, 401.

75. Malcolm X, "The Black Revolution," 51.

76. Manning Marable, ed., *The Portable Malcolm X Reader* (New York: Penguin, 2013), 184–90.

77. "Malcolm X, Rustin Debate Race Issue at Howard," *Carolina Times*, November 11, 1961, 6B.

78. See, e.g., Robert James Branham, "'I Was Gone on Debating': Malcolm X's Prison Debates and Public Confrontations," *Argumentation and Advocacy* 31 (Winter 1995): 117–37.

79. Michel Foucault, *Discipline and Punish: The Birth of the Prison*, trans. Alan Sheridan (New York: Vintage Books, 1972), 25–26.

80. Ossie Davis, "Malcolm Was a Man: Eulogy of Malcolm X," in *Life Lit by Some Large Vision: Selected Speeches and Writings* (New York: Simon and Schuster, 2006), 153.

81. James Tyner, *The Geography of Malcolm X: Black Radicalism and the Remaking of American Space* (New York: Routledge, 2006), 93.

82. Ossie Davis, "To Roger Price," in *Life Lit by Some Large Vision: Selected Speeches and Writings* (New York: Simon and Schuster, 2006), 227.

83. Malcolm X, "Interview," in *The Negro Protest*, by Kenneth B. Clark (Boston: Beacon Press, 1963), 26–27.

84. Malcolm X, "Interview," 26.

85. Cornel West, *Hope on a Tightrope: Words and Wisdom* (New York: Hay House, 2008).

86. Alexander G. Weheliye, *Habeas Viscus: Racializing Assemblages, Biopolitics, and Black Feminist Theories of the Human* (Durham, NC: Duke University Press, 2014), 2.

87. George Plimpton, "Miami Notebook: Cassius Clay and Malcolm X," *Harper's*, June 1964, 57.

88. Hans J. Massaquoi, "The Mystery of Malcolm X," *Ebony*, September 1964, 39.

89. Ahmed, *The Cultural Politics of Emotion*, 83.

90. Ahmed, *The Cultural Politics of Emotion*, 84. See also Donald L. Nathanson, *Shame and Pride: Affect, Sex, and the Birth of the Self* (New York: Norton, 1995).

91. Tomkins, in *Shame and Her Sisters*, 133–36.

92. Ahmed, *The Cultural Politics of Emotion*, 85.

93. Barbara Ritchie, *The Riot Report* (New York: Viking Press, 1969), 125.

94. Michael Eric Dyson, *Open Mike: Reflections on Philosophy, Race, Sex, Culture and Religion* (New York: Basic Books, 2003), 329.

95. Cornel West, "Malcolm X and Black Rage," in *Malcolm X: In Our Own Image*, ed. Joe Wood (New York: St. Martin's Press, 1992), 48.

96. Cornel West, "Malcolm X and Black Rage," 48.

97. Cornel West, "Malcolm X and Black Rage," 49.

98. Cornel West, "Malcolm X and Black Rage," 53.

99. Cornel West, *Race Matters* (Boston: Beacon Press, 1993), 103.

100. Thomas West, *Signs of Struggle*, 79.

101. Ahmed, *The Cultural Politics of Emotion*, 43.

102. Ahmed, *The Cultural Politics of Emotion*, 43.

103. J. Edgar Hoover, "Memo to Secret Service Chief," December 6, 1963, in *Malcolm X FBI File, The Portable Malcolm X Reader*, ed. Manning Marable and Garrett Felber (New York: Penguin, 2013), 180.

104. See, e.g., Jean Laplanche and Jean-Bertrand Pontalis, *The Language of Psycho-Analysis*, trans. Donald Nicholson-Smith (London: Karnac Books, 1988).

105. Lisa M. Corrigan, "Fifty Years Later: Commemorating the Life and Death of Malcolm X," *Howard Journal of Communications* 28, no. 2 (2017): 144–59.

106. bell hooks, *Killing Rage* (New York: Holt, 1996), 18.

107. hooks, *Killing Rage*, 13.

108. hooks, *Killing Rage*, 14.

109. hooks, *Killing Rage*, 15–16.

110. hooks, *Killing Rage*, 18.

111. hooks, *Killing Rage*, 18.

112. Amiri Baraka, "The Legacy of Malcolm X, and the Coming of the Black Nation," in *The LeRoi Jones / Amiri Baraka Reader*, ed. William J. Harris with Amiri Baraka (New York: Thunder's Mouth Press, 1991), 161.

113. Baraka, "The Legacy of Malcolm X," 166.

114. Miller, "Plymouth Rock Landed on Us," 217.

115. James Baldwin, *No Name in the Street* (New York: Dial, 1972), 97.

116. Baldwin, *No Name in the Street*, 98.

117. Berlant, "'68 or Something," 128.

118. Goldman, *Death and Life of Malcolm X*, 18.

119. Lester, "Angry Children of Malcolm X," 443.

120. William Van Deburg, *New Day in Babylon: The Black Power Movement and American Culture* (Chicago: University of Chicago Press, 1992), 51.

121. Van Deburg, *New Day in Babylon*, 51.

122. See Molefi K. Assante, *Malcolm X as Cultural Hero and Other Afrocentric Essays* (Trenton, NJ: Africa World Press, 1993).

123. Fanon, *Black Skin, White Masks*, 118.

124. Fanon, *Black Skin, White Masks*, 117.

125. Cornel West, "Malcolm X and Black Rage," 49.

126. On the despair and the dream deferred, see Mark Lawrence McPhail, *The Rhetoric of Racism Revisited: Reparations or Separation?* (Lanham, MD: Rowman and Littlefield, 2002), 140–41.

127. William W. Sales Jr., *From Civil Rights to Black Liberation: Malcolm X and the Organization of Afro-American Unity* (Boston: South End Press, 1984), 41.

Chapter Four: Feeling Riots: The Emotional Language of Urban Rebellion

1. Throughout the chapter, I use the terms *riot, rebellion, revolt*, and *uprising* synonymously. While I think that the phenomena described in this chapter are closer to rebellions or uprisings, *riot* is the prevalent term in the historical literature, and it carries with it the antiblack political connotations that I wish to explore here. Thus I have kept it here as a part of the rhetorical history of the moment and of the term.

2. "Violence Sends a Message," *Ebony*, September 1964, 140.

3. "Violence Sends a Message," 140.

4. Pronouncements like this about the plight of the urban poor inundated the American media in the spring and summer of 1964, making the Harlem riot even more salient. See, e.g., Robert Dalleck, *Flawed Giant: Lyndon Johnson and His Times* (Oxford: Oxford University Press, 1999), 108.

5. "Violence Sends a Message," 140.

6. "Violence Sends a Message," 140.

7. Cornel West, *Race Matters*, 14.

8. Lauren Berlant, "Slow Death (Sovereignty, Obesity, Lateral Agency)," *Critical Inquiry* 33, no. 4 (2007): 754.

9. See Cathy Lisa Schneider, *Police Power and Race Riots: Urban Unrest in Paris and New York* (Philadelphia: University of Pennsylvania Press, 2014).

10. Mbembe, *On the Postcolony*, 26–27.

11. Mbembe, *On the Postcolony*, 27.

12. Hubert Locke, *The Detroit Riot of 1967* (Detroit: Wayne State University Press, 2017), 23.

13. "Violence Sends a Message," 140.

14. "Violence Sends a Message," 140.

15. This period saw more than four hundred urban riots. See August Meier and Elliot Rudwick, *From Plantation to Ghetto*, 3rd ed. (1966; New York: Hill and Wang, 1976), 301. For detailed histories and timelines of the riots, see Fred C. Shapiro and James W. Sullivan, *Race Riots, New York, 1964* (New York: Crowell, 1964); David Boesel and Peter H. Rossi, eds., *Cities under Siege: An Anatomy of the Ghetto Riots, 1964–1968* (Princeton, NJ: Princeton University Press, 1971); Janet L. Abu-Lughod, *Race, Space and Riots in Chicago, New York, and Los Angeles* (New York: Oxford University Press, 2007); Max Arthur Herman, *Summer of Rage: An Oral History of the 1967 Newark and Detroit Riots* (New York: Peter Lang, 2013);

Michael Flamm, *In the Heat of the Summer: The New York Riots of 1964 and the War on Crime* (Philadelphia: University of Pennsylvania Press, 2016).

16. Gunnar Myrdal, *An American Dilemma: The Negro Problem and Modern Democracy* (New York: Harper and Row), 569.

17. See also Amber Jamilla Musser, *Sensational Flesh: Race, Power, and Masochism* (New York: New York University Press, 2014). Musser elaborates on Fanonian concepts of becoming-black through abjection.

18. Frantz Fanon, *A Dying Colonialism* (1959; New York: Grove Press, 1965), 44.

19. Frantz Fanon, *The Wretched of the Earth* (1963; New York: Grove Press, 2004), 8.

20. Fanon, *The Wretched of the Earth*, 17.

21. Paula Ioanide, *The Emotional Politics of Racism: How Feelings Trump Facts in an Era of Colorblindness* (Stanford, CA: Stanford University Press, 2015), 15.

22. Myrdal, *An American Dilemma*, 567.

23. Price Cobbs, "Journeys to Black Identity: Selma to Watts," *Negro Digest*, July 1967, 64.

24. Grier and Cobbs, *Black Rage*, 25.

25. Grier and Cobbs, *Black Rage*, 26.

26. Roy E. Finkenbine, "The Underground Railroad and Early Radical Violence," in *Detroit 1967: Origins, Impacts, Legacies*, ed. Joel Stone (Detroit: Wayne State University Press, 2017), 30. See also Malcolm McLaughlin, *Urban Rebellion in America: The Long Hot Summer of 1967* (New York: Palgrave Macmillan, 2014).

27. Bill McGraw, "Detroit's Forgotten History of Slavery," in *Detroit 1967: Origins, Impacts, Legacies*, ed. Joel Stone (Detroit: Wayne State University Press, 2017), 21.

28. Hubert G. Locke, *The Detroit Riot of 1967* (Detroit: Wayne State University Press, 2017), 23.

29. Gerald Horne, *Fire This Time: The Watts Uprising and the 1960s* (Charlottesville: University of Virginia Press, 1995), 30. Josh Sides adds, "Sparked and sustained by black anger at white America, the Watts riot also reflected the deepening political divide between the Great Migration generation and their children. Though casual observers assumed that the young rioters were recent arrivals from the South, the greatest numbers either had been born in Los Angeles or had moved to the city with their parents before 1960. Those rioting were not disappointed newcomers but rather young black men who had grown up disappointed, not only with the persistence of discrimination but also with their black leaders." Josh Sides, *L.A. City Limits: African American Los Angeles from the Great Depression to the Present* (Berkeley: University of California Press, 2003), 175.

30. Dalleck, *Flawed Giant*, 222–23.

31. Julius Lester, "The Angry Children of Malcolm X," in *Black Protest Thought in the Twentieth Century*, ed. August Meier et al. (New York: Bobbs-Merrill, 1971), 470.

32. *Black Power, White Backlash*, CBS News, September 27, 1966, http://www.cbsnews.com/videos/black-power-white-backlash.

33. Michael Herzfeld, *The Social Production of Indifference* (Chicago: University of Chicago Press, 1992).

34. Mbembe, *The Postcolony*, 17.

35. Martin Luther King Jr., *Where Do We Go from Here: Chaos or Community?* (New York: Penguin, 1968), 59.

36. Grier and Cobbs, *Black Rage*, 72.

37. Martin Luther King Jr., "Nonviolence: The Only Road to Freedom," *Ebony*, October 1966, 28.

38. For an analysis of race contagion and sex panic, see E. Patrick Johnson, *Appropriating Blackness: Performance and the Politics of Authenticity* (Durham, NC: Duke University Press, 2003).

39. Bryan J. McCann, *The Mark of Criminality: Rhetoric, Race, and Gangsta Rap in the War-on-Crime Era* (Tuscaloosa: University of Alabama Press, 2017).

40. King, "Nonviolence: The Only Road to Freedom," 28.

41. See Robert L. Scott and Donald K. Smith, "The Rhetoric of Confrontation," *Quarterly Journal of Speech* 55, no. 1 (1969): 1–8; Robert J. Doolittle, "Riots as Symbolic: A Criticism and Approach," *Central States Speech Journal* 27, no. 4 (1976): 310–17.

42. As the riot historian Peter Levy argues, one of the reasons that the riots of this period "were perceived as spontaneous and/or unexpected, and one of the reasons why the public has seen them either as unrelated to the civil rights movement or as a betrayal of the goals of the movement, is . . . because of our temporal configuration of the movement." Peter B. Levy, *The Great Uprising: Race Riots in Urban America during the 1960s* (New York: Cambridge University Press, 2018), 11.

43. Martin Luther King Jr., *The Autobiography of Martin Luther King, Jr.*, ed. Clayborne Carson (New York: Warner Books, 1998), 336.

44. In Otto Santa Ana, *Brown Tide Rising: Metaphors of Latinos in American Public Discourse* (Austin: University of Texas Press, 2002), 118. This section comes from an interview that Malcolm had with Claude Lewis in December 1964.

45. James Baldwin, "Fifth Avenue, Uptown," in *Nobody Knows My Name* (New York: Vintage, 1961), 67.

46. James Baldwin, "No Name in the Street," in *The Price of the Ticket: Collected Nonfiction, 1948–1985* (New York: St. Martin's Press, 1985), 550.

47. Martin Luther King Jr., "Our Struggle," in *A Testament of Hope: The Essential Writings and Speeches of Martin Luther King, Jr.*, ed. James M. Washington (New York: HarperCollins, 1986), 69; italics mine.

48. Martin Luther King Jr., "*Playboy* Interview: Martin Luther King Jr.," in *A Testament of Hope: The Essential Writings and Speeches of Martin Luther King, Jr.*, ed. James M. Washington (New York: HarperCollins, 1986), 363.

49. Donald R. Kinder and Lynn M. Sanders, *Divided by Color: Racial Politics and Democratic Ideals* (Chicago: University of Chicago Press, 1996), 104.

50. Randall Woods, *Prisoners of Hope: Lyndon B. Johnson, the Great Society, and the Limits of Liberalism* (New York: Basic Books, 2016), 318.

51. Gary Orfield, "Race and the Liberal Agenda: The Loss of the Integrationist Dream, 1965–1974," in *The Politics of Social Policy in the United States*, ed. Margaret Weir, Ann Shola Orloff, and Theda Skocpol (Princeton, NJ: Princeton University Press, 1988), 329.

52. Lawrence Samuel, *New York City 1964: A Cultural History* (New York: McFarland, 2014), 130.

53. Harry S. Scoble, "The McCone Commission and Social Science," *Phylon* 29, no. 2 (1968): 167–81.

54. LBJ and John McCone conversation, August 1965, WH Tapes, WH6508.05, Lyndon Baines Johnson Library.

55. Nathan Cohen, *The Los Angeles Riots: A Socio-Psychological Study* (Berkeley: University of California Press, 1970), 22.

56. California Labor Federation, AFL-CIO, *Reports of Executive Council and Executive Secretary-Treasurer to the Convention*, vol. 6 (August 1966), 55.

57. Gerald Horne, *Fire This Time: The Watts Uprising and the 1960s* (Charlottesville: University of Virginia Press, 1995), 181.

58. Connor Kilpatrick, "It's Not Just the Drug War," interview with Marie Gottschalk, *Jacobin*, March 2015, https://www.jacobinmag.com/2015/03/mass-incarceration-war-on -drugs.

59. Quoted in *The Black Panthers Speak*, ed. Philip S. Foner (Cambridge, MA: DeCapo Press, 2002),63.

60. "Seven Negro Leaders Issue a Statement of Principles Repudiating 'Black Power,'" *New York Times*, October 14, 1966, 27.

61. "Dr. King Endorses Racial Statement," *New York Times*, October 15, 1966, 14.

62. "A Negro 'No' on Black Power," *New York Times*, October 16, 1966, 2E.

63. Lindsey Lupo, *Flak-Catchers: One Hundred Years of Riot Commission Politics in America* (Lanham, MD: Lexington, 2011), 242.

64. Lupo, *Flak-Catchers*, 223.

65. Governor's Commission on the Los Angeles Riots, *McCone Commission Report* (Los Angeles: Kimtrex, 1965), 4.

66. *McCone Commission Report*, 4.

67. Kathryn Bond Stockton, *The Queer Child, or Growing Up Sideways in the Twentieth Century* (Durham, NC: Duke University Press, 2009), 31. See also Robin Bernstein, *Racial Innocence: Performing American Childhood from Slavery to Civil Rights* (New York: New York University Press, 2011).

68. *McCone Commission Report*, 3A.

69. *Report of the National Advisory Commission on Civil Disorders* (New York: Bantam, 1968), 1–2. *Newsweek* also commissioned a lengthy report on the 1967 riots that came to similar conclusions. See Osborn Elliott, "The Negro in America: What Must Be Done? A Program of Action," *Newsweek*, November 20, 1967, 1–25; and for a retrospective on the commission, see Fred R. Harris and Roger W. Wilkins, eds., *Quiet Riots: Race and Poverty in the United States* (New York: Pantheon, 1988).

70. Peniel E. Joseph, *Waiting 'til the Midnight Hour: A Narrative History of Black Power in America* (New York: Macmillan, 2007), 226–27.

71. Lupo, *Flak-Catchers*, 147.

72. Hugh Davis Graham, "On Riots and Riot Commissions: Civil Disorders in the 1960s," *Public Historian* 2, no. 4 (1980): 7–27.

73. Michael W. Flamm and David Steigerwald, *Debating the 1960s: Liberal, Conservative, and Radical Perspectives* (Lanham, MD: Rowman and Littlefield, 2008), 146.

74. Calvin L. Warren, *Ontological Terror: Blackness, Nihilism, and Emancipation* (Durham, NC: Duke University Press, 2018), 67.

75. Vesla M. Weaver, "Frontlash: Race and the Development of Punitive Crime Policy," *Studies in American Political Development* 21 (2007): 232.

76. Weaver, "Frontlash," 250.

77. Ritchie, *The Riot Report*, 184.

78. Ritchie, *The Riot Report*, 129.

79. Aida Hussen, "'Black Rage' and 'Useless Pain': Affect, Ambivalence, and Identity after King," *South Atlantic Quarterly* 112, no. 2 (2013): 306.

80. Richard M. Nixon, "Toward Freedom from Fear," remarks in New York City, May 8, 1968, archived online at the American Presidency Project, https://www.presidency.ucsb.edu/ documents/remarks-new-york-city-toward-freedom-from-fear.

81. Nixon, "Toward Freedom from Fear."

82. Wendy Brown, *States of Injury: Power and Freedom in Late Modernity* (Princeton, NJ: Princeton University Press, 1995), 59.

83. Martin Luther King Jr., "Showdown for Nonviolence," 68.

84. Jerry Gafio Watts, *Amiri Baraka: The Politics and Art of a Black Intellectual* (New York: New York University Press, 2001), 468.

85. Watts, *Amiri Baraka*, 468.

86. Hubert H. Humphrey, *Beyond Civil Rights: A New Day of Equality* (New York: Random House, 1968), 133.

87. On white rage and its manifestations, see Carol Anderson, *White Rage: The Unspoken Truth of Our Racial Divide* (New York: Bloomsbury, 2016); Martin Durham, *White Rage: The Extreme Right and American Politics* (New York: Routledge, 2007); Dan T. Carter, *The Politics of Rage: George Wallace, the Origins of the New Conservatism, and the Transformation of American Politics* (Baton Rouge: Louisiana State University Press, 1995).

Chapter Five: Mourning King: Memory, Affect, and the Shaping of Black Power

1. Elizabeth Hardwick, "The Apotheosis of Martin Luther King," *New York Review of Books*, May 9, 1968, https://www.nybooks.com/articles/1968/05/09/the-apotheosis-of-martin-luther-king.

2. Sara Ahmed, *The Promise of Happiness* (Durham, NC: Duke University Press, 2004), 121.

3. Stokely Carmichael (Kwame Toure), *Ready for Revolution: The Life and Struggles of Stokely Carmichael* (New York: Simon and Schuster, 2003), 659.

4. Carmichael, *Ready for Revolution*, 659.

5. Cleveland Sellers, *The River of No Return: The Autobiography of a Black Militant and the Life and Death of SNCC* (Jackson: University Press of Mississippi, 1990), 238.

6. "An Hour of Need," *Time*, April 12, 1968 (italics mine); archived online at http://swampland.time.com/2013/04/04/time-looks-back-martin-luther-kings-assassination/#ixzz2U87T3djL.

7. Jeffrey C. Alexander, "Toward a Theory of Cultural Trauma," in *Cultural Trauma and Collective Memory*, ed. Jeffrey C. Alexander et al. (Los Angeles: University of California Press, 2004), 1.

8. Grier and Cobbs, *Black Rage*, 210.

9. Alexander, "Toward a Theory of Cultural Trauma," 10.

10. Alexander, "Toward a Theory of Cultural Trauma," 11.

11. Alexander, "Toward a Theory of Cultural Trauma," 12.

12. Alexander, "Toward a Theory of Cultural Trauma," 12.

13. Alexander, "Toward a Theory of Cultural Trauma," 13–15.

14. Michael W. Schuyler, "Ghosts in the White House: LBJ, RFK and the Assassination of JFK," *Presidential Studies Quarterly* 17, no. 3 (1987): 2.

15. Michael Eric Dyson, *April 4, 1968: Martin Luther King Jr.'s Death and How It Changed America* (New York: Basic Books, 2008).

16. Martin Luther King Jr., "I See the Promised Land," April 3, 1968, in *A Testament of Hope: The Essential Writings and Speeches of Martin Luther King, Jr.*, ed. James M. Washington (New York: HarperCollins, 1986), 286.

17. Dyson, *April 4, 1968*, 40.

18. John H. Johnson, "Publisher's Statement," in *Black Power Revolt*, ed. Floyd B. Barbour (Boston, MA: Extending Horizons Books, 1968), vi–vii.

19. Alice Walker, "The Civil Rights Movement: What Good Was It?" in *In Search of Our Mothers' Gardens: Womanist Prose* (New York: Harcourt Brace, 1983), 124.

20. Alice Walker, "Choice: A Tribute to Martin Luther King Jr.," in *In Search of Our Mothers' Gardens: Womanist Prose* (New York: Harcourt Brace, 1983), 144.

21. Lauren Berlant, *Cruel Optimism* (Durham, NC: Duke University Press, 2011), 48.

22. Hussen, "'Black Rage' and 'Useless Pain,'" 307.

23. Warren, "Black Nihilism," 219.

24. Warren, "Black Nihilism," 221.

25. Martin Luther King, "Address at the Thirty-Sixth Annual Dinner of the War Resisters League," February 3, 1959, in *The Papers of Martin Luther King, Jr.: Threshold of a New Decade*, ed. Adrienne Clay, Tenisha Armstrong, and Clayborne Carson (Oakland: University of California Press, 2005), 123.

26. Adam Fairclough, *Martin Luther King, Jr.* (Athens: University of Georgia Press, 1995), 13. For a more in-depth discussion of King's politics of optimism, see Keith D. Miller, *Voice of Deliverance: The Language of Martin Luther King, Jr., and Its Sources* (Athens: University of Georgia Press, 1998), 51–58.

27. Carmichael, *Ready for Revolution*, 658.

28. *New York Times*, April 15, 1968, 26.

29. Timothy Raphael, "Mo(u)rning in America: Hamlet, Reagan, and the Rights of Memory," *Theatre Journal* 59 (2007): 2.

30. Sellers, *The River of No Return*, 253.

31. Martin Luther King Jr., "I Have a Dream," 217.

32. James Cone, *Martin and Malcolm and America: A Dream or a Nightmare* (Maryknoll, NY: Orbis Books, 1991), 196.

33. Malcolm X, "The Ballot or the Bullet," 40.

34. Malcolm X, "The Ballot or the Bullet," 26.

35. Ida E. Lewis, "The Rev. Dr. Martin Luther King Jr.: The Dream Endures Forever," *Crisis*, April–May 1998, 4.

36. Clarence Waldron, "King Remembered in Memphis Forty Years after Assassination," *Jet*, April 21, 2008, 6–7.

37. Harry Belafonte with Michael Shnayerson, *My Song: A Memoir* (New York: Knopf, 2011), 333.

38. Belafonte, *My Song*, 338.

39. Walker, "Civil Rights," 128–29.

40. Maya Angelou, interview with George Stroumboulopoulos, Canadian Broadcast Corporation, http://www.cbc.ca/strombo/videos/web-exclusive/maya-angelou-on-the-death-of-martin-luther-king-jr.-it-was-terrible (accessed July 14, 2014).

41. Nina Simone, *I Put a Spell on You: The Autobiography of Nina Simone* (New York: Da Capo Press, 2003), 114.

42. "*Time* Looks Back: The Assassination of Martin Luther King, Jr.," reprint of "An Hour of Need," April 4, 2003, http://swampland.time.com/2013/04/04/time-looks-back-martin-luther-kings-assassination.

43. Carmichael, *Ready for Revolution*, 227.

44. Eldridge Cleaver with Kathleen Cleaver, *Target Zero: A Life in Writing* (New York: Palgrave Macmillan, 2007), 83.

45. Cleaver, *Target Zero*, 83.

46. Cleaver, *Target Zero*, 83.

47. Berlant, *Cruel Optimism*, 25.

48. Berlant, *Cruel Optimism*, 25.

49. Berlant, *Cruel Optimism*, 27.

50. Berlant, *Cruel Optimism*, 27.

51. Cleaver, *Target Zero*, 84.

52. Berlant, *Cruel Optimism*, 24.

53. Berlant, *Cruel Optimism*, 1.

54. Berlant, *Cruel Optimism*, 23.

55. Berlant, *Cruel Optimism*, 24.

56. "*Time* Looks Back."

57. Harry Reed, "History and Memory: Reflections on Dreams and Silences," *Journal of Negro History* 84, no. 2 (1999): 155.

58. Thomas F. Jackson, *From Civil Rights to Human Rights: Martin Luther King, Jr., and the Struggle for Economic Justice* (State College: Pennsylvania State University Press, 2011), 2.

59. Berlant, *Cruel Optimism*, 45.

60. Garth Pauley, *The Modern Presidency and Civil Rights* (College Station: Texas A&M Press, 2001), 16.

61. Cleaver, *Target Zero*, 72.

62. Warren, "Black Nihilism," 233.

63. Cleaver, *Target Zero*, 87–88.

64. Cleaver, *Target Zero*, 68–69.

65. See J. Samuel Walker, *Most of 14th Street Is Gone: The Washington, DC, Riots of 1968* (New York: Oxford University Press, 2018); Jason Sokol, *The Heavens Might Crack: The Death and Legacy of Martin Luther King, Jr.* (New York: Hachette/Basic Books, 2018); Rebecca Burns, *Burial for a King: Martin Luther King, Jr.'s Funeral and the Week That Transformed Atlanta and Rocked the Nation* (New York: Simon and Schuster, 2011).

66. Newton, *Revolutionary Suicide*, 201.

67. David Hilliard, *This Side of Glory: The Autobiography of David Hilliard and the Story of the Black Panther Party* (Chicago: Lawrence Hill, 2001), 182.

68. Burns, *Burial for a King*, 49. See also Clay Risen, *A Nation on Fire: America in the Wake of the King Assassination* (Hoboken, NJ: Wiley, 2009).

69. Devorah Heitner, *Black Power TV* (Durham, NC: Duke University Press, 2013), 1–2.

70. James Forman, *The Making of Black Revolutionaries* (Seattle: University of Washington Press, 1997), 526.

71. Forman, *The Making of Black Revolutionaries*, 526.

72. Bobby Seale, "Interview—Eyes on the Prize," November 4, 1988, Washington University Digital Gateway Texts, http://digital.wustl.edu/e/eii/eiiweb/sea5427.0172.147bobbyseale .html.

73. Reed, "History and Memory," 150.

74. Vincent Harding, "Beyond Amnesia: Martin Luther King, Jr., and the Future of America," *Journal of American History* 74, no. 2 (1987): 468–69.

75. Harding, "Beyond Amnesia," 469.

76. Harding, "Beyond Amnesia," 470.

77. Ron Eyerman, *The Cultural Sociology of Political Assassination: From MLK and RFK to Fortuyn and Van Gogh* (New York: Palgrave Macmillan, 2011), 52.

78. Hardwick, "The Apotheosis of King."

79. Arthur Dudden, "Nostalgia and the American," *Journal of the History of Ideas* 22, no. 4 (1961): 517.

80. Dudden, "Nostalgia and the American," 517.

Chapter Six: Revolutionary Suicide: Necromimesis, Radical Agency, and Black Ontology

1. Huey Newton, "A Prison Interview," in *The New Left Reader*, ed. Carl Oglesby (New York: Grove Press, 1969), 224.

2. Newton, "A Prison Interview," 225–26.

3. Newton, "A Prison Interview," 227.

4. Huey Newton, *To Die for the People* (San Francisco: City Lights, 2009), 17.

5. Butler, *Precarious Life*, 29.

6. Huey Newton, *Revolutionary Suicide* (1973; New York: Penguin, 2009), 163.

7. Frank Wilderson, "The Prison Slave as Hegemony's (Silent) Scandal," *Social Justice* 30, no. 2 (2010): 80.

8. Donna Murch, *Living for the City: Migration, Education, and the Rise of the Black Panther Party in Oakland, California* (Chapel Hill: University of North Carolina Press, 2010), 167–68.

9. James Baldwin, *No Name in the Street* (1972; New York: Vintage Books, 2007), 165.

10. Antonio Viego has traced similar phenomena among Latinx populations, writing about the psychic production of "dead subjects." See Viego, *Dead Subjects: Toward a Politics of Loss in Latino Studies* (Durham, NC: Duke University Press, 2007).

11. See Achille Mbembe, *Necropolitics*, trans. Libby Meintjes, *Public Culture* 15, no. 1 (2003): 11–40.

12. Mbembe, *Critique of Black Reason*, 28.

13. Wendy Brown, *States of Injury: Power and Freedom in Late Modernity* (Princeton, NJ: Princeton University Press, 1995), 6.

14. Alex Houen, "Sacrificial Militancy and the War on Terror," in *Terror and the Postcolonial: A Concise Companion* (New York: Wiley, 2015), 134.

15. Kenneth O'Reilly, *Racial Matters: The FBI's Secret War on Black America, 1960–1972* (New York: Free Press, 1991); Ward Churchill and Jim Vander Wall, *The COINTELPRO Papers: Documents from the FBI's Secret Wars against Dissent in the United States* (Boston: South End Press, 1990); Nelson Blackstock, *COINTELPRO: The FBI's Secret War on Political Freedom* (Atlanta: Pathfinder Press, 1988).

16. Newton, *Revolutionary Suicide*, 2.

17. Newton, *Revolutionary Suicide*, 2–3.

18. Grier and Cobbs, *Black Rage*, 157.

19. Mbembe, *Critique of Black Reason*, 78.

20. Tommy J. Curry, *The Man-Not: Race, Class, Genre and the Dilemmas of Black Manhood* (Philadelphia: Temple University Press, 2017), 104–36. See also James B. Stewart, "The Political Economy of Black Male Suicides," *Journal of Black Studies* 11, no. 2 (1980): 249–61; James B. Stewart and Joseph W. Scott, "The Institutional Decimation of Black American Males," *Western Journal of Black Studies* 2, no. 2 (1978): 82–92.

21. Mbembe, *Critique of Black Reason*, 78.

22. David Hilliard, *This Side of Glory: The Autobiography of David Hilliard and the Story of the Black Panther Party* (New York: Little, Brown, 1993), 182.

23. Eldridge Cleaver, "The Death of Martin Luther King, Jr.: Requiem for a Dream," in *Post-Prison Writings and Speeches* (New York: Random House, 1969), 74.

24. Peniel E. Joseph, *The Black Power Movement: Rethinking the Civil Rights–Black Power Era* (New York: Routledge, 2006).

25. Michele Kennerly and Damien Pfister, "*Poiēsis, Genesis, and Mimēsis*: Toward a Less Selfish Genealogy of Memes," in *Ancient Rhetorics and Digital Networks*, ed. Michele Kennerly and Damien Pfister (Tuscaloosa: University of Alabama Press, 2018), 207.

26. Baldwin, *No Name in the Street*, 165.

27. Fredrika Newton, "Preface," in *Revolutionary Suicide* (1973; New York: Penguin, 2009), xvi.

28. Thomas B. Farrell, *Norms of Rhetorical Culture* (New Haven, CT: Yale University Press, 1995), 118.

29. Farrell, *Norms of Rhetorical Culture*, 134.

30. Hans Robert Jauss, *Aesthetic Experience and Literary Hermeneutics*, trans. M. Shaw (Minneapolis: University of Minnesota Press, 1982), 35.

31. Michel Foucault, "Space, Knowledge, and Power," interview by Paul Rabinow, in *The Foucault Reader*, ed. Paul Rabinow (New York: Pantheon, 1984), 245.

32. William E. Connolly, *Identity/Difference: Democratic Negotiations of Political Paradox* (Minneapolis: University of Minnesota Press, 1991), 17.

33. Karlyn Kohrs Campbell and Kathleen Hall Jamieson, *Deeds Done in Words: Presidential Rhetoric and the Genres of Governance* (Chicago: University of Chicago Press, 1990), 37.

34. Newton, *To Die for the People*, 234.

35. Mbembe, *Critique of Black Reason*, 100–101.

36. George Jackson, *Soledad Brother: The Prison Letters of George Jackson* (1970; Chicago: Lawrence Hill, 1994), 14.

37. Grier and Cobbs, *Black Rage*, 152.

38. Fred Moten, *Black and Blur* (Durham, NC: Duke University Press, 2017), 69.

39. Paul Gilroy, *The Black Atlantic: Modernity and Double-Consciousness* (Cambridge, MA: Harvard University Press, 1993), 57.

40. Huey Newton, "Eulogy for George Jackson," in *The Huey P. Newton Reader*, ed. David Hilliard and Donald Weise (New York: Seven Stories, 2002), 245.

41. Moten, *Black and Blur*, 69.

42. Lisa M. Corrigan, "Theorizing Black Power in Prison: The Writings of George Jackson and Angela Davis," in *Social Controversy and Public Address in the 1960s and Early 1970s: A Rhetorical History of the United States, Vol. IX*, ed. Richard Jensen (Lansing: Michigan State University Press, 2017), 39–82. That doctrine suspended civil rights for the imprisoned. In California during the late 1960s and 1970s, a broad coalition of activists worked to upend the "civil death" doctrine. They ultimately reinstated Penal Code 2600, which preserved those civil rights for inmates. As America's most celebrated political prisoner, Jackson inspired inmates to view themselves as a "class of civil constituents" whose experience and information could challenge the carceral regime. See Doran Larson, "Abolition from Within: Enabling the Citizen Convict," *Radical Teacher* 91 (2001): 11.

43. Saidiya V. Hartman, *Scenes of Subjection: Terror, Slavery, and Self-Making in Nineteenth-Century America* (Oxford: Oxford University Press, 1997), 24.

44. Katherine Stanutz, "'Dying but Fighting Back': George Jackson's Modes of Mourning," *MELUS* 42, no. 1 (2017): 33.

45. Frank B. Wilderson III, *Red, White, and Black: Cinema and the Structure of U.S. Antagonisms* (Durham, NC: Duke University Press, 2010), 142.

46. Mbembe, *Critique of Black Reason*, 28.

47. Michelle Koerner, "Line of Escape: Gilles Deleuze's Encounter with George Jackson," *Genre* 44, no. 2 (2011): 164.

48. Newton, "Eulogy for George Jackson," 245.

49. Newton, "Eulogy for George Jackson," 245.

50. Gilbert Moore, *A Special Rage* (New York: Harper and Row, 1971), 87–88.

51. Joe Street, "The Shadow of the Soul Breaker: Solitary Confinement, Cocaine, and the Decline of Huey P. Newton," *Pacific Historical Review* 84, no. 3 (2015): 337.

52. Hortense Spillers, "Mama's Baby, Papa's Maybe: An American Grammar Book," *Diacritics* 17, no. 2 (1987): 67.

53. J. Herman Blake, "The Caged Panther: The Prison Years of Huey P. Newton," *Journal of African American Studies* 16, no. 2 (2012): 236–48.

54. Newton, *Revolutionary Suicide*, 3.

55. Newton, *Revolutionary Suicide*, 3.

56. Newton, *Revolutionary Suicide*, 3.

57. Newton, *Revolutionary Suicide*, 3.

58. Mbembe, "Necropolitics," 13.

59. Newton, *Revolutionary Suicide*, 116–17.

60. Jacques Derrida, *Specters of Marx: The State of the Debt, the Work of Mourning, and the New International*, trans. Peggy Kamuf (New York: Routledge, 1994), 120.

61. Scott and Smith, "The Rhetoric of Confrontation," 5.

62. Scott and Smith, "The Rhetoric of Confrontation," 5.

63. Innerarity, *The Future and Its Enemies*, 36.

64. Warren, "Black Nihilism," 223.

65. Newton, *Revolutionary Suicide*, 355.

66. Houen, "Sacrificial Militancy," 131.

67. Winters, *Hope Draped in Black*, 72.

68. Street, "Shadow of the Soul Breaker," 338.

69. Turner, "The Sociology of Black Nationalism," 26.

Conclusion

1. Wilber C. Rich, "Introduction: Barack Obama and the Transformational Impulse," in *Looking Back on Barack Obama's Legacy: Hope and Change* (New York: Palgrave Macmillan, 2018), 3. Likewise, Jonathan Chait's book *Audacity: How Barack Obama Defied His Critics and Created a Legacy That Will Prevail* (New York: HarperCollins, 2017) tackles Obama's centrism (what Chait describes as an impulse toward liberal Republicanism) and his record of accomplishment.

2. Barack Obama, *The Audacity of Hope: Thoughts on Reclaiming the American Dream* (New York: Vintage, 2008). Obama explains, "If anything, what struck me was just how modest people's hopes were, and how much of what they believed seemed to hold constant across race, region, religion, and class" (7).

3. Obama, *The Audacity of Hope*, 25.

4. Obama, *The Audacity of Hope*, 356.

5. Obama, *The Audacity of Hope*, 356.

6. For an extended discussion of how irony functions as an exclusionary discourse, see Linda Hutcheon, *Irony's Edge: The Theory and Politics of Irony* (New York: Routledge, 1994).

For the psychoanalytic perspective on irony, see Frank Stringfellow, *The Meaning of Irony: A Psychoanalytic Investigation* (Albany: State University of New York Press, 1994).

7. Darryl Pinckney and Joan Didion, "Obama: In the Irony-Free Zone," *New York Review of Books*, December 18, 2008, https://www.nybooks.com/articles/2008/12/18/obama-in-the-irony-free-zone.

8. See Spike Lee and Aaron Perry-Zucker, eds., *Design for Obama: Posters for Change; A Grassroots Anthology* (Cologne: Taschen, 2009).

9. Richard Wolffe, *Renegade: The Making of a President* (New York: Crown/Random House, 2010), 107.

10. "Presidential Approval Ratings—George W. Bush," Gallup, https://news.gallup.com/poll/116500/presidential-approval-ratings-george-bush.aspx.

11. Barack Obama, "Announcement of Presidential Campaign," February 10, 2007, transcript at CBS News, https://www.cbsnews.com/news/transcript-of-barack-obamas-speech.

12. Barack H. Obama, "Inaugural Address," January 21, 2009, https://obamawhitehouse.archives.gov/blog/2009/01/21/president-barack-obamas-inaugural-address.

13. Obama for America, *Change We Can Believe In: Barack Obama's Plan to Renew America's Promise* (New York: Three Rivers Press, 2008), 240.

14. Obama for America, *Change We Can Believe In*, 246.

15. See Stacey K. Sowards, *Sí, Ella Puede! The Rhetorical Legacy of Dolores Huerta and the United Farm Workers* (Austin: University of Texas Press, 2019).

16. William Chaloupka, *Everybody Knows: Cynicism in America* (Minneapolis: University of Minnesota Press, 1999), 8.

17. Tony Monchinski, *Education in Hope: Critical Pedagogies and the Ethic of Care* (New York: Peter Lang, 2010), 138.

18. Obama for America, *Change We Can Believe In*, 212.

19. Brown, *States of Injury*, 75n42. See also *Keep Hope Alive: Jesse Jackson's 1988 Presidential Campaign*, ed. Frank Clemente and Frank Watkins (Boston: South End Press, 1989).

20. Joe Klein, "Why Barack Obama Could Be the Next President," *Time*, October 23, 2006, http://content.time.com/time/covers/0,16641,20061023,00.html.

21. Gerald Early, "The Two Worlds of Race Revisited: A Meditation on Race in the Age of Obama," *Daedalus*, Winter 2011, https://www.amacad.org/publication/two-worlds-race-revisited-meditation-race-age-obama#A2.

22. Tim Dickinson, "The Fierce Urgency of Now," *Rolling Stone*, November 3, 2007, https://www.rollingstone.com/politics/politics-news/the-fierce-urgency-of-now-180031.

23. James T. Kloppenberg, *Reading Obama: Dreams, Hopes, and the American Political Tradition* (Princeton, NJ: Princeton University Press, 2010), 225.

24. Obama, *The Audacity of Hope*, 247.

25. Rachel E. Dobrofsky, "Authentic Trump: Yearning for Civility," *Television and New Media* 17, no. 7 (2016): 663–66.

26. Jonathan Capehart, "If Steve Bannon Gets a Pass, Why Was Jeremiah Wright Demonized?" *Chicago Tribune*, November 21 2016, https://www.chicagotribune.com/opinion/commentary/ct-steve-bannon-jeremiah-wright-20161121-story.html.

27. Michael Fletcher, "The Speech on Race That Saved Obama's Candidacy," *Washington Post*, April 22, 2016, https://www.washingtonpost.com/graphics/national/obama-legacy/jeremiah-wright-2008-philadelphia-race-speech.html.

28. Barack Obama, "A More Perfect Union," March 18, 2008, https://www.npr.org/templates/story/story.php?storyId=88478467.

29. Obama, "A More Perfect Union."

30. Obama, "A More Perfect Union."

31. Obama, "A More Perfect Union."

32. Obama, "A More Perfect Union."

33. Ebony Utley and Amy L. Heyse, "Barack Obama's (Im)Perfect Union: An Analysis of the Strategic Successes and Failures in His Speech on Race," *Western Journal of Black Studies* 33, no. 3 (2009): 154.

34. See Barbara Ransby, *Making All Black Lives Matter: Reimagining Freedom in the Twenty-First Century* (Los Angeles: University of California Press, 2018); Patrisse Khan-Cullors and Asha Bandele, *When They Call You a Terrorist: A Black Lives Matter Memoir* (New York: St. Martin's Press, 2018); Amanda Nell Edgar and Andre Johnson, *The Struggle over Black Lives Matter and All Lives Matter* (Lanham, MD: Lexington Books, 2018); Keeanga-Yamahtta Taylor, *From #BlackLivesMatter to Black Liberation* (New York: Haymarket, 2016).

35. Adia Harvey Wingfield and Joe R. Feagin, *Yes We Can? White Racial Framing and the Obama Presidency* (New York: Routledge, 2013), 192.

36. Eduardo Bonilla-Silva, "The Structure of Racism in Color-Blind, 'Post-Racial' America," *American Behavioral Scientist* 59, no. 11 (2015): 1358–1376. See also Eduardo Bonilla-Silva, *Racism without Racists: Color-Blind Racism and the Persistence of Racial Inequality in the United States* (New York: Rowman and Littlefield, 2013).

37. Ian F. Haney López, "Is the 'Post' in Post-Racial the 'Blind' in Colorblind?" *Cardozo Law Review* 32, no. 3 (2010): 808.

38. Haney López, "Is the 'Post' in Post-Racial," 808.

39. P. J. Brendese, "The Race of a More Perfect Union: James Baldwin, Segregated Memory, and the Presidential Race," in *The Political Companion to James Baldwin*, ed. Susan J. McWilliams (Lexington: University Press of Kentucky, 2017), 71.

40. Brendese, "Race of a More Perfect Union," 71.

41. Lee Glendinning, "What Jesse Jackson Really Said about Barack Obama," *Guardian*, July 17, 2008, https://www.theguardian.com/world/deadlineusa/2008/jul/17/newonethe fullforceofjess.

42. Suzanne Goldenberg, "US Election 2008: 'I Want to Cut His Nuts Out'—Jackson Gaffe Turns Focus on Obama's Move to the Right," *Guardian*, July 10, 2008, https://www.theguardian.com/world/2008/jul/11/barackobama.uselections2008.

43. The turn of phrase was made even more ironic because Jackson's book *Legal Lynching: The Death Penalty and America's Future* (1997) offered dense arguments about capital punishment as a structural erasure of black community, and Obama's positions on crime were a far departure from Jackson's.

44. "Blacks Upbeat about Black Progress, Prospects," Pew Research Center Report, January 21, 2010, https://www.pewsocialtrends.org/2010/01/12/blacks-upbeat-about-black-progress-prospects.

45. Michael Tesler, *Post-Racial or Most-Racial? Race and Politics in the Obama Era* (Chicago: University of Chicago Press, 2016), 5.

46. Matt Bai, "Is Obama the End of Black Politics?" *New York Times*, August 6, 2008, https://www.nytimes.com/2008/08/10/magazine/10politics-t.html.

47. Joshua Foa Dienstag, *Pessimism: Philosophy, Ethic, Spirit* (Princeton, NJ: Princeton University Press, 2006), 5.

48. Carol Anderson, *White Rage: The Unspoken Truth of Our Racial Divide* (New York: Bloomsbury, 2016), 2.

49. Anderson, *White Rage*, 2.

50. Curry, *The Man-Not*, 19.

51. Anderson, *White Rage*, 3.

52. Anderson, *White Rage*, 3.

53. Antoine J. Banks, *Anger and Racial Politics: The Emotional Foundation of Racial Attitudes* (New York: Cambridge University Press, 2014), 27.

54. Banks, *Anger and Racial Politics*, 14.

55. David L. Eng and Shinhee Han, *Racial Melancholia, Racial Dissociation: On the Social and Psychic Lives of Asian Americans* (Durham, NC: Duke University Press, 2019), 24.

56. Eric King Watts, "Postracial Fantasies, Blackness, and Zombies," *Communication and Critical/Cultural Studies* 14, no. 4 (2017): 317–33.

57. Ta-Nehisi Coates, "The Case for Reparations," *Atlantic*, June 2014, https://www.theatlantic.com/magazine/archive/2014/06/the-case-for-reparations/361631.

58. Cheryl I. Harris, "Whiteness as Property," *Harvard Law Review* 106, no. 8 (June 1993): 1707–91.

59. Michael C. Dawson, *Black Visions: The Roots of Contemporary African-American Political Ideologies* (Chicago: University of Chicago Press, 2001), 324.

60. Mbembe, *Critique of Black Reason*, 5.

61. Gianni Vattimo, *Nihilism and Emancipation*, ed. Santiago Zabala, trans. William McCuaig (New York: Columbia University Press, 2004), 49–50.

INDEX

ABOUT THE AUTHOR

Lisa M. Corrigan is associate professor of communication, director of the gender studies program, and affiliate faculty in African and African American studies and in Latin American and Latino studies at the University of Arkansas. She is author of the award-winning *Prison Power: How Prison Influenced the Movement for Black Liberation*, published by University Press of Mississippi.

CPSIA information can be obtained
at www.ICGtesting.com
Printed in the USA
BVHW071922250220
573275BV00001BA/2